Heavenly Visions in Photos

Cynthia Meyers-Hanson

Copyright 2022

Heavenly Visions in Photos

First Edition 2022

By: Cynthia Meyers-Hanson

All rights reserved. No portion of this book may be reproduced or utilized in any form or by any means, electronic or mechanical including photocopying, without permission in writing from the author. Inquiries should be addressed online @ mchanson714@yahoo.com

Dedication

To God because He created it all. To my fans and self for staying the course...

Disclaimer

Names may be changed to give people anonymity as well as to protect my innocence in any and all of these stories.

Cover from 8/12/21

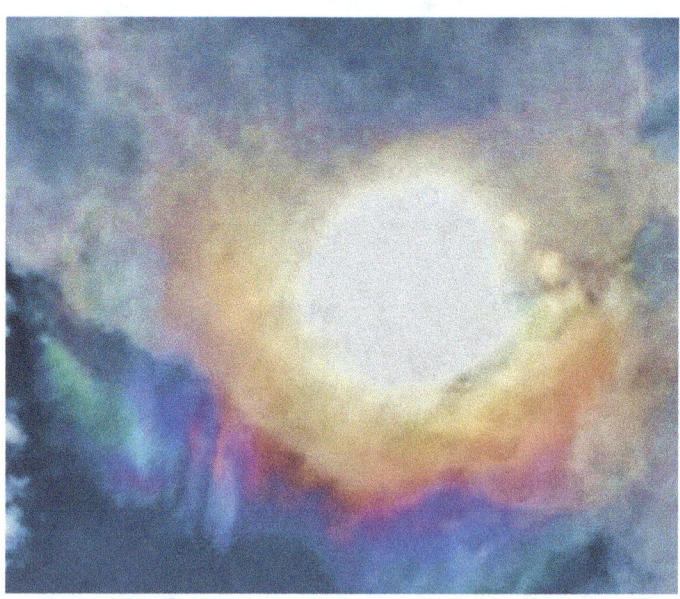

Heavenly Visions in Photos- Table of Contents

Table of Contents

Helpful Book Summaries 5

Introduction: God's Communication Continues 7

Chapter 1: The Light Helps Beauty Shine 9

   The Lights 10

      Sundog(s) 10

      Sunbows or Sun Halos 12

      Sun Halo accompanied by a Circumzenithal Arc 14

      Sun Coronas 14

      Iridescent Clouds 16

      Moonlight 17

Chapter 2: God's Signs, Symbols, Skywriting, and Ideas 20

   The Creator is 20

   Rainbows 24

   Twin Rainbows 25

   The Creator's Skywriting 26

   Meaningful Numbers 27

   Misty Symbols such as: a Lion, an Elephant, The Wise Old Owl, and Santa 27

   The Messiah Arrived to… 29

   Symbols for Jesus The Christ include: A Lamb, Bunny, Fish, and Bread 29

   Skywriting Including "T" or "t", "E' or "e", "v", and "IV" 30

   The Ever-present Nature of God's Holy Spirit 32

   A "3" and a Triangle Can Explain The Trinity 34

   The Role of God's Angels 35

   Mary's Role in The Christian Church 36

Chapter 3: Some Photos from Holy Days 38

   A Special Note 42

Chapter 4: After Years of Looking Up at The 7th Heaven 45

   Antisolar Sunrays 58

Chapter 5: Vacations before Heaven's Paradise 61

Chapter 6: The Book of Life 67

- *Don't Worry Before It's Time to Do It* 67
- *Stairway to Heaven* 67
- *Mom's on the Roof and I Can't Get Her Down* 70
- *World Ends* 70
- *The Last Judgement* 70
- *Signs in The Heavens* 71
- *The Rescue* 72
- *Co-authoring a Book with Wavie* 74
- *Who Wins?* 75
- *Face It* 81
- *Be not Afraid* 82
- *The Sun Beams* 82
- *Heaven Reflects on The Earth* 84
- *The End or New Beginning* 85
- *Sunrise* 85
- *Sunset* 86
- *Leave the Light On* 87
- *Skywriting that Turns a Mind's Light On* 88
- *Go Figure(s)* 88
- *My Word* 89
- *Heaven, Thanks* 89
- *Is this Random Skywriting?* 90
- *Every Picture Tells a Story; Don't it?* 90

Helpful Book Summaries

There are things the reader needs to know to understand this book. Ideally, they should read my nonfiction stories in the following order.

Mom's on the Roof and I Can't Get Her Down has the backdrop of terminal cancer as well as Christianity. It is a tale about life after death. By the way, some of the unfinished prophecy mom brought from Heaven happened after the copyright date, which proves God's Hand is in the story.

The Evans Terrace Girls reveals small miracles in grief recovery after a bunch of young females believed in helping a mourning friend. Some people thought their neighborhood was cursed when seven or more parents died of unrelated issues within two years; the girls believed in spiritual wonders and God's version of magic. After reading their anecdotal proof, you may as well.

Stacey's Song follows the little miracles that helped pull the young girl through her grief recovery. I was her guardian after she lost two generations of parents starting with her natural ones and ending with her grandparents' deaths. Those events led to her twice orphaned status and then to my home.

Through the Storms- HE Performs is a book I coproduced with a friend. She out lived a "Jaws of Life" necessary, car accident while pregnant. Her coma lasted fourteen days, and a team of physicians declared her brain dead. While her husband fretted over his wife and their unborn child, while comatose, Wavie Green met with God as well as vividly tracked her hospital room visitors. She came back to great adversity but remained in communion with The Lord. Read her testimony to find out what The Almighty told her about life and His Dominion. (This nonfiction is out of print but I have access.)

The Presence- the Presents explains my aunt's recoveries from breast cancer, strokes, kidney failure, heart attacks, and other ailments. One April Fools' Day, her physician said that a stroke medicine she took produced a bleed out condition that would take her life. Her doctors could do nothing to stop the accompanying fever and other things driving that diagnosis. As the hospital provided comfort care, Anne awaited death but God added years to her life with her miraculous healings. Read her saga via this book. (This nonfiction is out of print but I have access.)

My ArmOr explains the unbelievable trauma endured when I almost lost my left arm. From that saga, I describe the wonders of life as well as how I used my past to propel me through my limb's rehabilitation. My "can do" attitude prevailed after the doctor and physical or occupational therapists gave up on that arm. The book contains some answers to the unfinished prophecy contained in book one on this list.

The Vision provides a description of being born legally blind and growing in vision. Based on a true story, the main character discusses infirmities including learning disabilities. In addition, she reveals the ramifications of her father's Bipolar Disease with its impact on her family and her psyche. In short, she reveals the lessons that varied adversities taught her.

God News provides answers to some questions. "Is there a God? Is there an Afterlife? Does The Creator of Heaven and Earth interact with humans?"

God News in Photos is a companion book for God News. My camera took most of the images between Father's Day in June of 2015 and the same day in 2016. The storyline reveals God is alive and communicating with this realm. In this case, He talks via clouds interacting with the sun. He uses skywriting among other ways to convey His messages across the miles. Keep looking up.

HIS Story in Photos is a companion book for God News and God New in Photos. For this photo journal or my second, picture diary, most of the imagery arrived in The Heavens between July 2016 and July 2017 aka my birthday month. The storyline reveals that God is alive and still communicating with humanity. In this case, He talks using sunlight and clouds. The Creator, also, finds other ways to convey His messages across the miles. Keep looking up.

Humor-US (with God's Artistry) is the third picture, storybook about things created in The Heavens or God inspired skywriting. HIS Story in Photos and God New in Photos are companion books for this nonfiction. For this photo journal or my third, picture diary- I snapped the camera's "freeze frames" because the storyline continues to reveal that God is alive and communicating with humans. In this case, He talks via The Heavens. The Creator, also, finds other ways to convey His messages across the miles. By now, I bet you are hooked on clouds.

It's a Celebration (with God's Artistry) is the fourth storybook about images in The Heavens aka God's inspired skywriting. HIS Story in Photos, God New in Photos, and Humor-US (with God's Artistry) are companion books to this nonfiction. My camera's pictures and the storyline continue to reveal that God is alive and still communicating with this place using the sky as His canvass. By now, I bet you are hooked on clouds.

God's Skywriting in Photos (The Celebration Continues...) covers the threshold of January 2018 through September 2018. This nonfiction is the fifth storybook about images in The Heavens aka God's inspired skywriting. HIS Story in Photos, God New in Photos, Humor-US (with God's Artistry), and It's a Celebration (with God's Artistry) are similar books to this nonfiction. My camera's pictures and the storyline continue to reveal that God is alive and still communicating with this place using the sky and The Earth as His canvass. By now, I bet you are hooked on His Creativity and Artistry.

God's Present in Photos contains images from October 2018 through June 22, 2019. This nonfiction is the sixth storybook about images in The Heavens aka God's inspired skywriting. HIS Story in Photos, God New in Photos, Humor-US (with God's Artistry), It's a Celebration (with God's Artistry) and God's Skywriting in Photos are similar books to this nonfiction. My camera's pictures and the storyline continue to reveal that God is alive and still communicating with this place using the sky and The Earth as His canvass. By now, I bet you are hooked on His Creativity and Artistry.

Stare Way to Heaven via Photos contains images and diary entries explaining The Heavens and signs from God starting from 6/23/2019 through 4/31/2020.

Keep Looking Up Via Photos contains imagery in The Heavens sent by God starting on 5/1/2020 through the end of 2020. It's the eighth book in a series; that is the biblical number of new beginnings. So, the journey begins, again.

Don't Stop Believing in Photographic Memories The best daze are yet to come. This was written from New Year's 2021 through June 2021.

Heavenly Visions in Photos These pictures should help point out the way to The Loving and Eternal Heaven. The content of this nonfiction goes from July 2021 through June 2022.

Introduction: God's Communication Continues

I am Cindy; my pen name is Cynthia Meyers-Hanson for nonfictions and children's storybooks. While writing with poetic license and exaggerating realities, my "nom de plume" is Sydney S. Song. Please, note that two, inspirational tales (that I helped author) are out of print but are summarized in some of my other narratives.

What started my writing journey? In 1991, after a miracle filled experience that ended with my mom losing her battle with breast cancer, in order to put rumors to rest, I explained what transpired in Lake Mary, Florida. The truth is chronicled in my first published nonfiction entitled <u>Mom's on the Roof and I Can't Get Her Down</u>.

Photographing cloudscapes started on 6/22/2015 or the day after Father's Day. A friend and religious mentor died before dawn that day; I knew she was dying because Wavie was terminal. In addition, I sensed she left this world because a thunderstorm lit the area during the darkest hours of the night. Fully awake, I saw her face in a vision while looking out my kitchen window at about 3AM. The book we composed together before her death was entitled <u>Through the Storms He Performs.</u>

That same day, at dusk, my eyes detected a lone cloud that looked like a Centurion; I felt that vision was an encounter with The Lord. From 6/22/2015 through most of July, August, and September- I waited in the Florida heat for more of God's skywriting. I almost gave up the search for signs from The Almighty above my head; and then, at sunset, while turning to walk off my dock to enjoy the air-conditioner inside my home, an angelic cloud appeared on the Western horizon. The date that I shot up the sky while gathering photos was 9/22/2015; I was hooked. In spite of the seasonal heat, my soul was on fire to capture more pictures of The Heavens. On 9/25/2015, the vision was a heart-shaped, white, misty area- which I captured for posterity, too. Soon, I began writing about God's communications tied to my pictures.

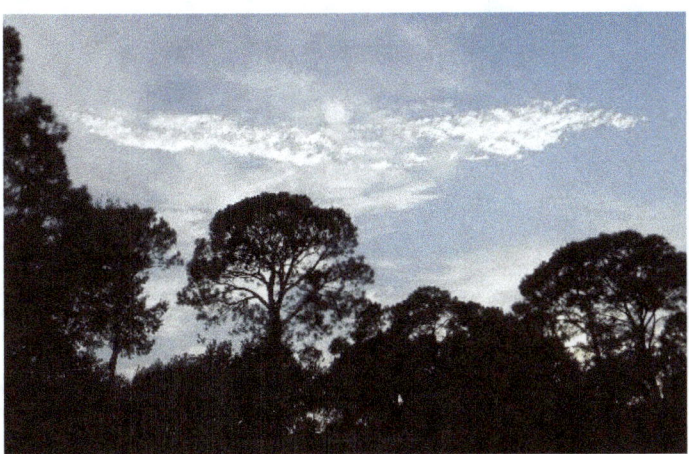 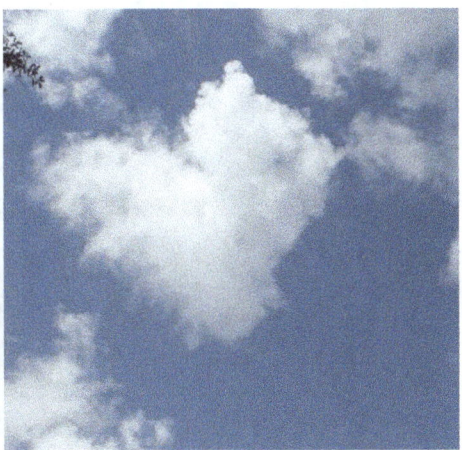

This is the tenth book in my photographic journey series of nonfictions; the snapshots and narrative starts in July of 2021. The original book in the series started on Father's Day 6/21/2015. The basis of my photo journals is to save and share heavenly visions for posterity. With that objective in mind, this narrative continues the ongoing pictorial and written narrative. Photographing the cloudy visions above my head was certainly a new thing for me in 2015. Now, people think I have a misty-scenery habit; I do not. It is too hot in Florida to seek these images outdoors for hours. Thus, I simply look up when The Spirit moves me; and I am blessed.

As I finish each picture diary about skywriting and cloudy images, symbols, or signs- I feel God's messages will stop. In reality, the truth is that He communicates anywhere with humans while using every way imaginable. Therefore, keep looking up via my photos or using your eyes, soul, heart, mind, psyche, and whole Being. In short, let His Spirit guide including with my verbiage that is corroborated with my pictures of my mostly heavenly-based journey of the past "7" years, which is perfect. If nothing else, hopefully, this nonfiction contains some awe-inspiring and miraculous scenes. Along the path to Eternal Paradise, to see more of His Story and visions search the sky as well as all your surroundings including nature with its inborn, intrinsic, deep-rooted, inherent, wonders for life's meaning with or without my guidance.

As you look up into the sky, never peek directly at the sun; or you may ruin your physical vision. Use your camera's lens to help you snap photos for posterity. A picture paints a thousand words; thus, this product will have more photos than words in many chapters; some of my previous books may fill in the gaps with explanations. According to The Bible God is The Light and Love. This book contains some glimpses into His version of Resting In Peace for Eternity in Paradise. If the bottom of Heaven is this beautiful, can you imagine the rest?

Chapter 1: The Light Helps Beauty Shine

"Everything is beautiful in its own way," are some lyrics from a pop song from ages ago. The Heavens are not only stunning but they may speak to the heart and soul of the viewer. Another tune may set the tone forever in your heart; "You are so beautiful to me."

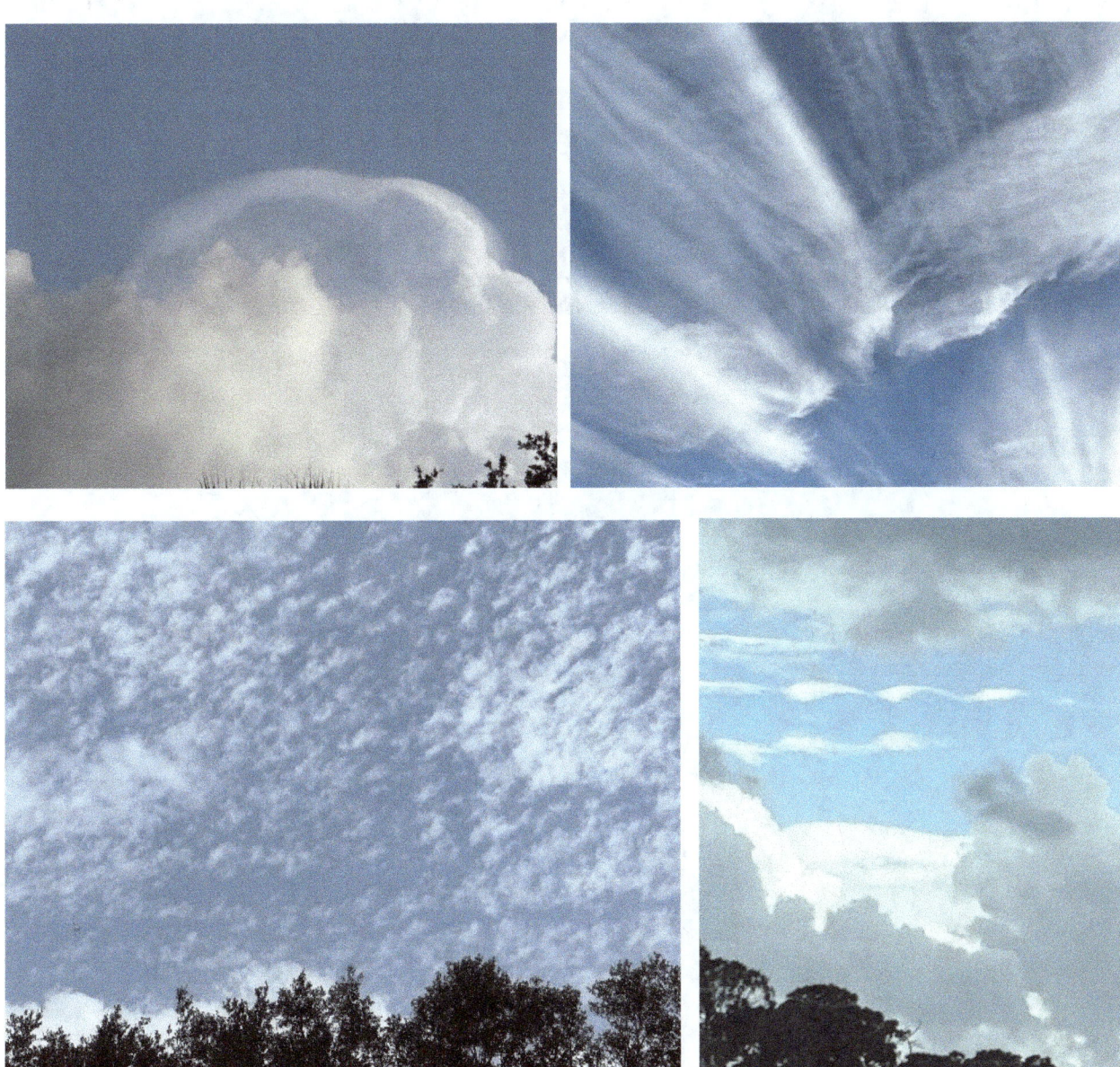

12/6: After a long list of chores completed, I informed my hubby; "I'm going outside to snap... the sun." I remind myself often, to prevent blindness, never look directly into the fireball; instead, point the camera lens to capture the sky visions. As I walked down the stairs from my porch deck, after turning West towards the slowly setting sun and rounding a bend, I peeked because the main light hid behind thick bamboo. I noticed a sun corona blending into another area in The Heavens, which created more, colorful, iridescent clouds. The scene grew into a sunbow often referred to as a fire bow due to its extreme color. The photos are saved for posterity, here.

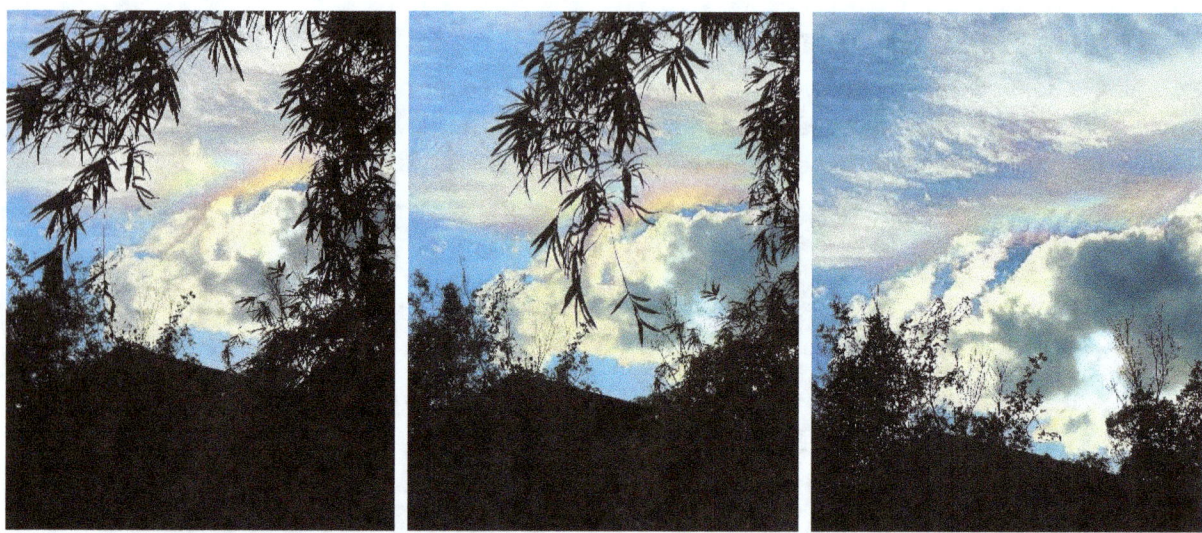

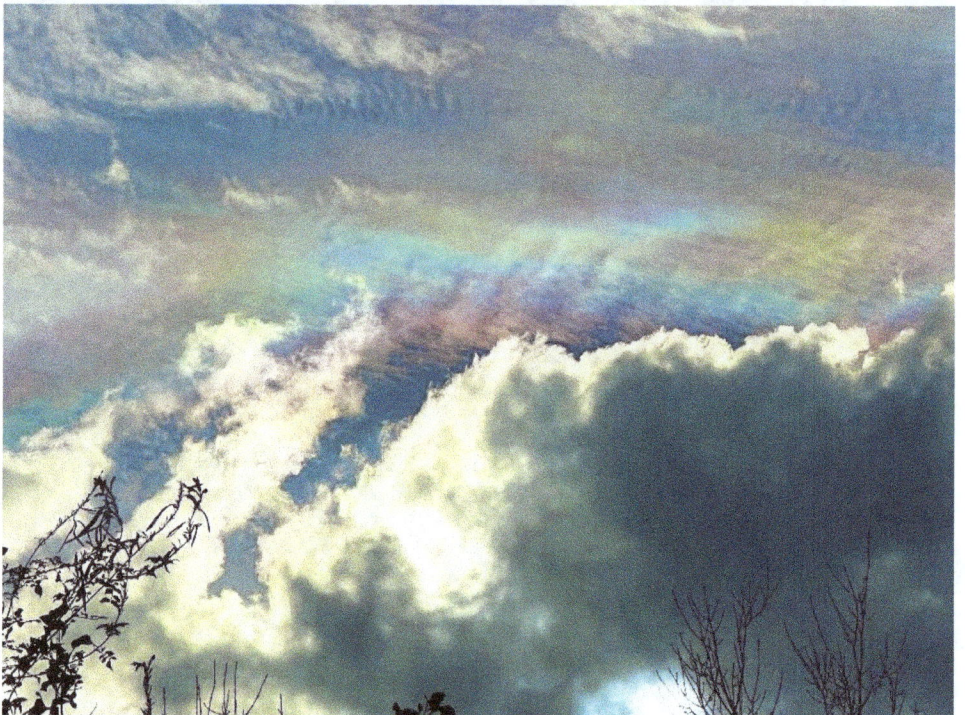

The Lights

Sundog(s)

The Alpha and Omega is The Creator of The Light; in The Bible, Yahweh is referred to as The Light as well. During a sermon, I learned what Epiphany means in the Christian realm. It's translation from Greek is "a light shining in the darkness." Meanwhile, *Sundogs are b*right spots; they are bursts or sparks of color appearing in the same part of the sky as the well-lit center of this Universe. This phenomenon in The Heavens reminds humans of The Man Upstairs and His control of everything; He is Omnipotent.

On a side note, reversing the last three letters of sundog creates the word God. As mentioned in previous books as well as within this nonfiction, an earthbound dog is referred to as man's best friend. For mankind, The Supreme Being is the best friend and most merciful, forgiving spirit in existence.

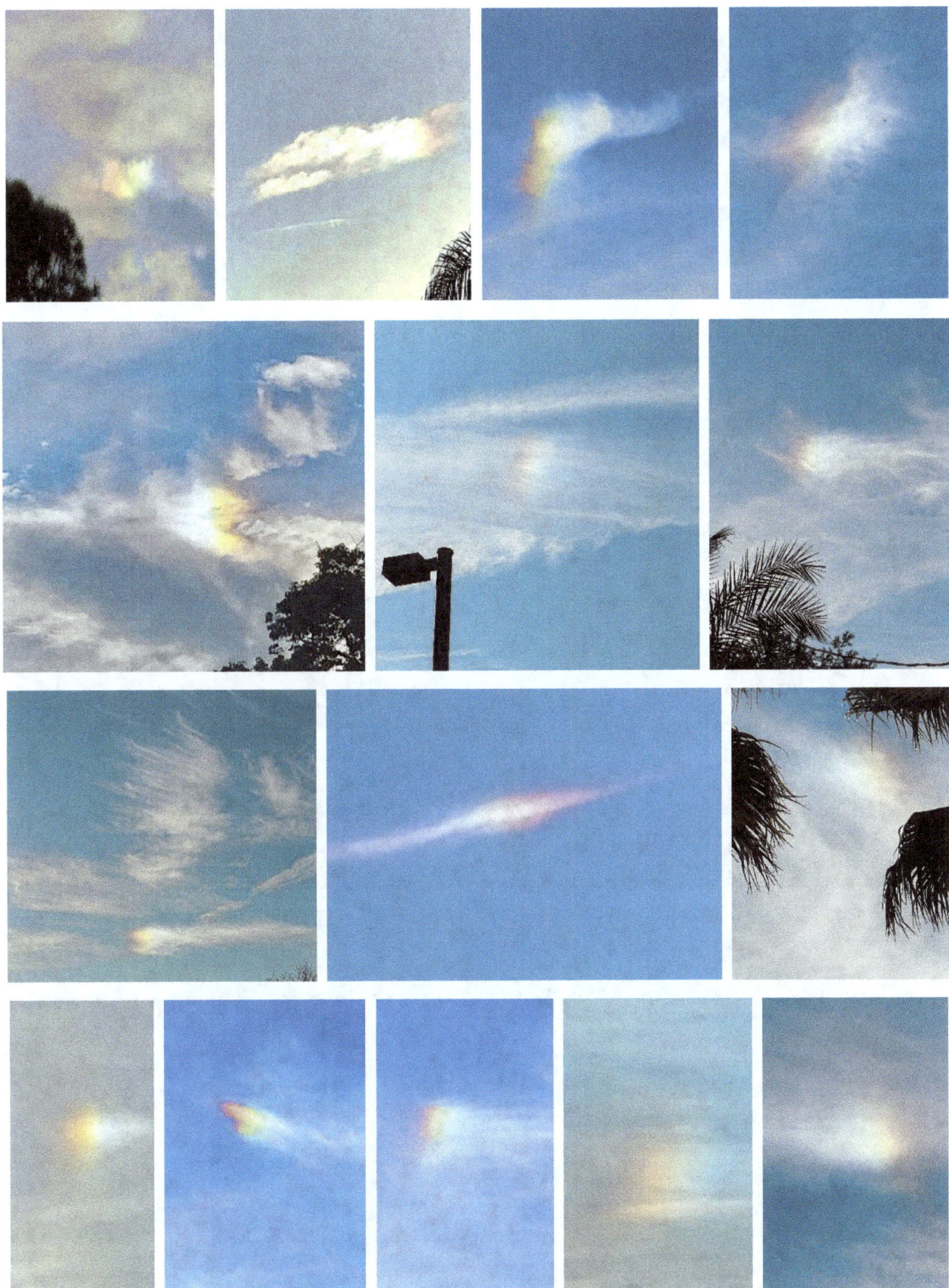

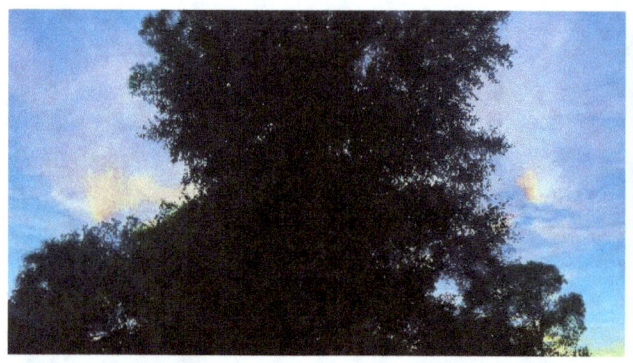 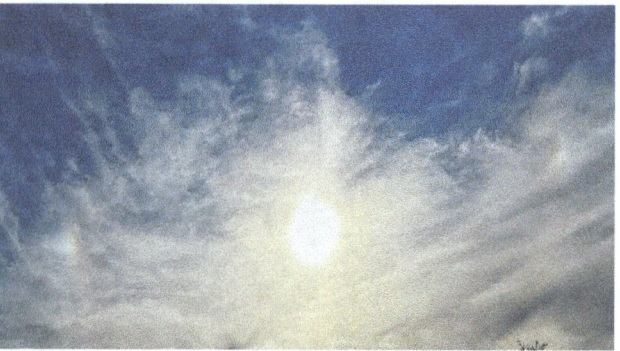

Sunbows or Sun Halos

The visions below have two names, which are sunbows or halos. They are circular areas surrounding The Center of The Universe. Halos and crowns are traditionally worn by the hierarchy or royalty in this world. This phenomenon may be meant to remind humans of the presence of Heavenly Crowned heads aka The King of kings and His Son The Prince of Peace.

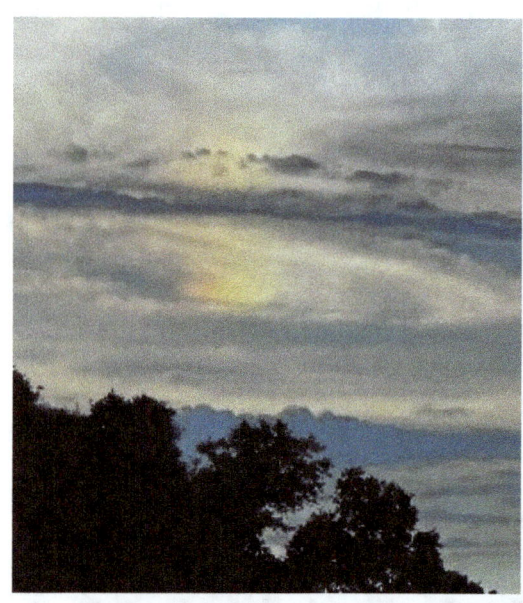 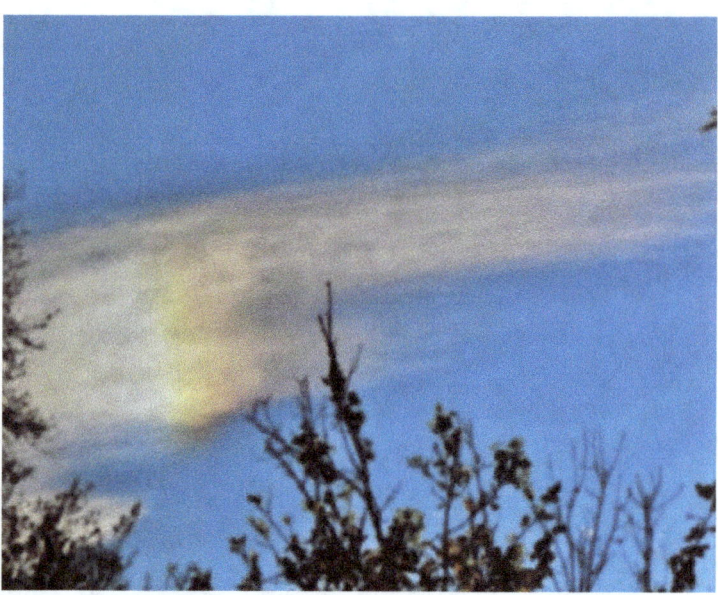

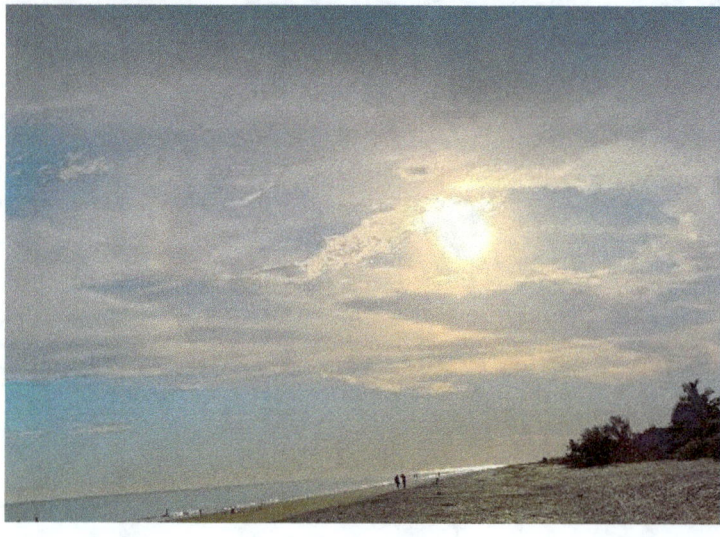 

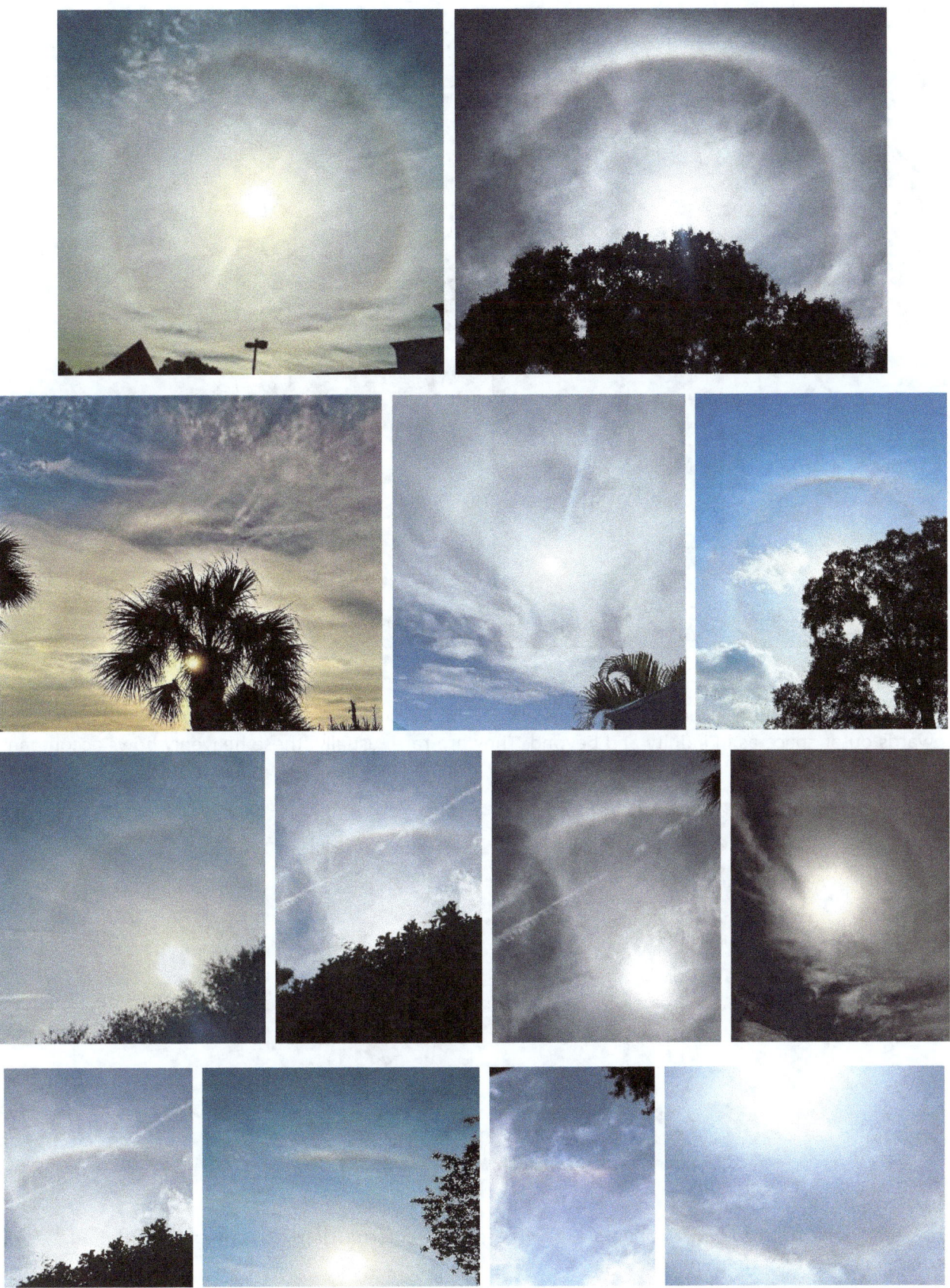

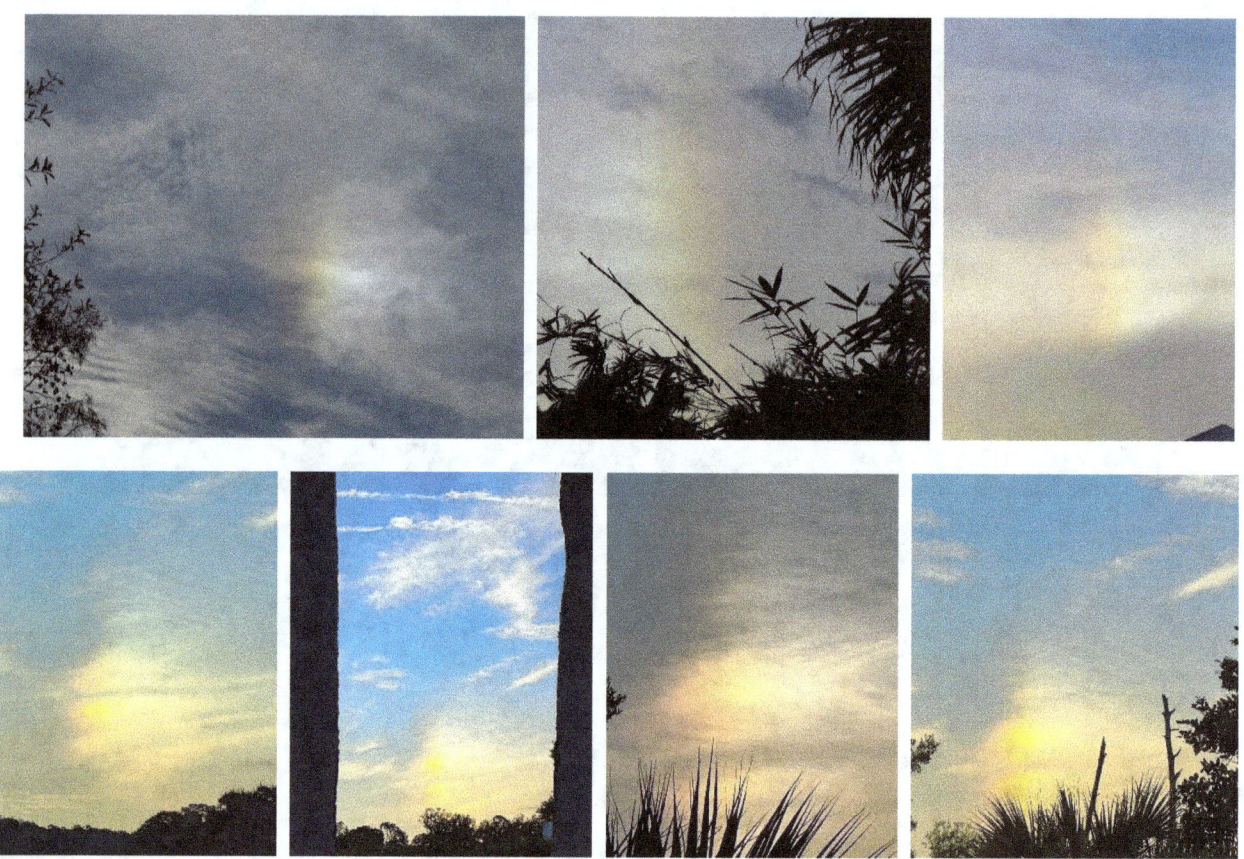

Sun Halo accompanied by a Circumzenithal Arc

Circumzenithal Arcs are inverted semicircles above The Center of The Universe; their open ends point towards outer space as in infinity and beyond. They are rare; usually, these heavenly bows accompany sunbows or halos.

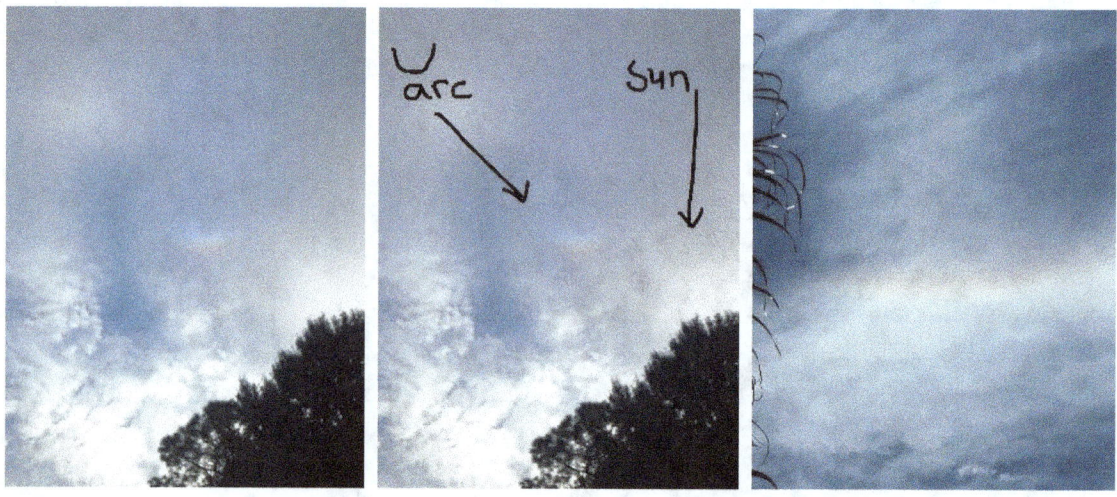

Sun Coronas

These rainbow-like, heavenly wonders are witnessed as colorful rings directly around the sun. They project the beauty of Heaven.

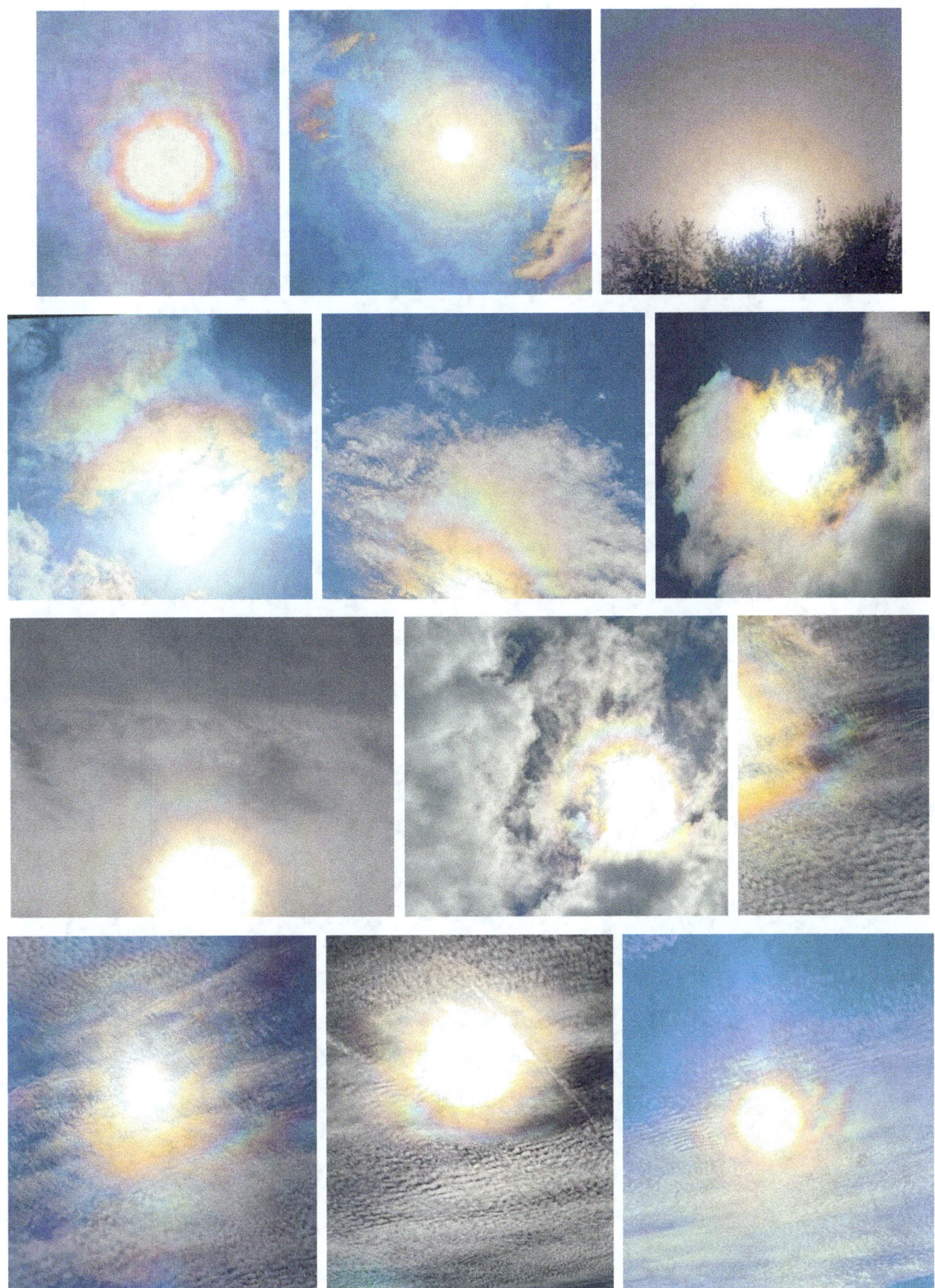

Iridescent Clouds
These misty areas have irregular colors pouring out into clouds near the sun. The Light does wonderous things in the sky above The Earth. Can you imagine the beauty of The Supreme Being's Kingdom?

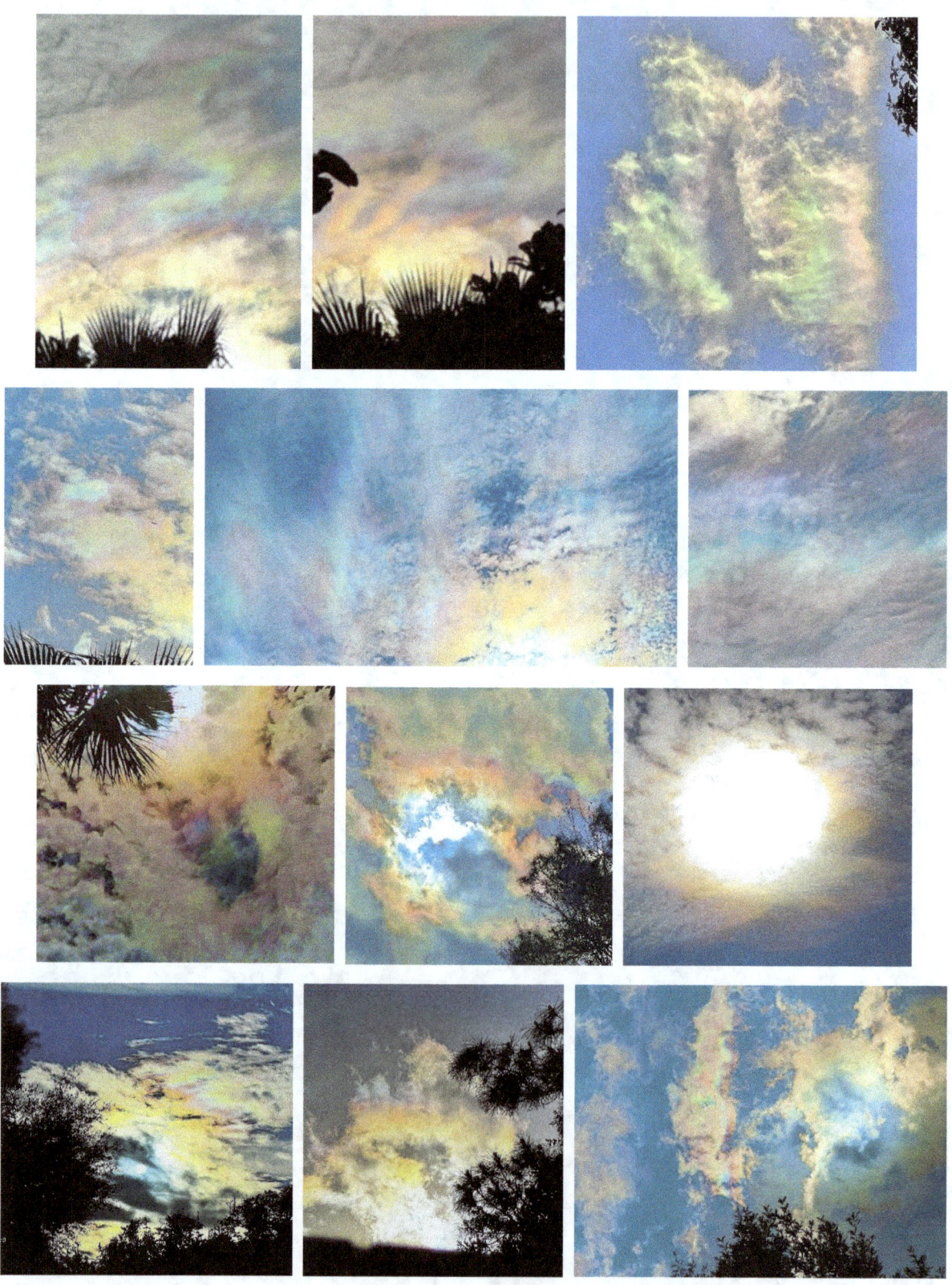

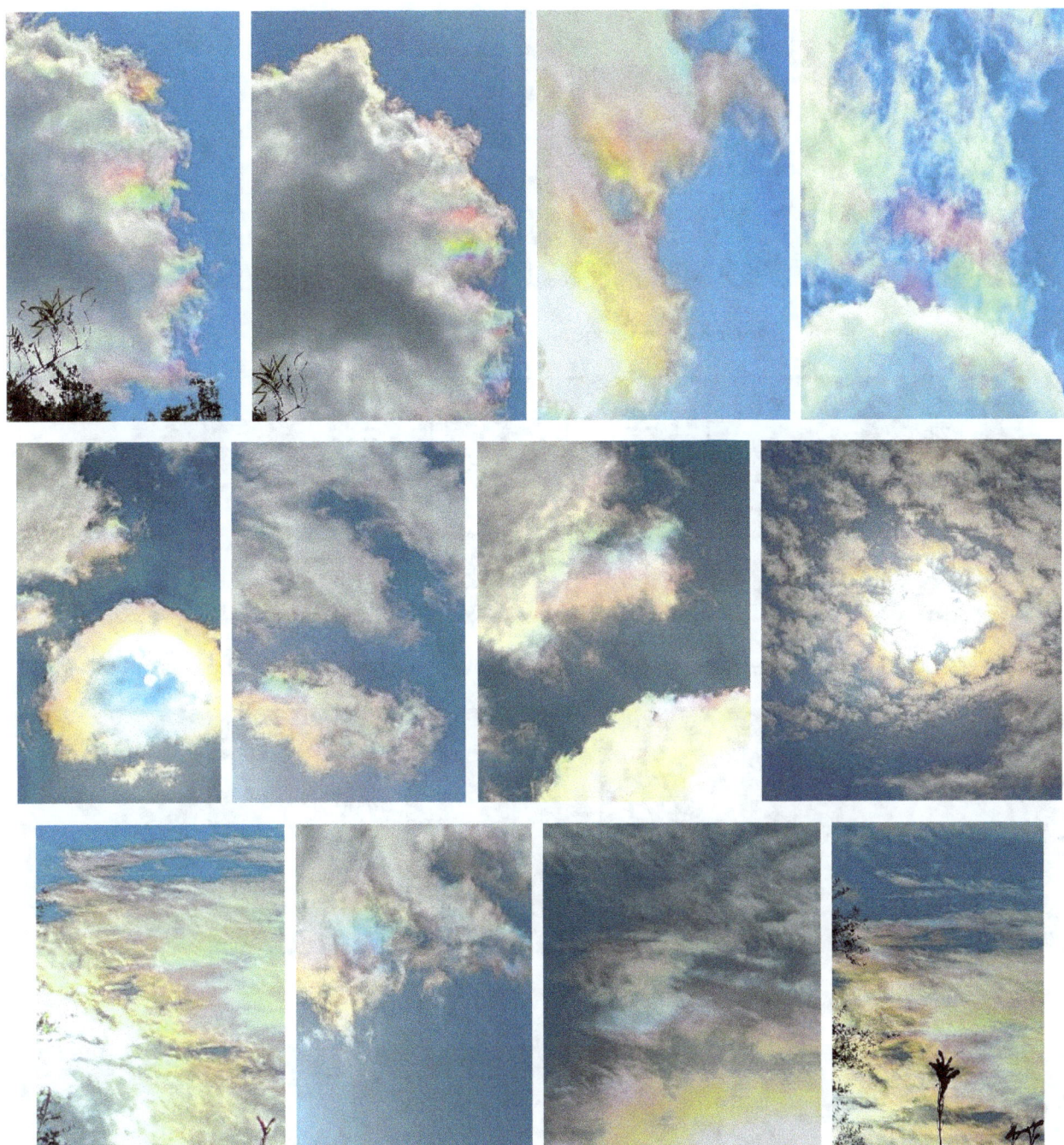

Moonlight
The Central Light of The Universe is mirrored on the moon. In addition, God's Son manifested His Father's goals via The Lords's life in action, words, and compassion for mankind; that man reflected The Almighty's nature. The Prince of Peace came to teach the way towards reconciliation with The Father and others using goodwill, kindness, helpfulness, benevolence, generosity, and caring in this world and The Afterlife. Jesus lived and personified The Law of Love aka The Golden Rule as in the 10 Commandments, which should be activated in real life circumstances and actions by an individual or society. (Matthew 7:12; Luke 6:31)

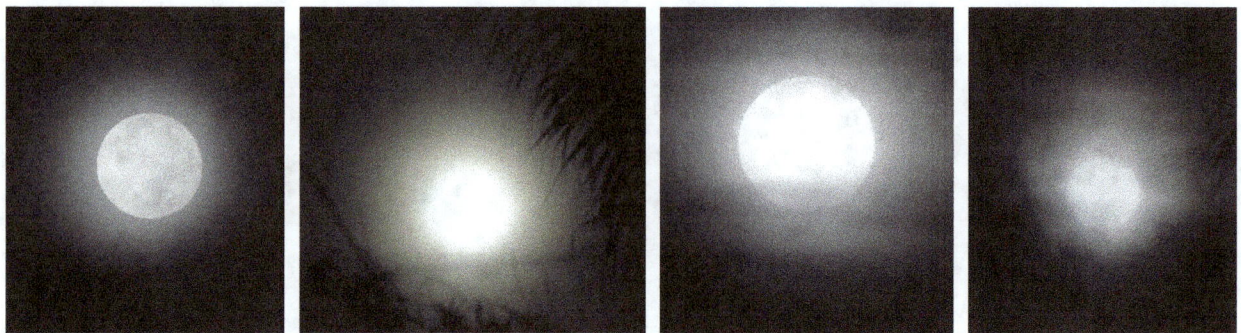

Moon auras or coronas and moon rays can happen.

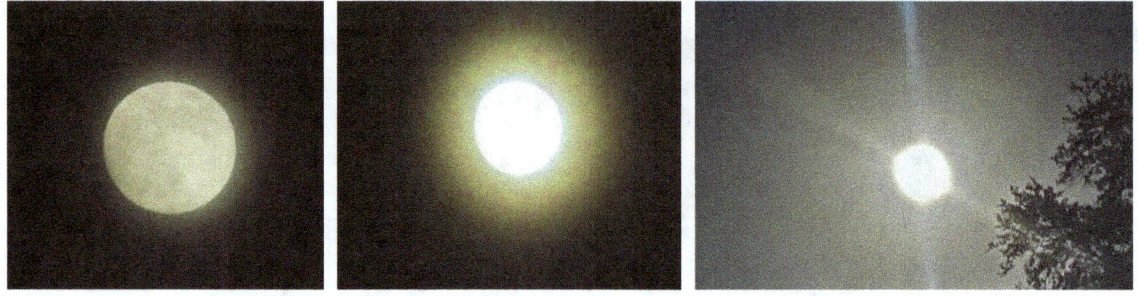

8/20: My granddaughter told her mom to tell me that I'd love the moon, tonight. She was right!

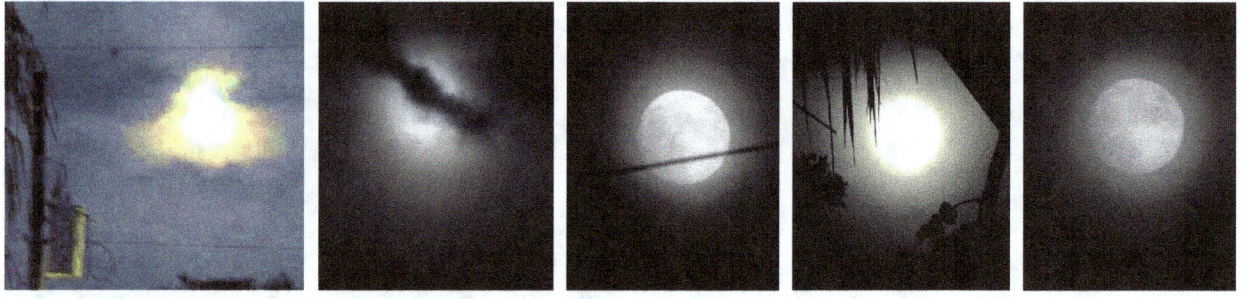

Is this The Man or boy in the moon? That answer may arrive later, Gator.

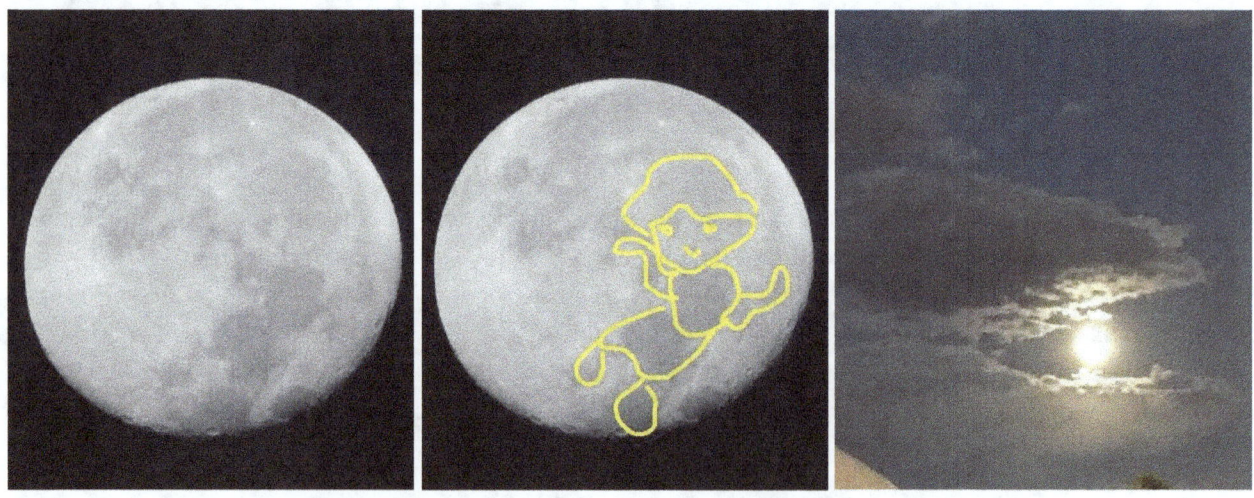

12/18: When The Light reflects its sunrays onto the moon and the interaction is visible to the world, there is hope. In short, there is no reason to curse the darkness. When beauty shines, Emmauel, which means God is with us, brings the generosity of Christmas to lives and inspires the soul to spread The Good News of love. it's a wonderful life. Or, as Mr. Roger's might sing; "It's a beautiful day in the neighborhood..." The scene below arrived near The Lord's birth day (birthday). Combining forces with The Almighty Father bring about perfection on this planet aka peace on Earth and goodwill to mankind. Keep looking up as well as all around you to find the beauty in this world.

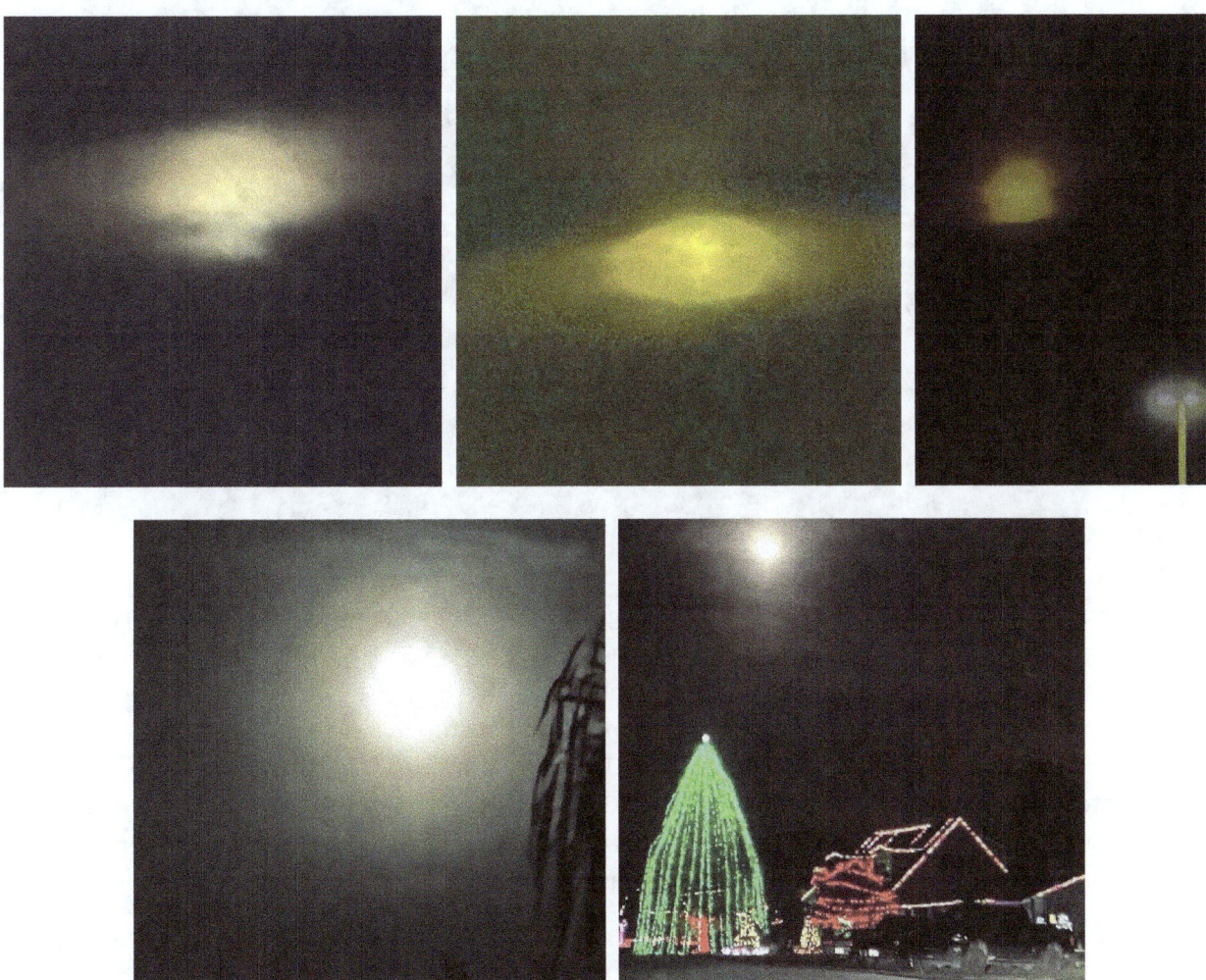

Chapter 2: God's Signs, Symbols, Skywriting, and Ideas

According to The Bible, God is Love, which includes mercy and compassion for the world beneath Him. "I AM" is The best, benevolent ruler ever. During the writing of this nonfiction, the next photos were taken and seem to point to Yahweh's plan. According to some misty arrows, That Supreme Being is here, there, and everywhere seeking a good and loving relationship with mankind.

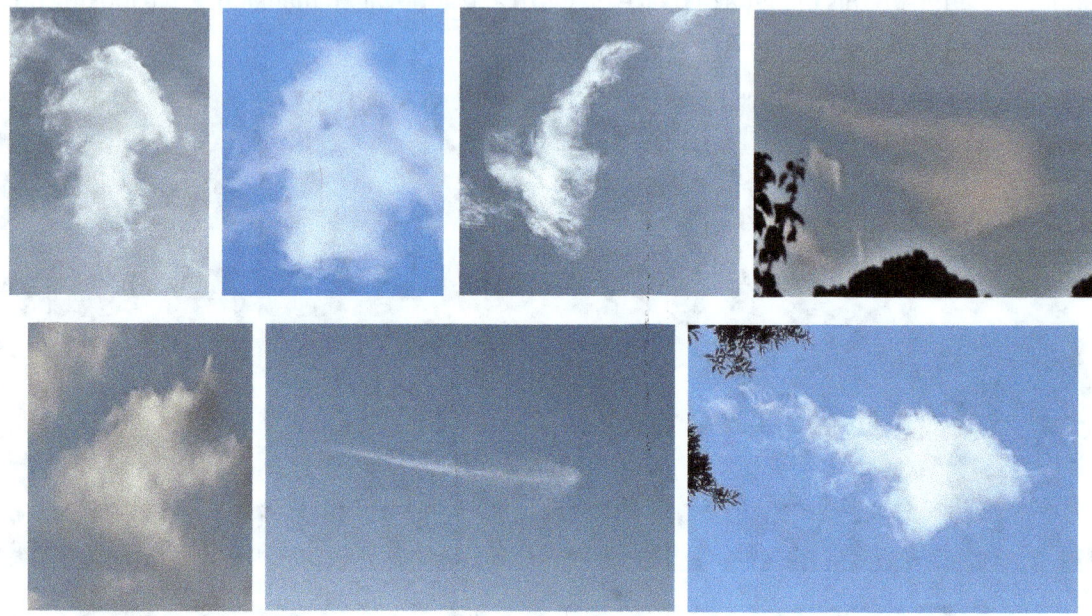

The Creator is

The Maker of Heaven and Earth is The Supreme Being and The Light radiating empathy and mercy to those souls willing to enter into a healthy relationship with Him. (Genesis 1:3) That's True or Heaven-sent Love. Via cloudbanks, it appears that The Alpha and Omega of The Universe symbolically draws "I heart" meaning "I Love." The multitude of hearts, that I captured for posterity, reveal His unlimited affection for the world; His fondness for mankind unveils using The skywriting. The Almighty appears to be inviting humans into a healthy relationship with Him. The Clouds, also, seem to indicate Heaven welcomes its followers with open arms. The Power of Love might be reminding mankind through misty signs that The Almighty has mountains of affection to share with His Creations.

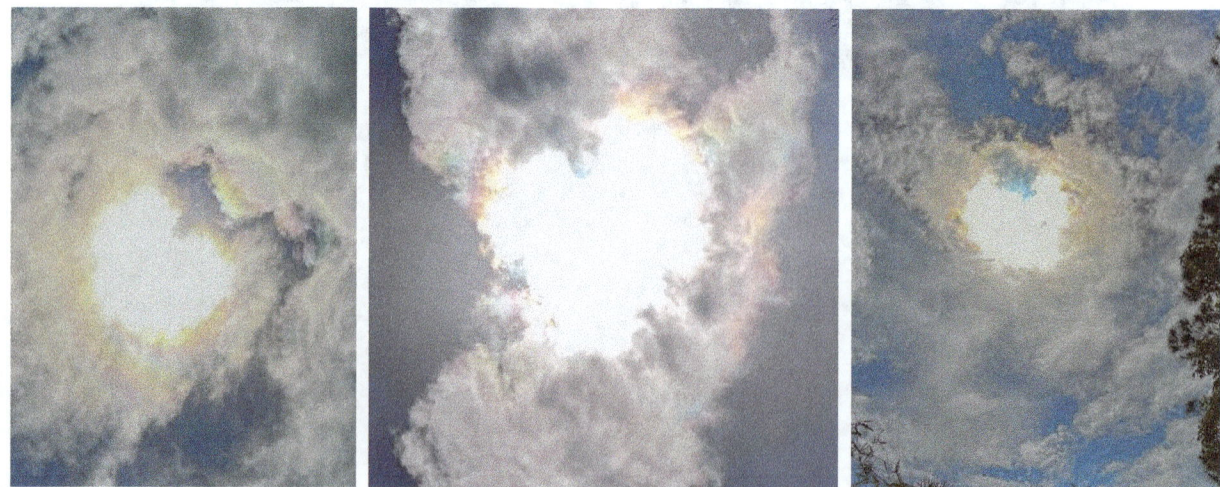

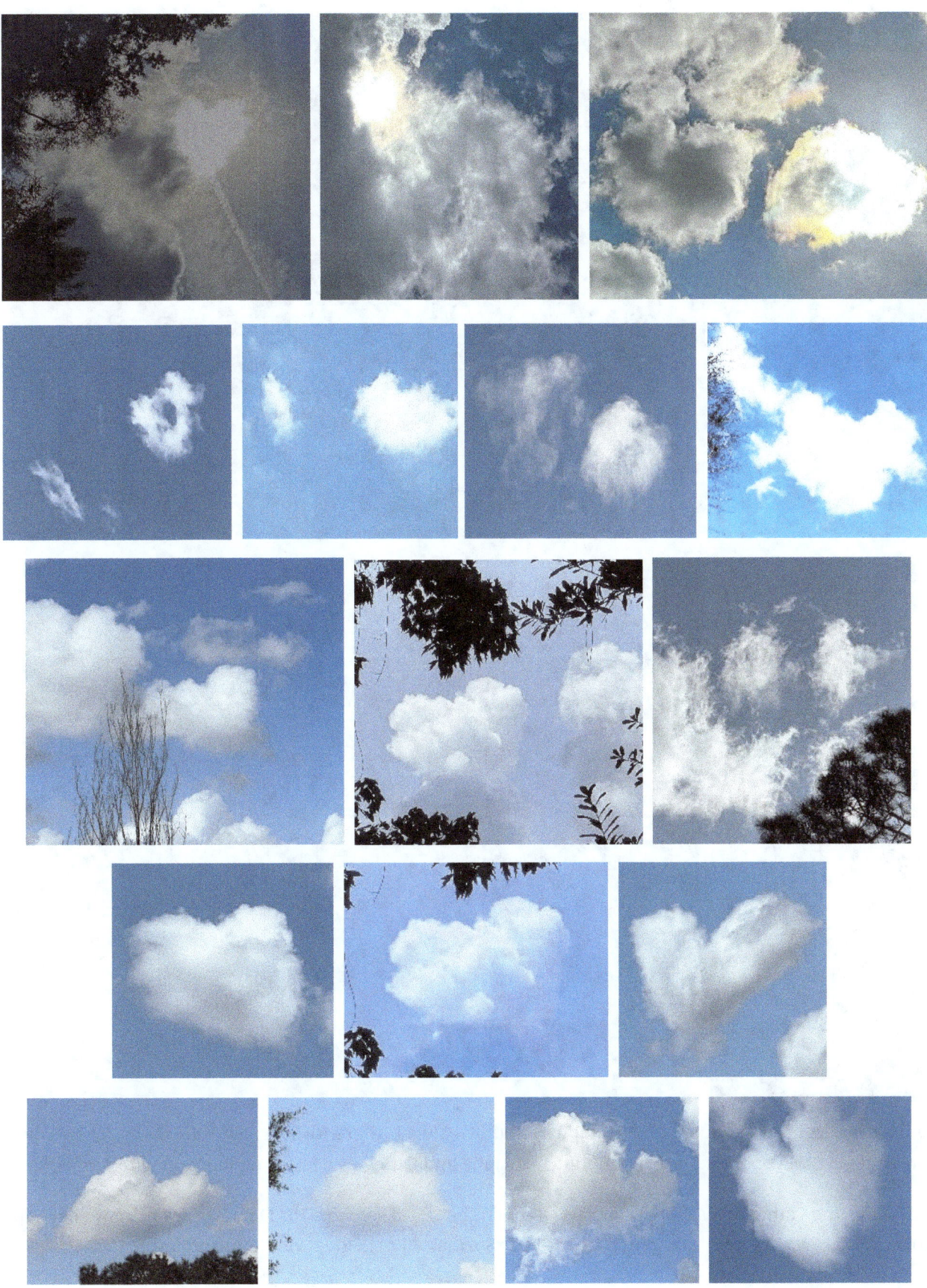

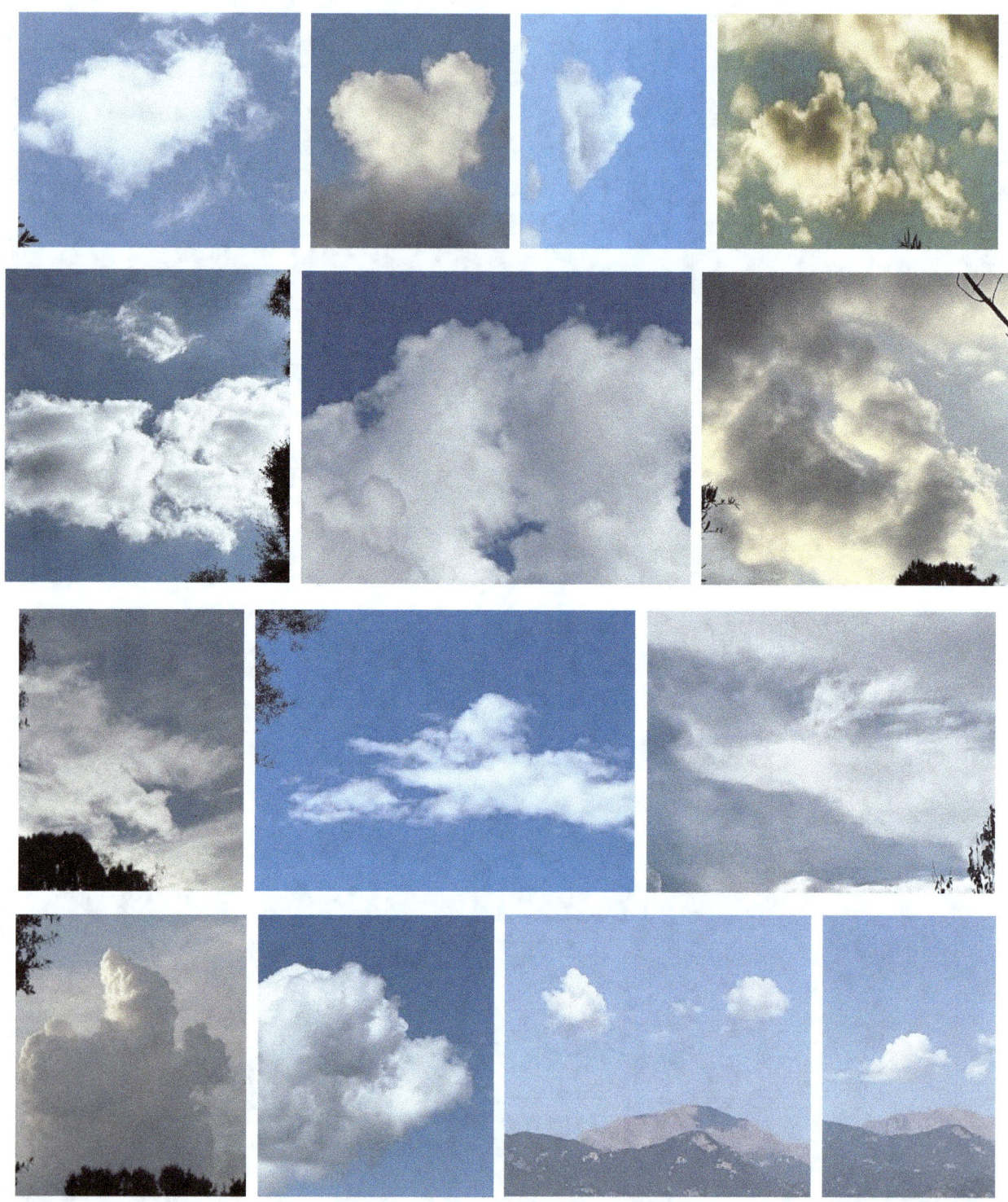

Sometimes, its hard to understand or find Love but it's always there for The Faithful. Let His light shine and your eyes will open to The Truth about The Alpha and Omega's desired connection with mankind.

8/17: God The Father loves all His children so much that He'd sacrifice His Only Begotten Son to save the world. The skywriting with two joined clouds seems to say, "I'm in love with 'C'hrist my son." "I AM' is The

King of kings while Jesus The Christ is The "P"rince of "P"eace that was sent to illuminate, exemplify, and live the personification of The Law of Love aka The Golden Rule aka The 10 Commandments.

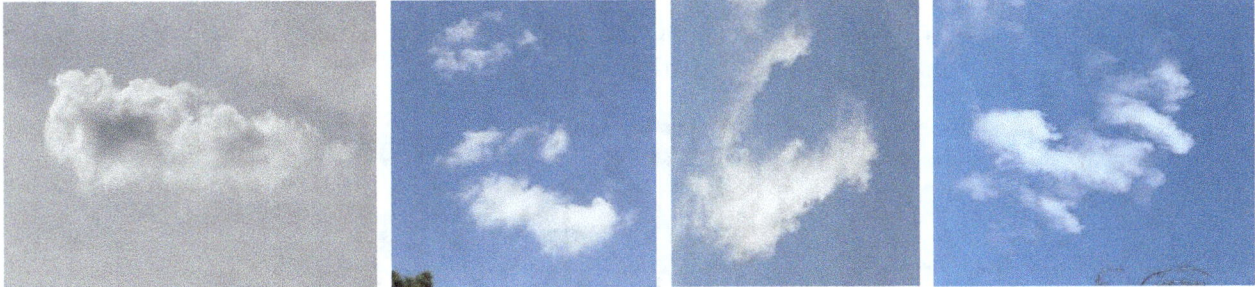

Other related images arrived in The sky and cloudbanks during the writing of this book.

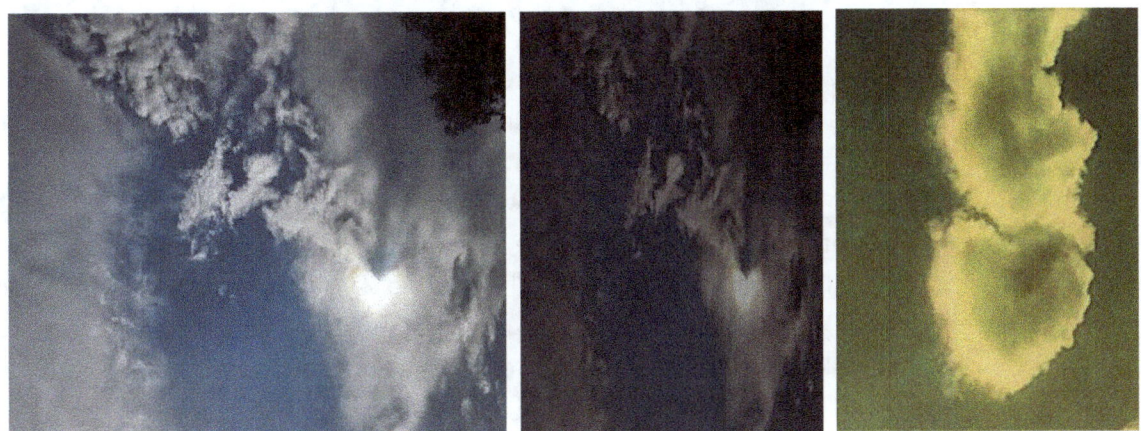

9/24: A day before the 6th anniversary of my first, love cloud spotting- God provided a Valentine's Day type of a heart. Perhaps, His main message to this world is that His affection for humans prevails. Keep looking up through the haze in order to see the splendor as well as The Almighty's messages and goals for mankind. Is the last photo in this series showing Moses with The 10 Commandment Tablets as in Yahweh's ten guidelines to a better life on Earth as well as in The Afterlife? Or, is that misty vision depicting some Being holding The Book of Life that is read on Judgement Day? The tablets of The 10 Commandments explain His Will. If you truly love someone, something, or some place- then- you show honor and respect. You, also, try hard to keep from doing any harm. The end goal is to enjoy Eternal Paradise with The Originator of merciful and compassionate behavior aka The Alpha and Omega.

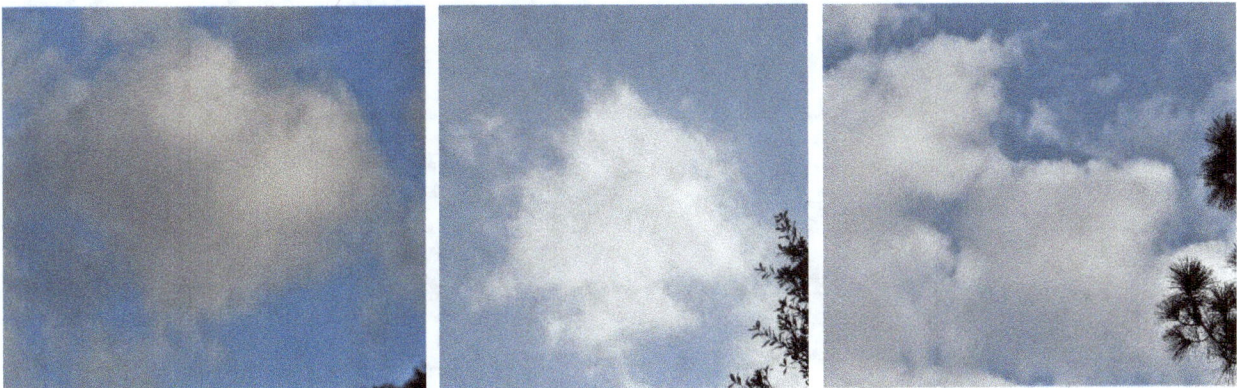

Rainbows

10/4: My youngest granddaughter and I went to the back porch after an early morning shower. She asked what I was looking for; when I said that my eyes were searching for a rainbow, she brought me a stool. She proved that God is here, there, and everywhere and not limited by human vision or simply living in Heavenly thoughts while unaware of this world. It's that simple.

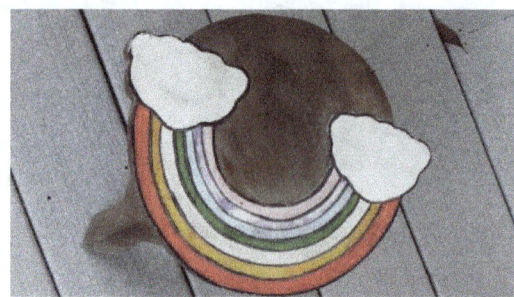

Most people know that rainbows arrive in the sky opposite the sun; they are normally a colorful arch or a double type. The pinker ones arrive near dawn or dusk. In reality, bows as well as vibrant colors can be found all over the sky as The Almighty unveiled via my photos on countless occasions; some of that beauty is chronicled in my nonfictions including this one. Meanwhile, historically, every Hebrew and Christian knows about Noah's Ark and his covenant with God. The Supreme Being promised never again to flood the world or kill off hordes of its inhabitants. The colorful arc in the sky reminds mankind of that simple promise and the eternal love The Maker of Heaven and Earth has for His creations. (Genesis 9:16-18) Sometimes, people have to look hard to see the rainbow or promise of God being fulfilled or completed. In short, don't stop believing in The Almighty's mercy and compassion.

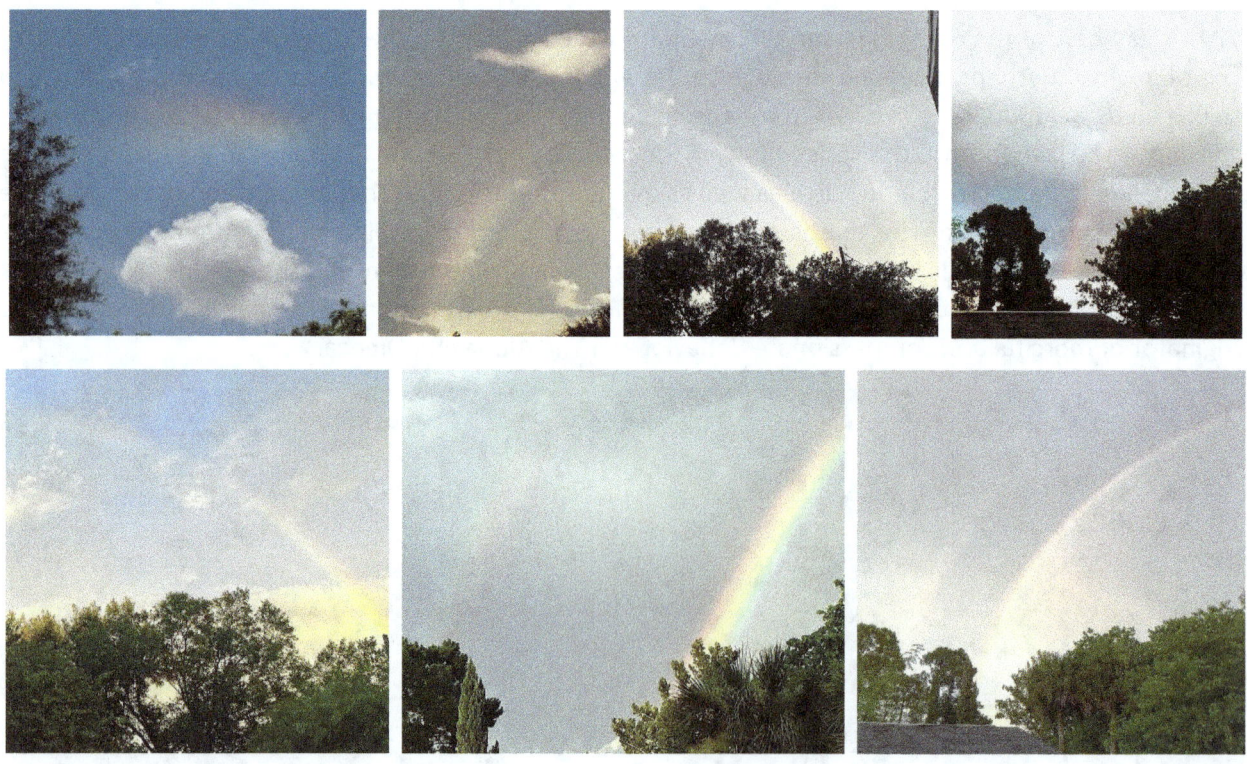

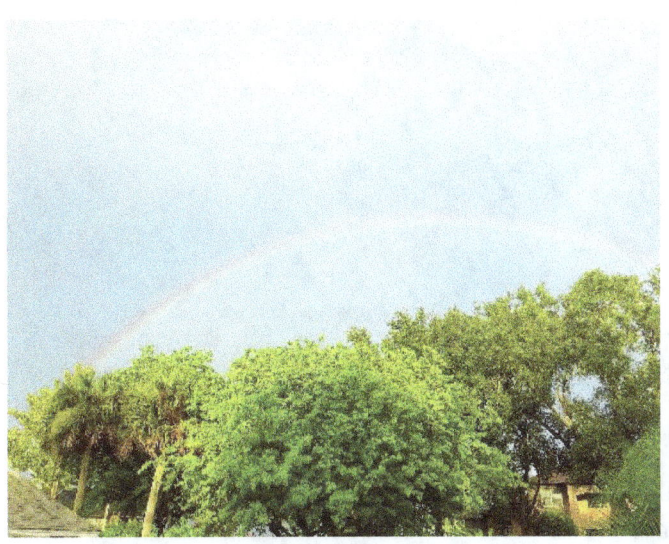
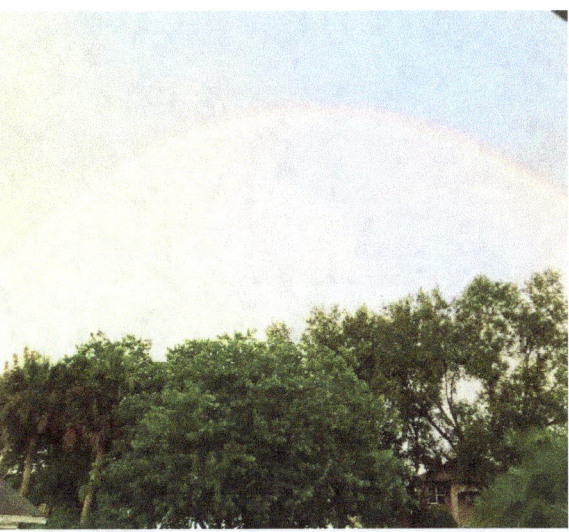
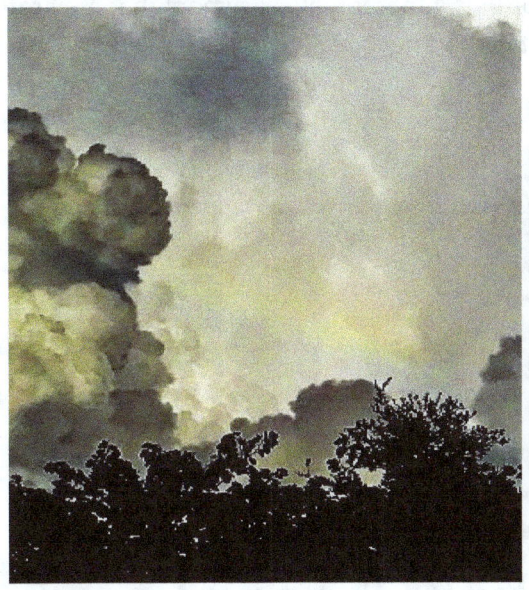
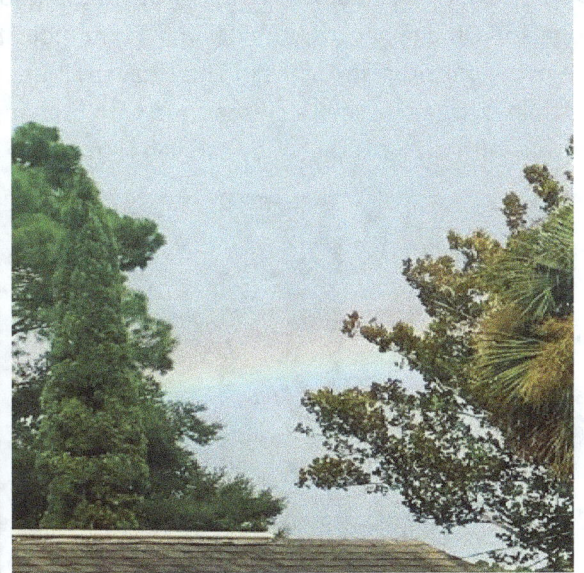

Twin Rainbows

A very uncommon vision happens in the sky when two different sized raindrops fall during a storm. That irregular precipitation can cause a colorful semicircle to overlay or overlap another multihued arc or the primary or dominant arch allowing a "Twin Rainbow" to materialize. This is not a double rainbow because the colors are not reversed and usually they blend into a single vision that almost appears to be a normal, simple rainbow to an observer. People unaware of the possible, weather phenomenon may simply marvel at the fatter than normal semicircle.

On 9/14, while in Colorado, a rare, Twin Rainbow appeared right as someone mentioned that the rain in the front of the patio had much larger droplets and seemed heavier than the misty other side of that area. In the next photos, the lighter or less obvious curve is skewed a bit down while over the larger, colorful semicircle. It's an extraordinary Twin Rainbow. Is Yahweh reminding this world of the Noah promise as well as the pledge Jesus The Christ made that one day He'd return to this world to finish what He started? We are privileged to have at least two promises from The Triune God or Trinity.

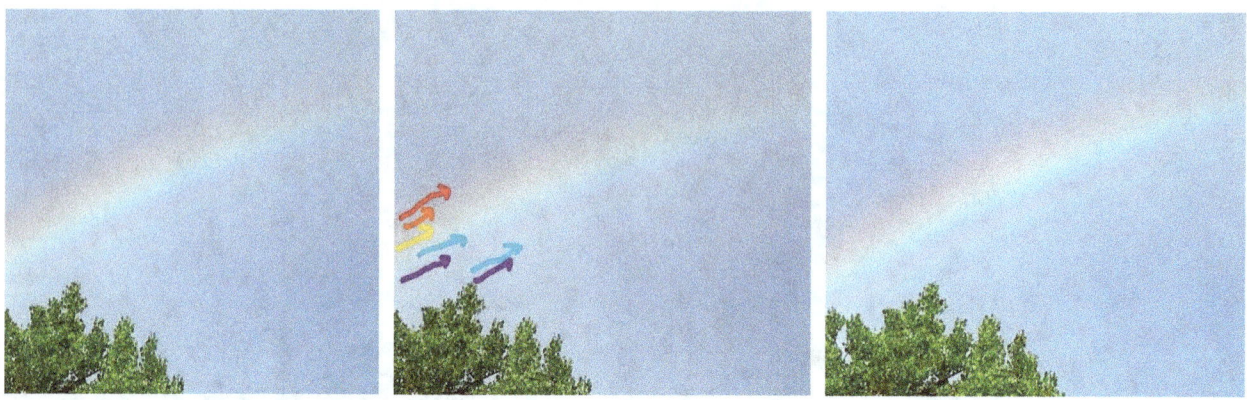

The Creator's Skywriting

Sometimes, skywriting appears in The Heavens without the help of planes. In some photos, the letter "g" or "G" may point to a "g"ood thing or be a "G"od indicator. A letter "F" probably means God The "F"ather. The Supreme Being is, also, known as "Y"ahweh. Phi or PI is a mathematical symbol that may reference The Alpha and Omega because the decimal point indicates that the right side is infinite like Him. According to some misty patterns and signs in The Heaven, it appears The Supreme Being might be communicating with earthlings. Does He seek a closer bond with humans? It seems like The Almighty wants a close enough relationship with humans that they can call Him by the nickname Al.

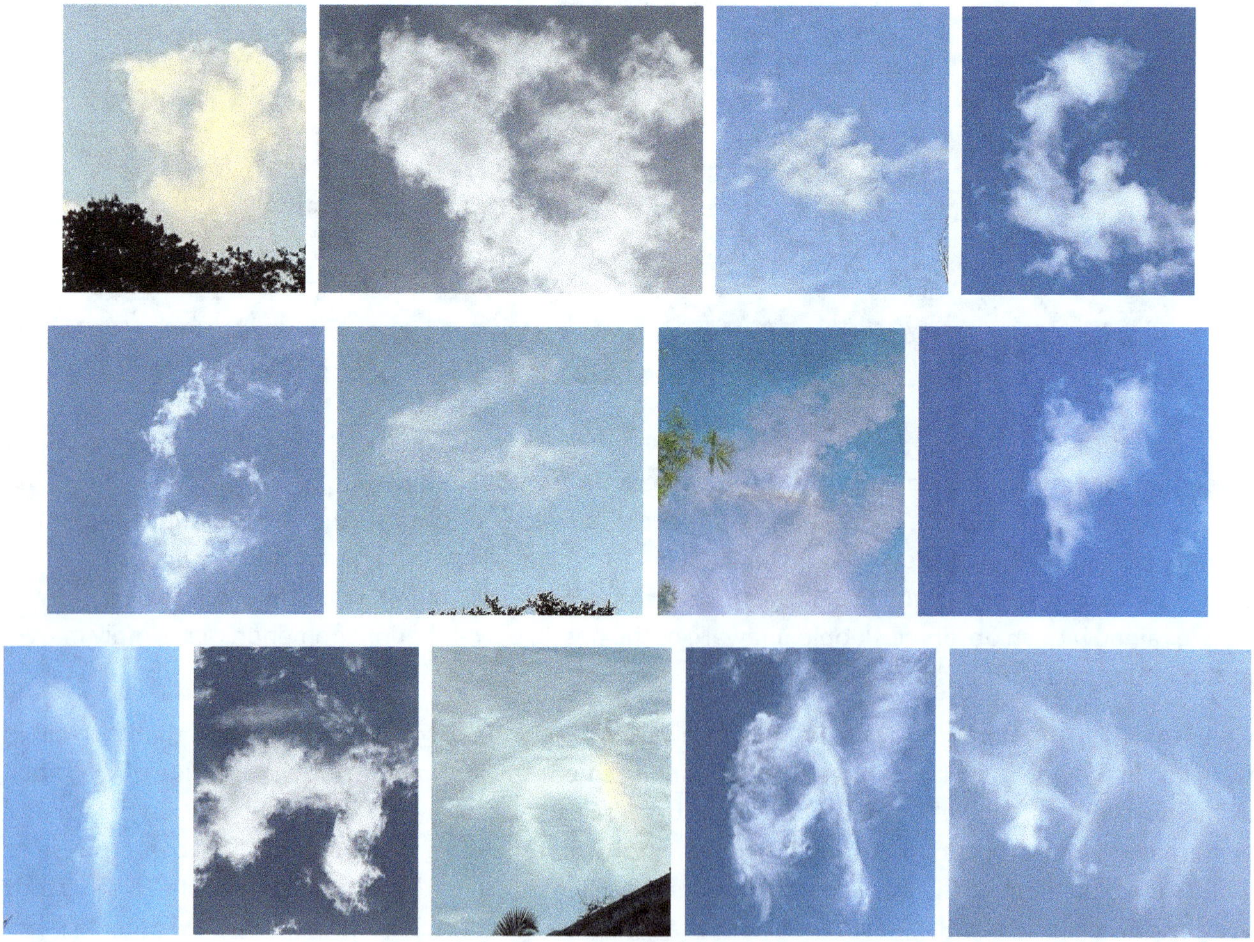

Meaningful Numbers

The Alpha and Omega desires a good relationship with His creations including humans. The number "5" refers to wholesome and respectable interactions and associations. When I snapped a "High 5" cloud, more than likely, the vision points to The Almighty's desire for healthy connections between man and Him as well as humans with one another. That would make a perfect world or be heavenly. Biblically, the number "7" represents God's perfection and excellence. For instance, there are seven days in the week that cycle the years and seasons in an easy and mathematically manageable style. The Designer believed that The Universe was beautiful as well as picture-perfect; that's probably one reason why The Supreme Being rested on the last day of the week to enjoy His creations.

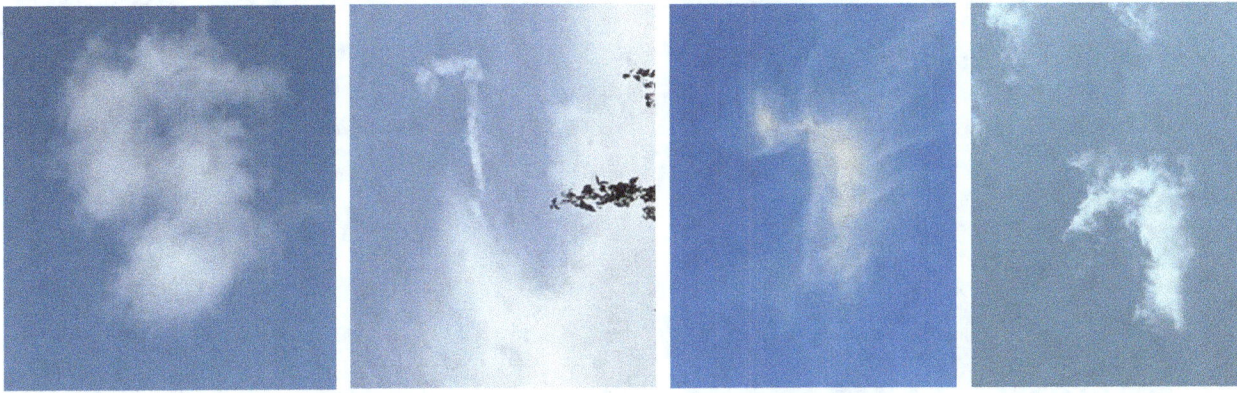

Misty Symbols such as: a Lion, an Elephant, The Wise Old Owl, and Santa

There are many cloudy signs of God; more than likely, the imagery drawn by Him in The Heavens is a part of His communications with this place. That Supreme Being is similar to a lion or king of the Jungle; The Master of The Universe is The King of all kings.

Similar to an elephant, The Almighty never forgets His own; He's that smart. Some people refer to The Maker as The Wise Old Owl.

By the way, He is, also, like Santa because He sees it all; and He knows when a soul is naughty or nice.

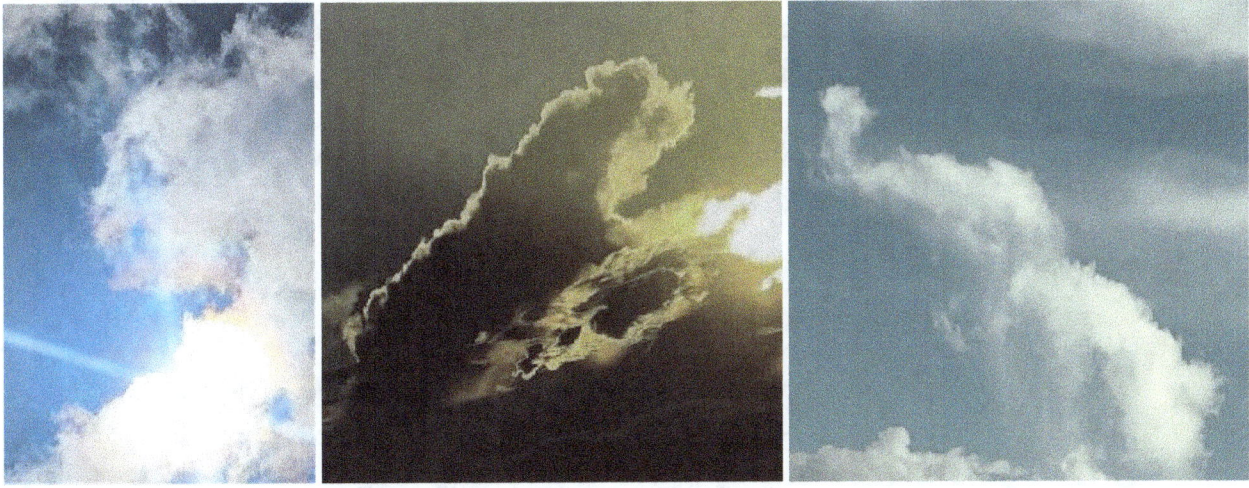

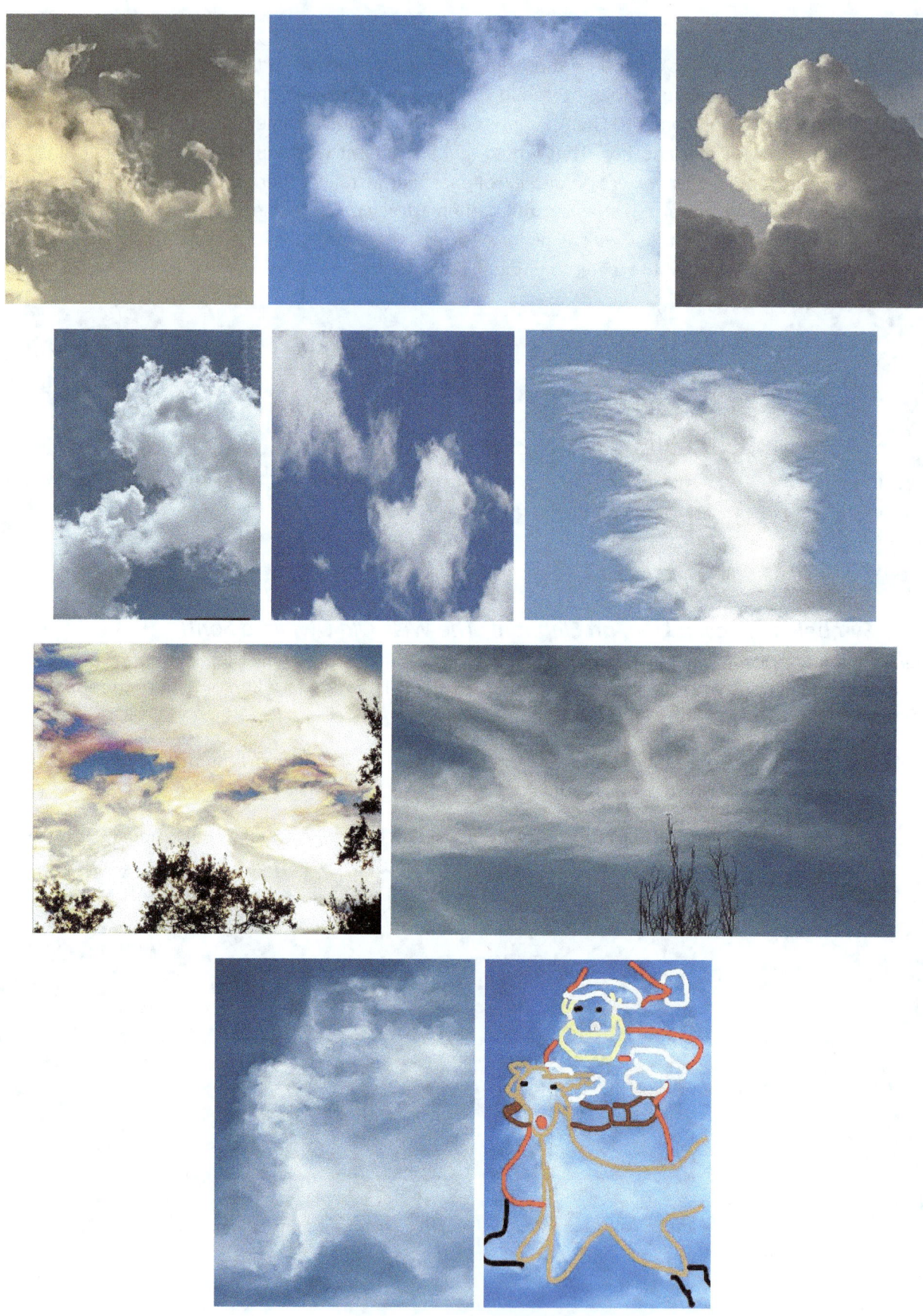

The Messiah Arrived to...
Jesus The Christ came to bring sinners out of darkness brought on by the evil in this world.

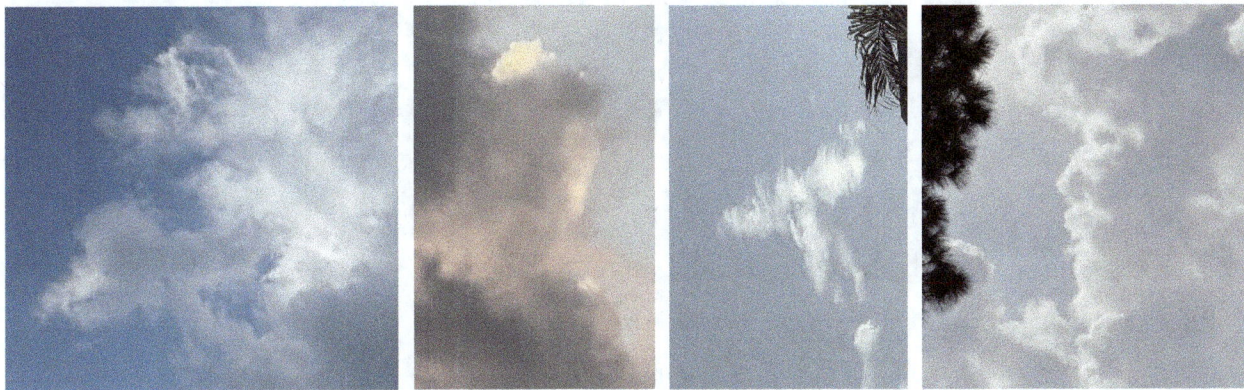

Symbols for Jesus The Christ include: A Lamb, Bunny, Fish, and Bread
In Sacred Scripture, Jesus is the Sacrificial Lamb of God due to His willing acceptance of His Cross to bear. Some misty clouds may be there to remind us that this world is near the threshold to Heaven. In photo number one, do you see a lamb? There are other visions that point to Jesus aka The Prince of Peace. For example, a bunny is passive similar to Jesus. In addition, Christ called himself The Bread of Life; in one picture, a sundog highlights that thought. Along with loaves of bread, a fish in the clouds reminds Christians of one of many miracles that The Lord performed while in human form. He multiplied a meal that included bread and fish to feed the masses arriving to hear His sermons. In a miraculous way, The Good Shepherd fed His flock or followers.

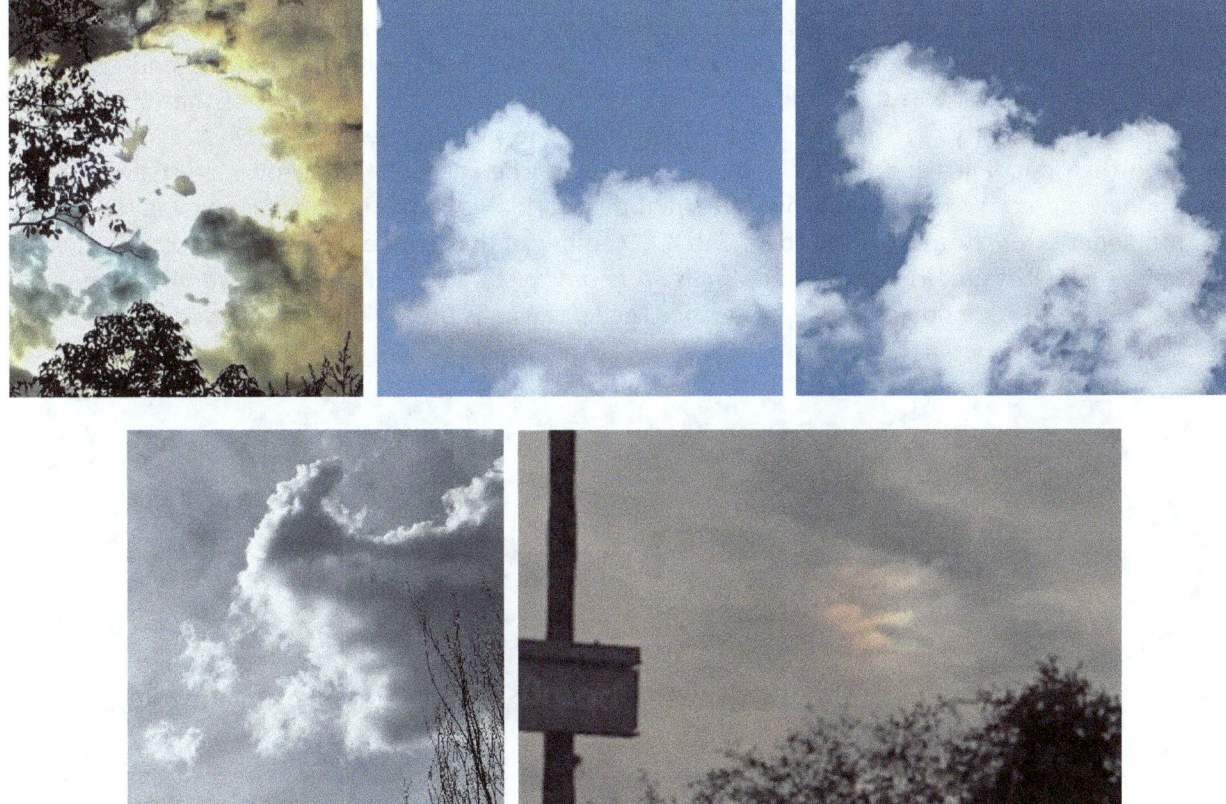

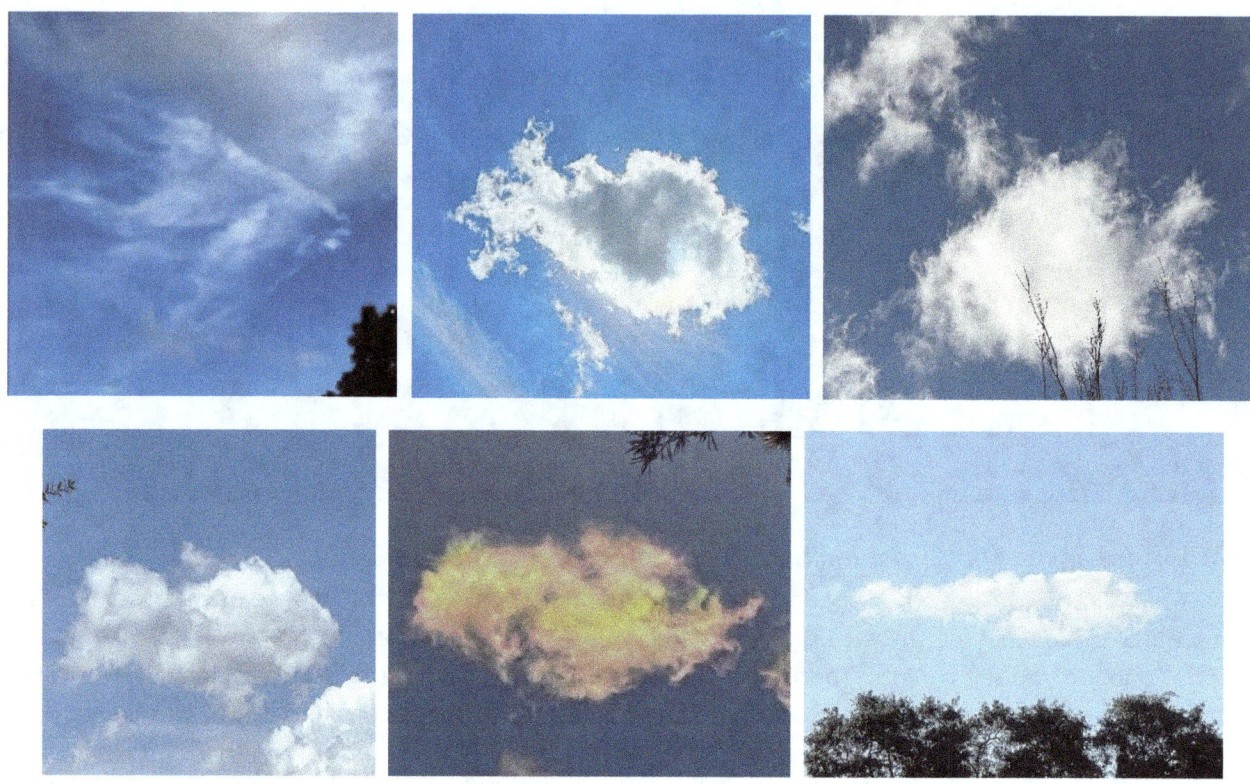

Skywriting Including "T" or "t", "E' or "e", "v", and "IV"

A cross could simply be a letter in the sky; without the "t" in the beginning, all you have is rust. It appears that some of the skywriting photographed for posterity points to The Christian Savior. Meanwhile, a capital "T" may represent the Tau Cross of Jesus, which is a variation in how it is presented symbolically. It reminds people that The Redeemer sacrificed His life to save Homo sapiens from evil and give every individual a chance at The Best, Afterlife. A letter "e" or "E" may be an indicator of that Eternity; The Cornerstone of Humanity aka The Christian Messiah reopenned The Pearly Gates to HIs faithful followers. Reflect on that idea. Furthermore, a cloudy "V" proclaims The Lord's "v"ictory over eternal death and damnation. It represents His triumph over the sin of this world. His Father in Heaven unveiled His plans to heal this planet through His Son; and then, The 2nd Member of that Triune God showed humans the way to conquer the evil of sin. His examples are in His Story or Christ's life. That human personified The Will of God for The Earth to see how to live as man-kind. The Lord was/is the "IV' meant to save the world from its sick and sinful ways.

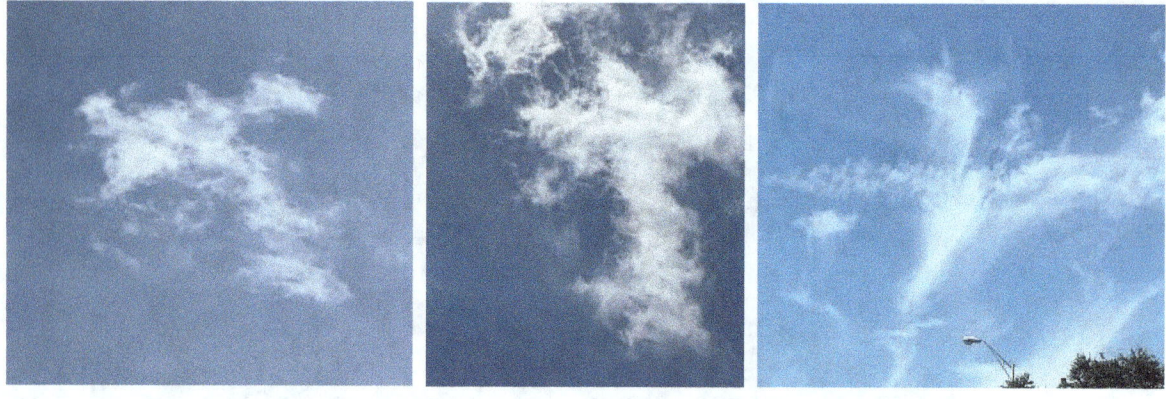

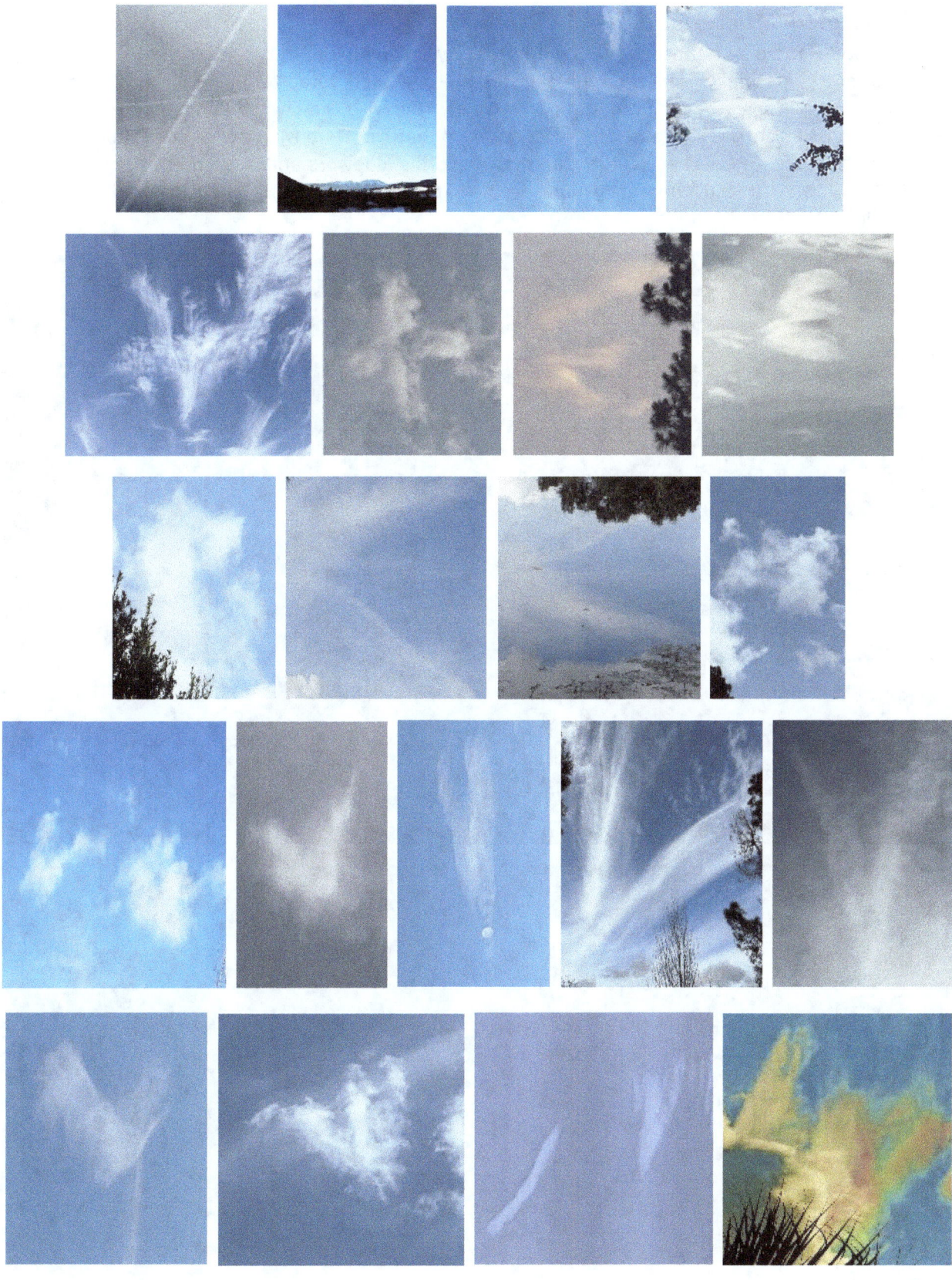

The Ever-present Nature of God's Holy Spirit

An "s" shaped cloud may represent The Spirit in the Sky. In The Bible, that 3rd Member of The Trinity's role is that of a guide while a soul is on the path to The Love-filled Hereafter in Paradise. His symbol is a bird or more specifically a Dove. Even in modern times, The Wise Old Owl still appears to be watching over The Earth. In fact, The Redeemer or Christ revealed that The Third Member of The Trinity or Helper would be left behind to direct as well as comfort The Lord's followers until the end of the world as we know it. The Holy Spirit leads those individuals to the pathway to Everlasting Life in Yahweh's, Unending Domain. (John 15:26)

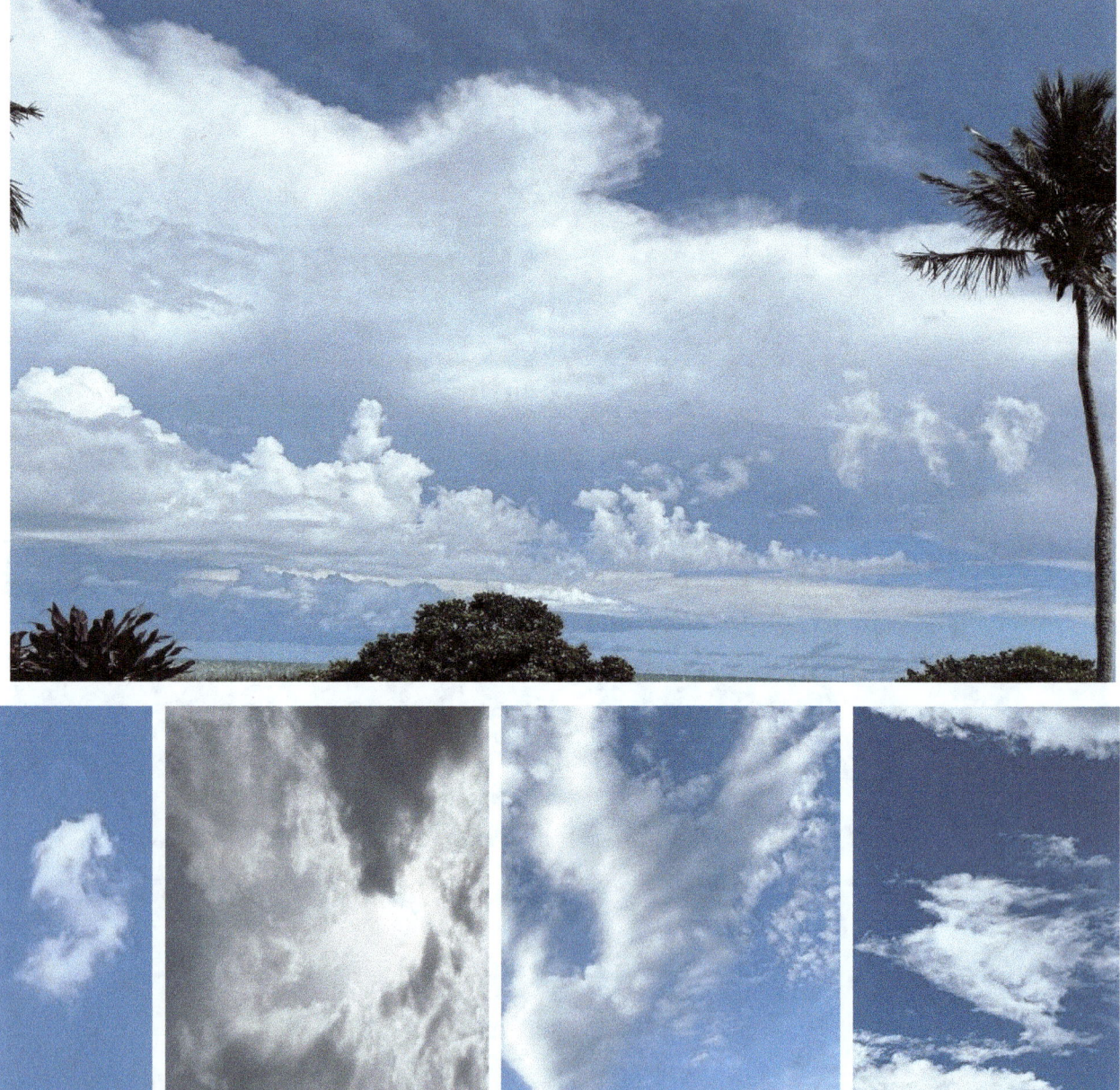

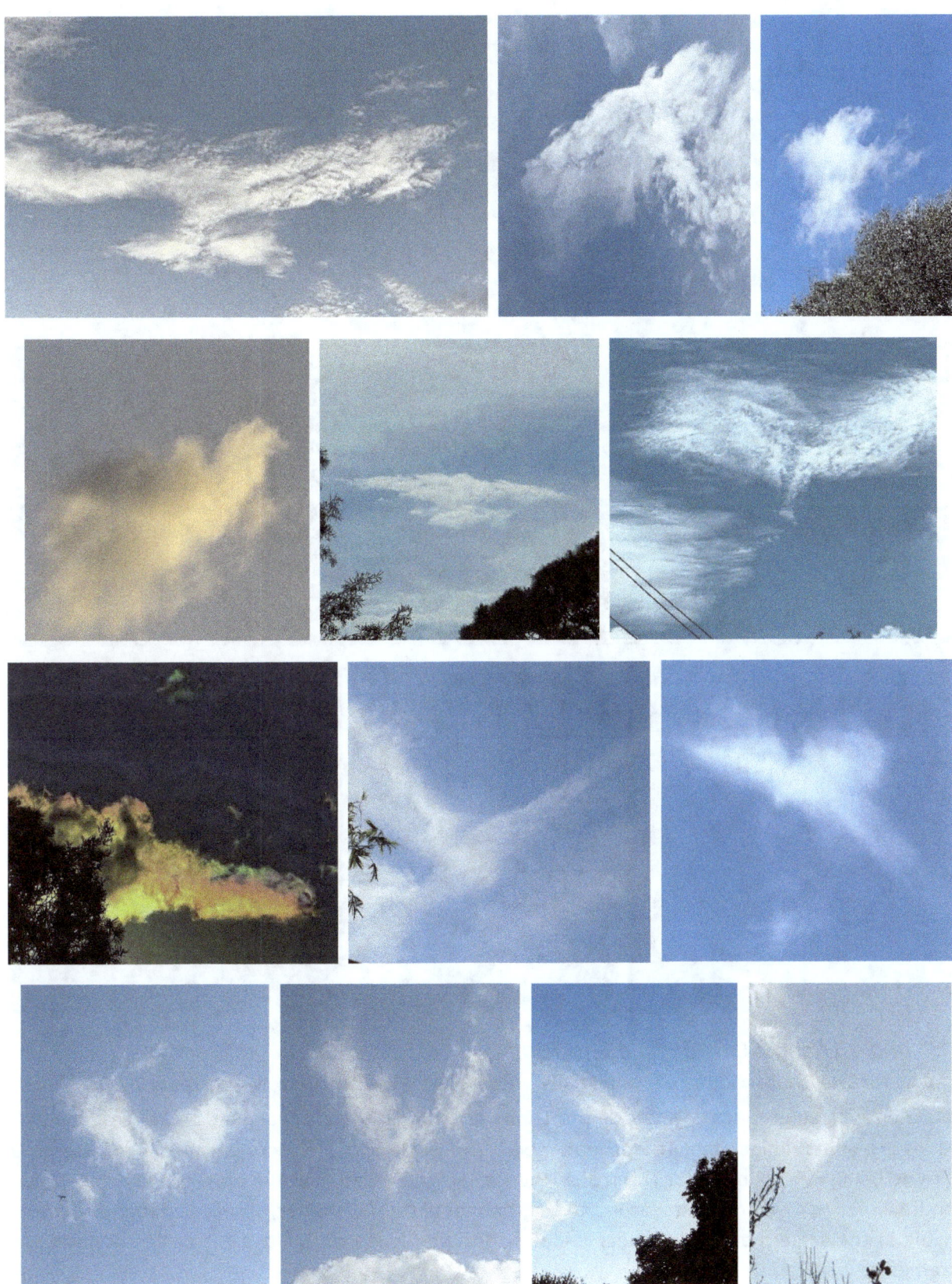

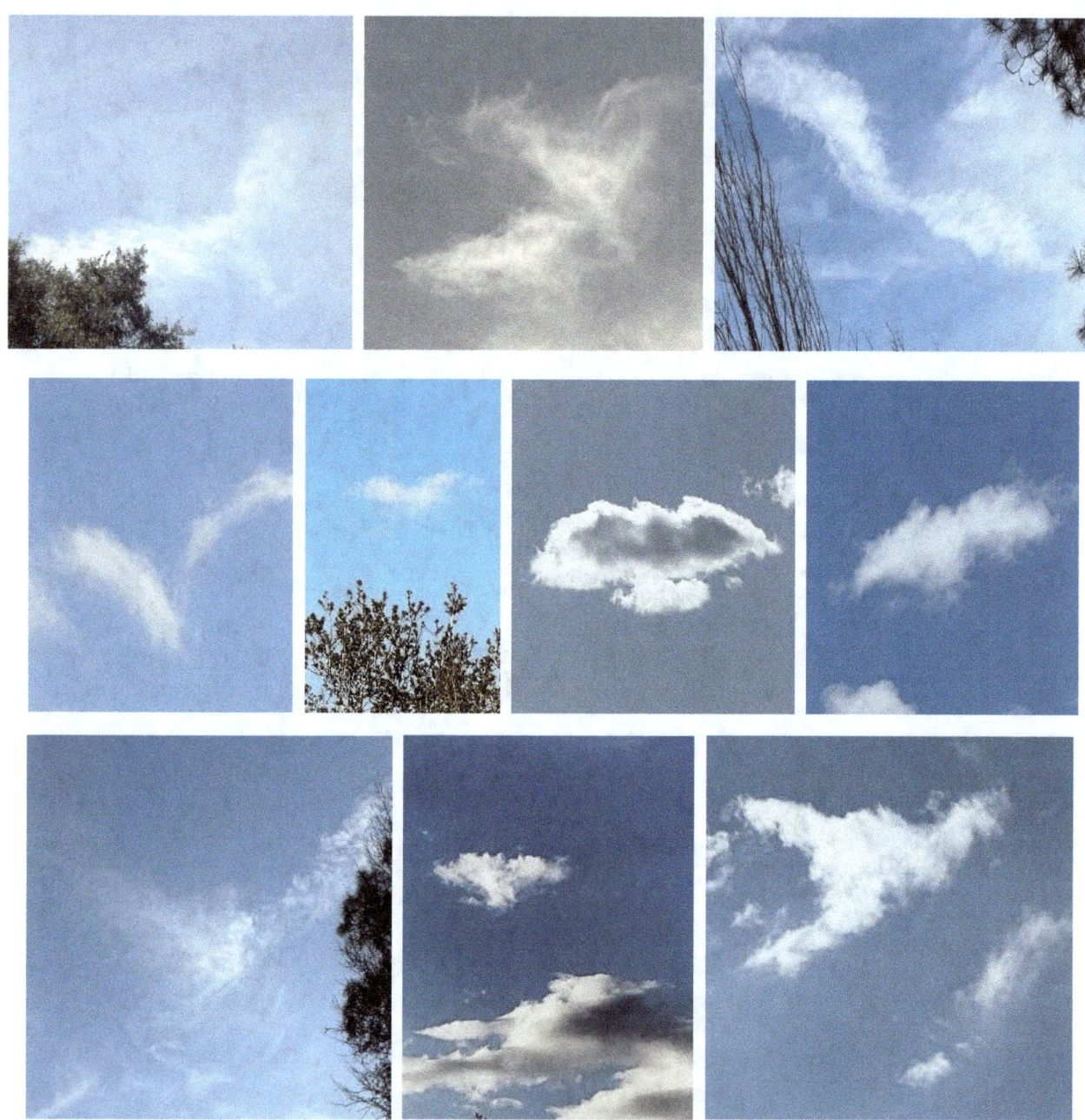

A "3" and a Triangle Can Explain The Trinity
Symbols for The Triune God appear in cloudy visions that were captured for posterity by my camera's lens. The Alpha and Omega is a part of The Trinity as symbolized by a triangle. The "1" group with "3" entities are united in lockstep. Thus, the number "13" is blessed and lucky because it represents The Supreme Being. Meanwhile, The Trio led by The Father Figure designed the perfection of the 13 lunar months as well as 4 well-defined seasons; the continuous pattern of Winter, Spring, Summer, and Autumn arriving in the same months each year is due to the perfection of "7" and His design done in week increments.

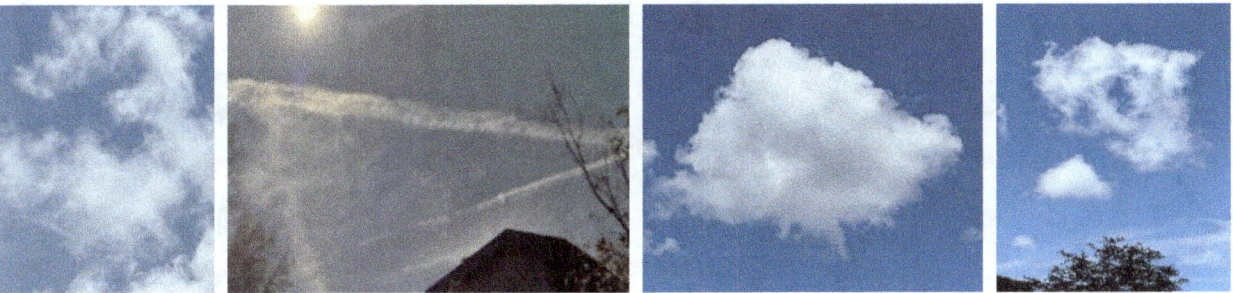

The Role of God's Angels

Some celestial Beings are messengers of The Almighty; these angels appear to be winged humans. This symbolically allows Yahweh's heralds and representatives to be less intimidating to the people they guide. Along with The Holy Spirit of God, they bring The Truth to this planet. In addition, a guardian angel looks after a human from the beginning to the end of that soul's earthly life.

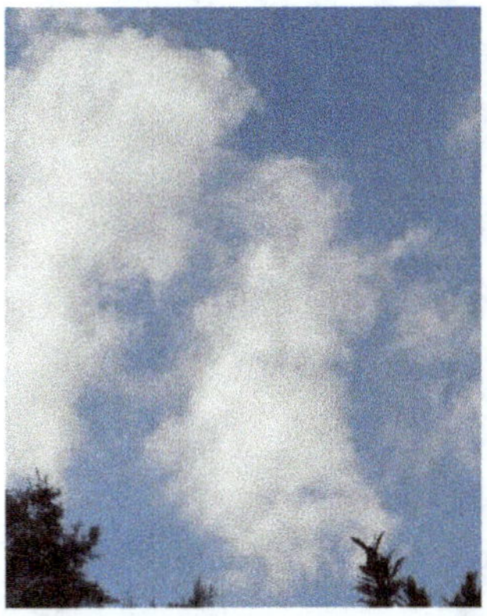

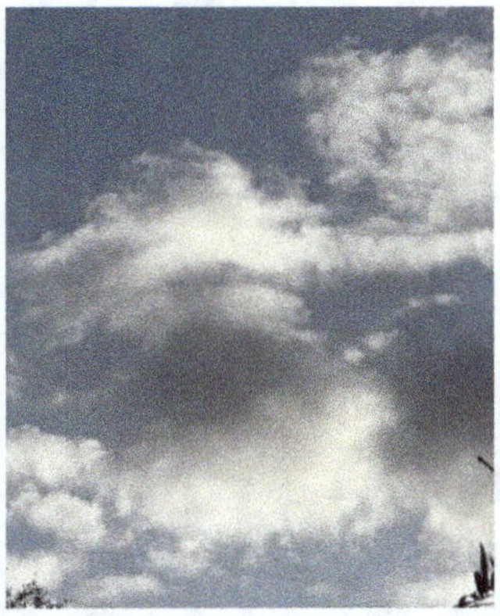

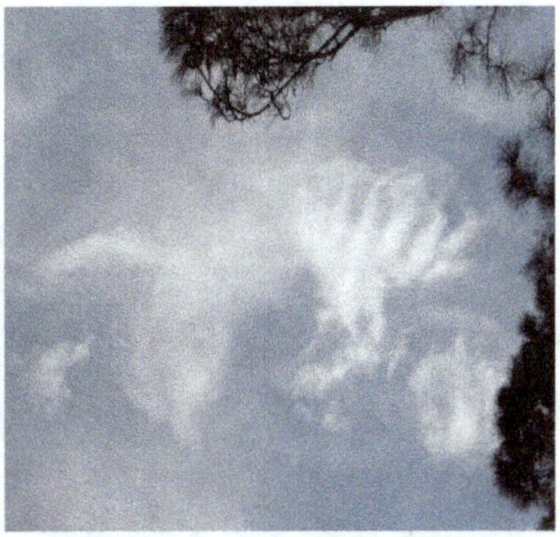

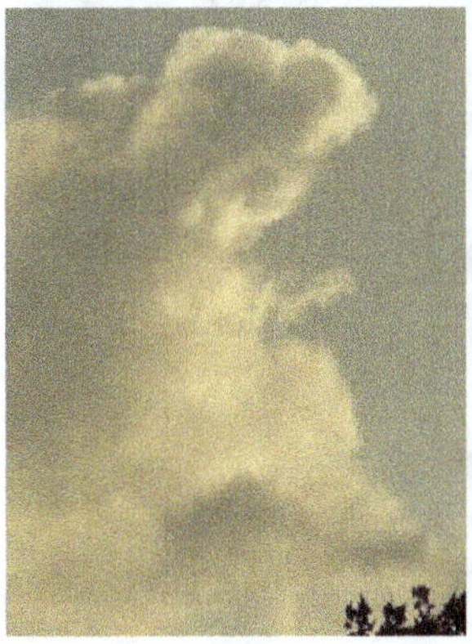

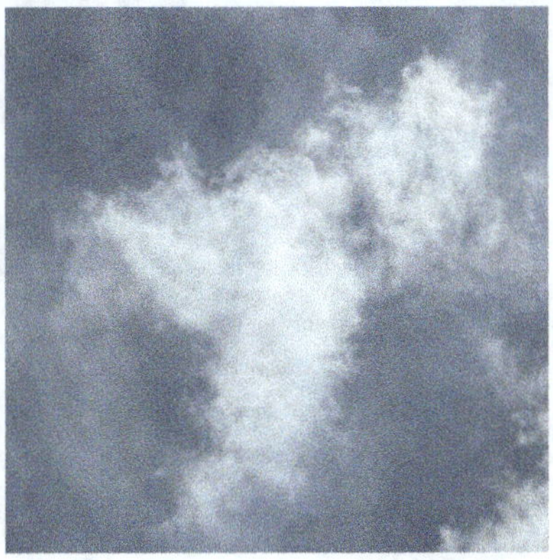

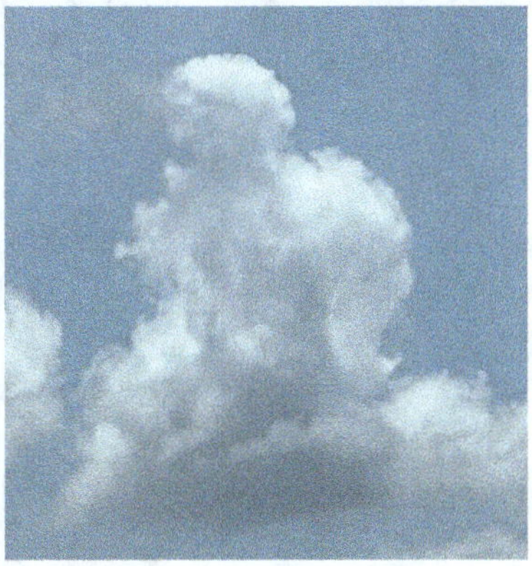

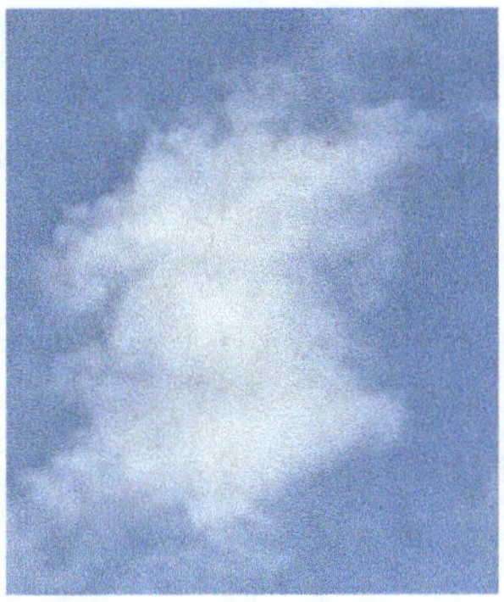

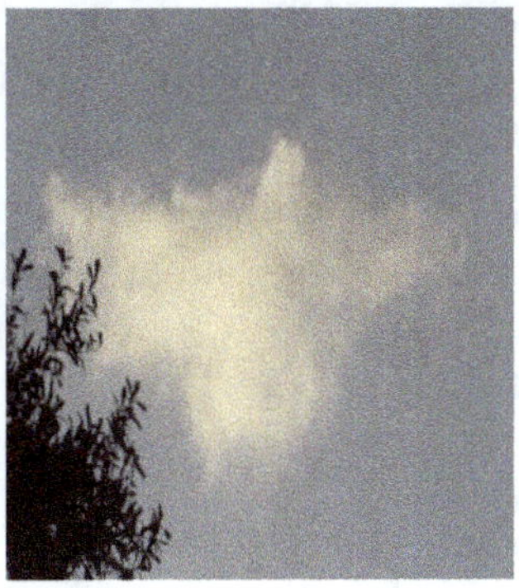

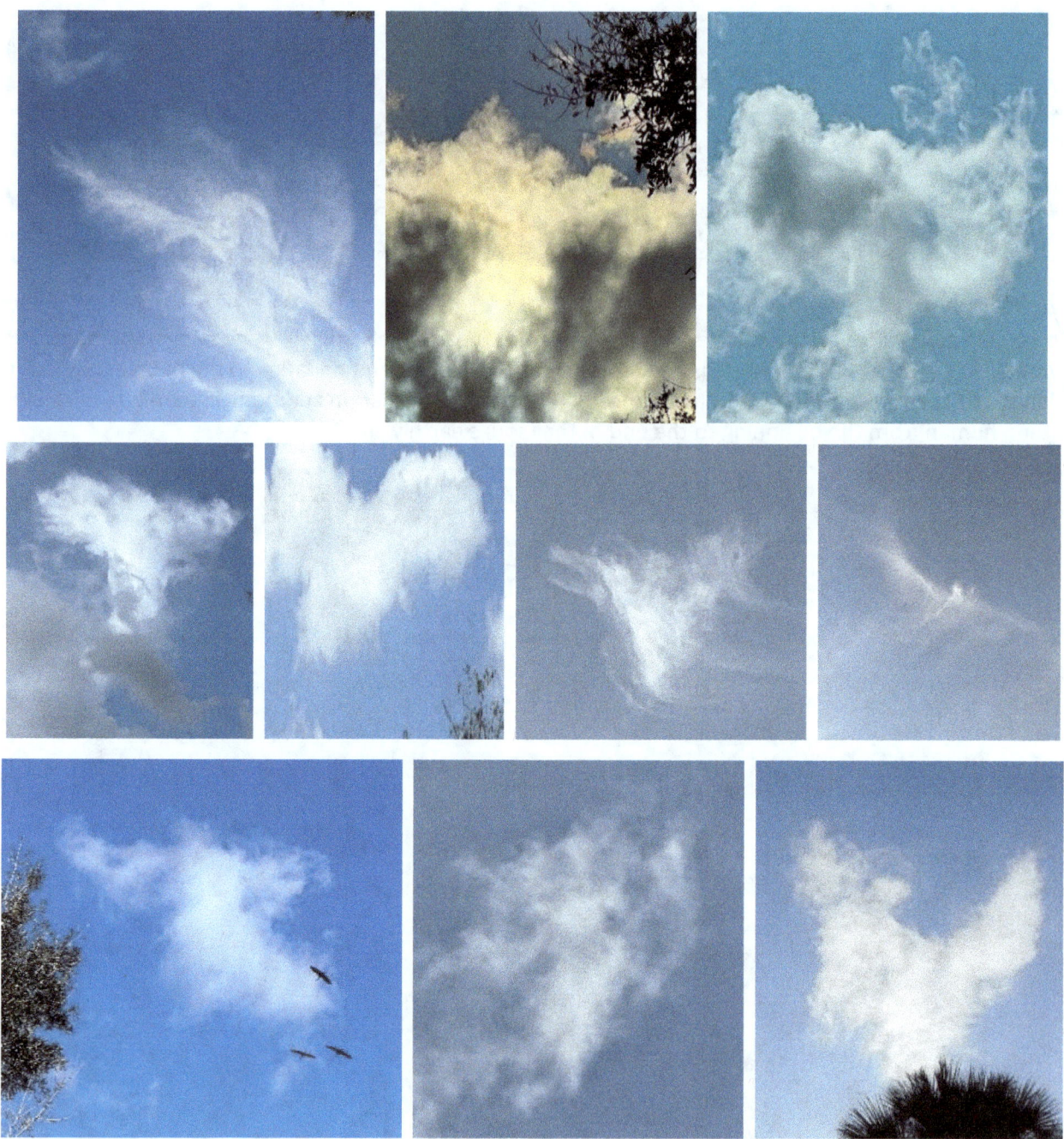

Mary's Role in The Christian Church

Christ's female parent is Heaven's Mother Figure; The Queen of The Universe is Mary. On The Cross, The Lord gave His mom to the world calling her everyone's Mother. In The Bible, in John 19:26-27, the passage reads as follows. When Jesus saw His mother standing there beside the disciple He loved, he said to her, "Dear woman, here is your son." And he said to this disciple, "Here is your mother." And from then on this disciple took her into his home. In short, without that Lady's role in Salvation History, everybody would still be awaiting The Messiah.

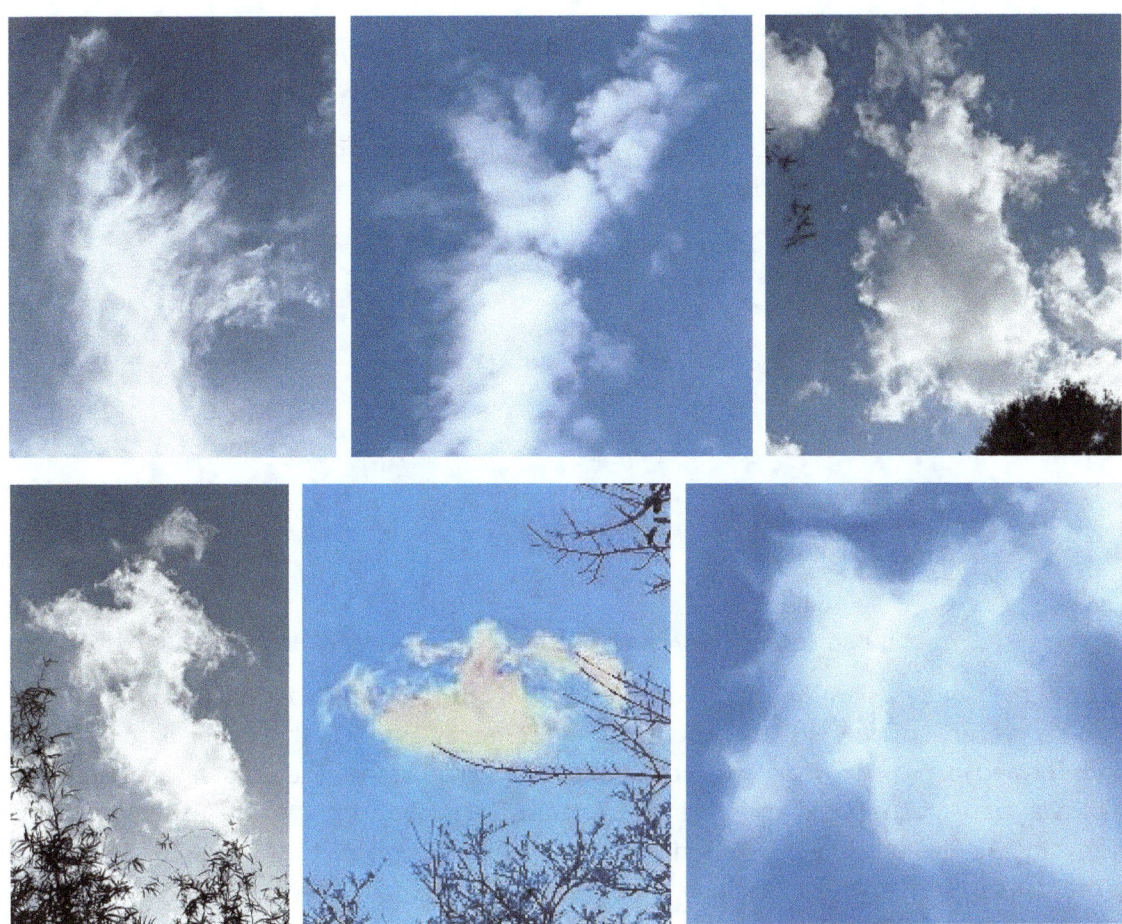

That last photo reminds me of my first encounter with a Mary cloud. It fluttered in as my heart raced. My IPhone and camera failed multiple times to grab the photo for posterity as my devices shot up the sky. I snapped aloud quarrelling with myself about my incompetence; then, I asked for the vision to enter my camera's lens. God must have -immediately and mysteriously- answered my prayers as the shutters on both devices continued to malfunction; surprisingly, once at my computer, Mary The Queen of The Universe was there- on the screen.

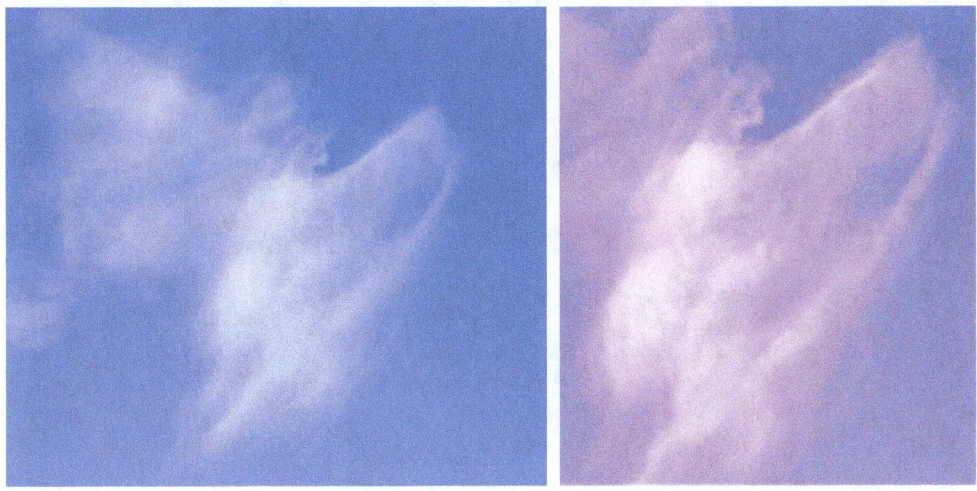

Chapter 3: Some Photos from Holy Days

Often, holidays include vacations; holy days normally point to Eternal Paradise in God's Kingdom.

12/8: On the Feast Day of The Immaculate Conception, my lens captured a quick photo as I race to the car to go babysit my grandchildren. Go figure.

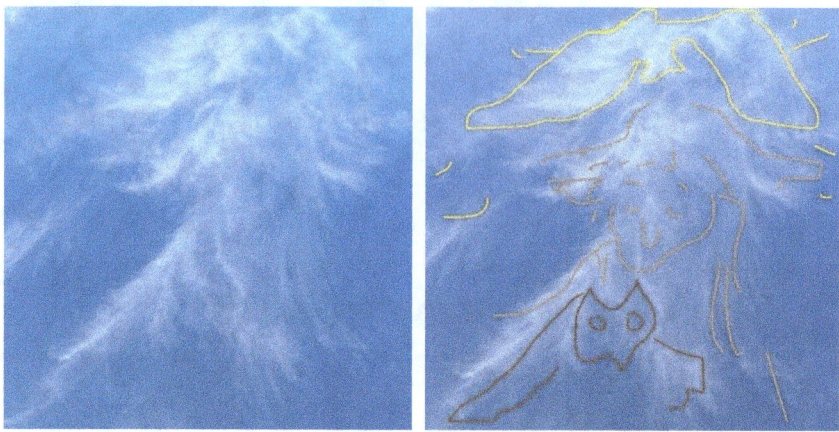

3/3: Many of the cloudy visions on this 3rd day of the 3rd month appear to agree with a thought that The Triune God is in charge of how His Story continues and someday ends. On this strong date for The Trinity, the clouds formed many pure-white, winged messengers indicating that The Creator is communicating to His people via every means possible including His angels. The sunbow or halo implies the communication is from royalty aka The King of kings. A bird head near a sun halo seems to say that The Dove can lead a soul up the stairs to True Love aka The Supreme Being. The last photo reminds the viewer that the number "5" speaks about forming good relationships with God and humans. The skywriting captured for posterity indicates that an "A"ngel as well as a Dove bring a message of hope that relationships (5) will originate from "G"od and spread The Love. If anyone interprets the vision as "1" and "3" instead of as a bird and a "5", the message would still be Heavenly because "13" points to "1" in "3" entities aka The Godhead of Christianity. Therefore, that number is not necessarily a bad sign.

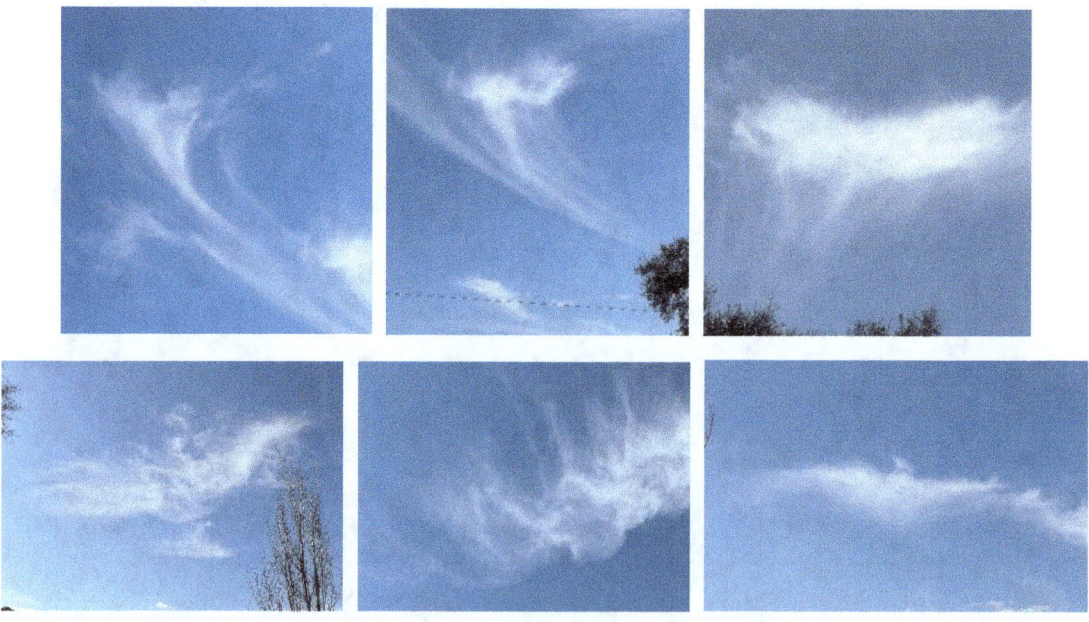

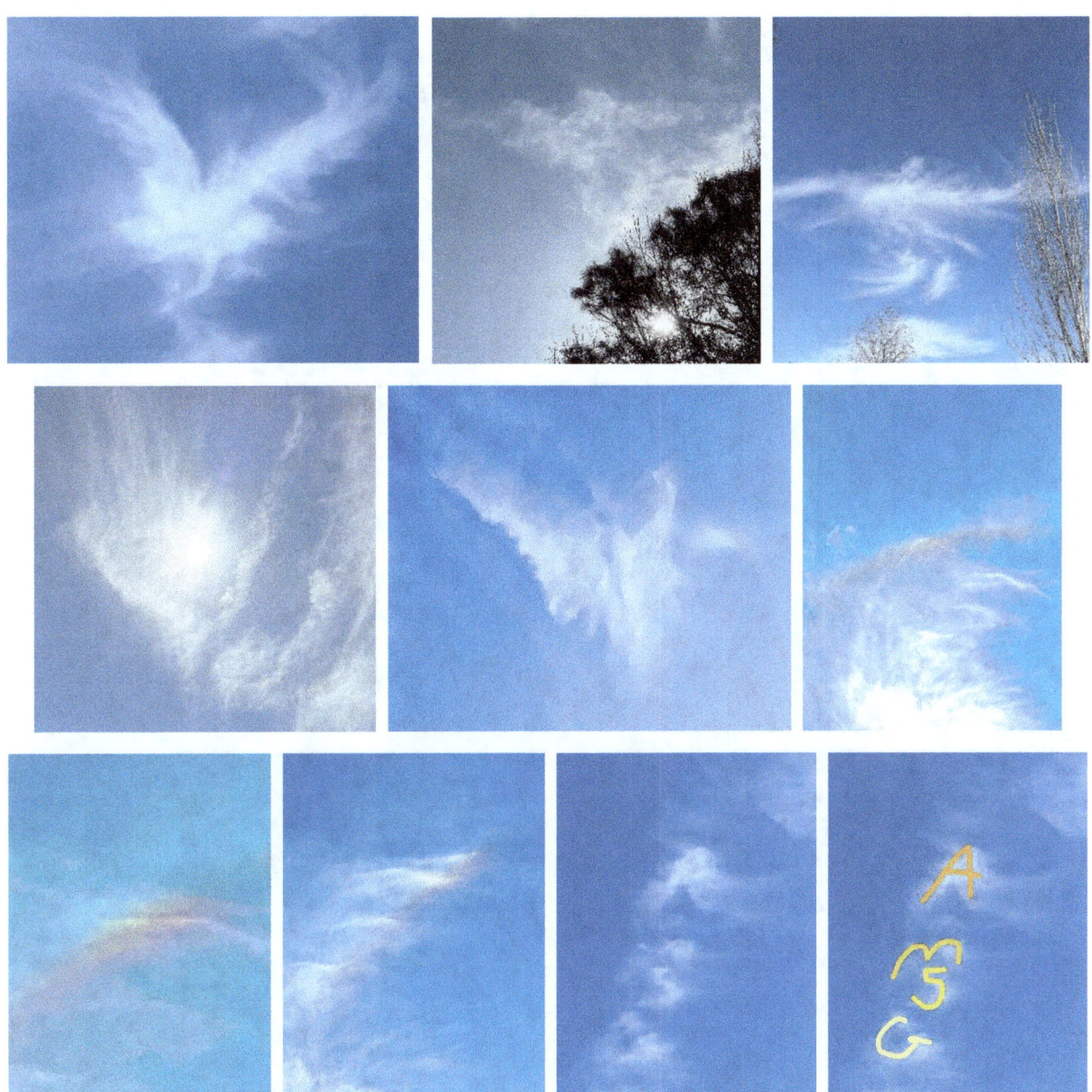

4/4: A triangle represents The Trinity; that Triune God is The Chief Engineer of life on The Earth. The Supreme Being aka The Father and eternally Wise Old Man is The Perfect Creator of things such as "7" days in a week. In the cloudy-face picture, do you see that number in the man's beard?

One of the snapshots appears to be a lion or elephant, which would point to God either way. The Man Upstairs is The King of Kings. Like an elephant, He never forgets His own people or the chosen especially His Loving and Obedient Son, Jesus The Christ or Jesus The Anointed One. He is, also, called The Messiah, The Christians' Savior or this world's Redeemer, and The Sacrificial Lamb. As represented via that animal's picture, His message continues on this planet, which is that The Lord and Prince of Peace died on The Cross to save humanity from The Devil's evil ways. He sacrificed Himself to teach people the way to live the words "I love" symbolized by the misty, "I heart" vision captured by my camera lens for posterity.

It seems apropos during Lent that the following skywriting and puffy mist occurred over my head.

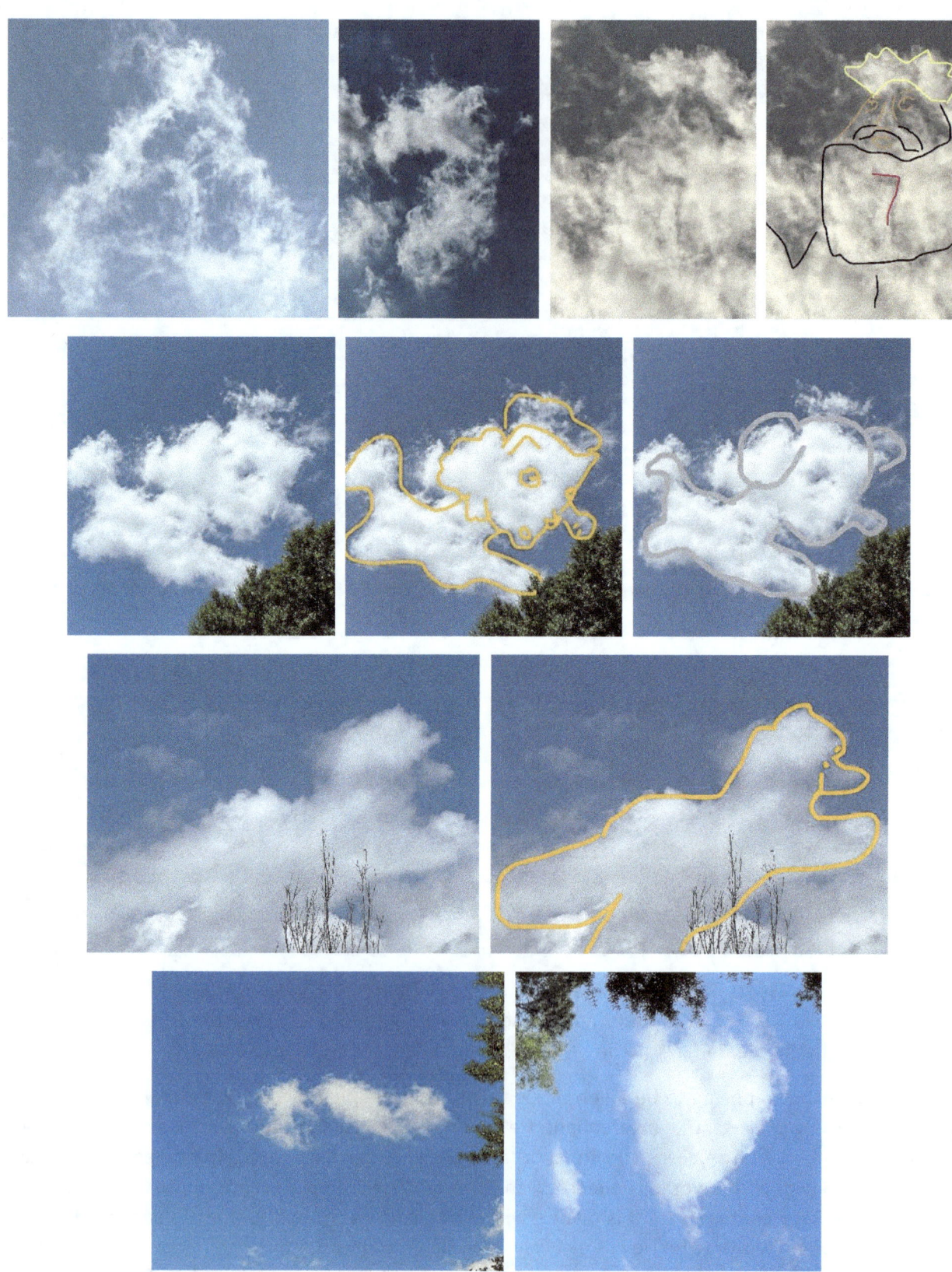

4/15: It was Good Friday, and The Almighty had much to say near 3PM. I was outside when the wind picked up, and some clouds raced through the sky. Just when it seems The Heavens have nothing left to say, God appears to be persistently communicating. Is His Story shortening before Judgement Day? That's a rhetorical question because each day that passes brings this world closer to Him- for better or worse. In short, when in misery or doubt know that this too will pass.

What do you see in these photos? What do I think the scenes mean that were flying over my head? Phi, The Lion King of kings, or God along with Mary brought The Father's Son aka Jesus The Christ to The Earth in order to set up the rescue of humans from sin. Emmanuel or "The Creator is with us" tried to move humans away from the worst possible judgement for mankind's sin when this world ends- in the future. After Jesus The Christ's Resurrection into Eternal Paradise, after His death on The Cross, and after Easter or Resurrection Sunday- The Holy Spirit took over the guidance and message of love of The Supreme Being. Love can and will cure this world as communicated through the cloudy skywriting letters of "IV," which stands for life-support in medicine. Or, "I'm victorious "as The Christian Messiah and The Savior incarnate (in person). During Lent or Holy Week, the continuing thought from Jesus seems to be "reflect on The Redeemer's mission for mankind" as in "reflect on Me, The Good Shepherd. I won't mislead you into Hell or the worst possible Afterlife."

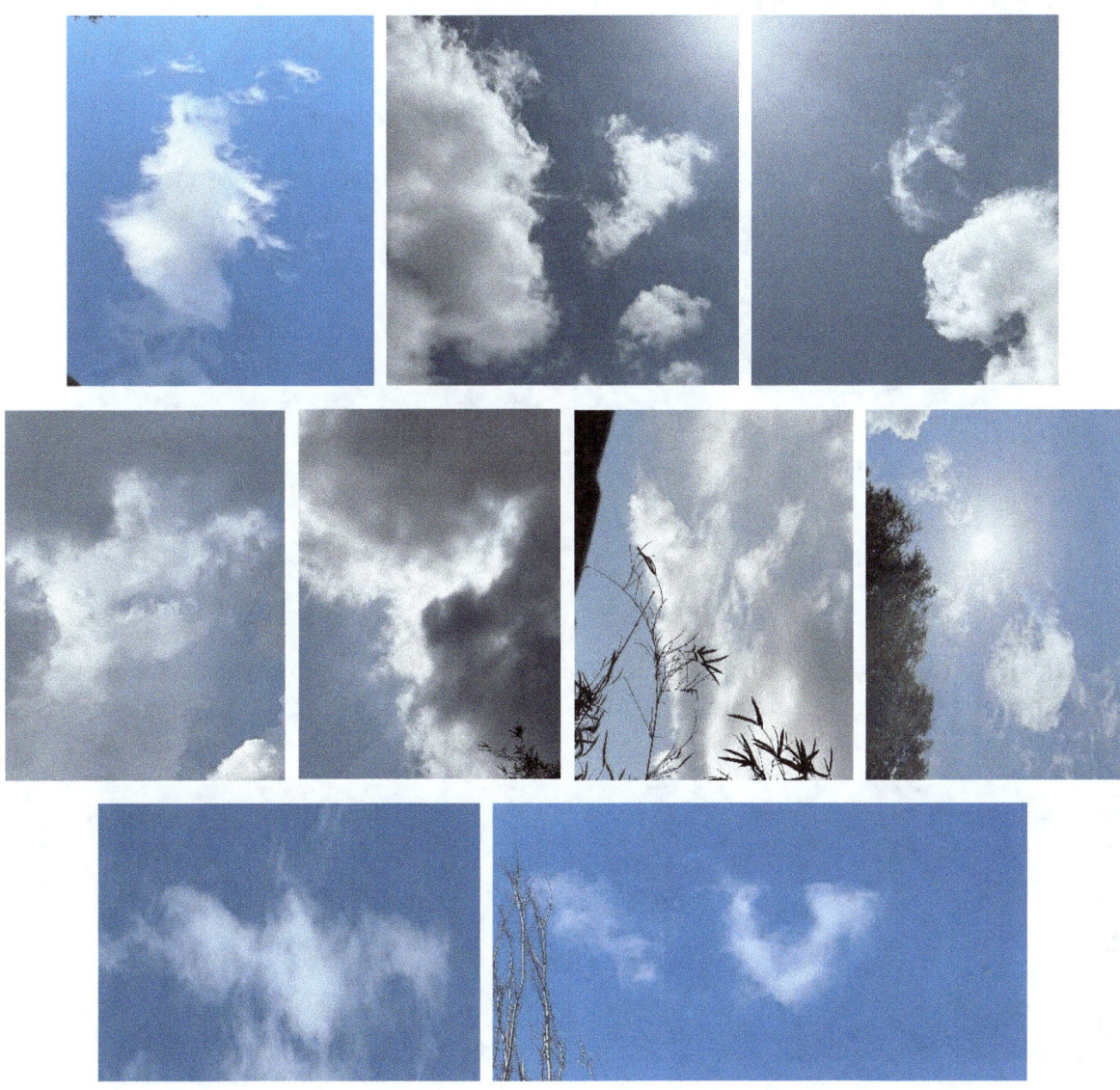

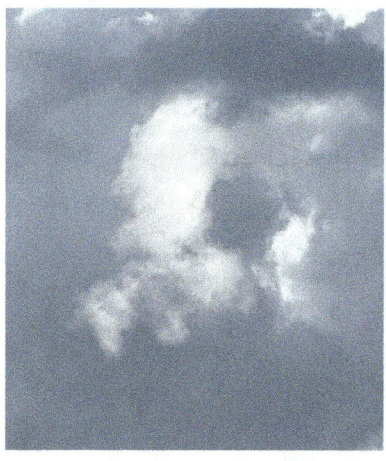 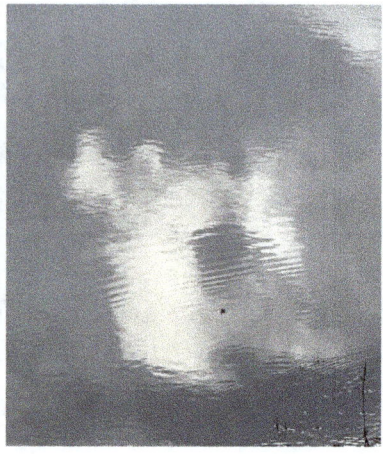

A Special Note

On Holy Saturday 2022, a friend asked. "Why do I keep seeing insects like roaches and beetles in the images in the clouds? What does it mean?"

I jested; "They are bugging you!"

She wrote; "You made me literally 'lol.'" Then, she sent a for instance photo.

I slightly repositioned the image texting that picture. "I wondered if that 'j' meant Jesus? So, I rotated the picture. Voila! The bug is actually Christ as The Good Shepherd's image in The Heavens."

"My heart skipped a beat!" She responded.

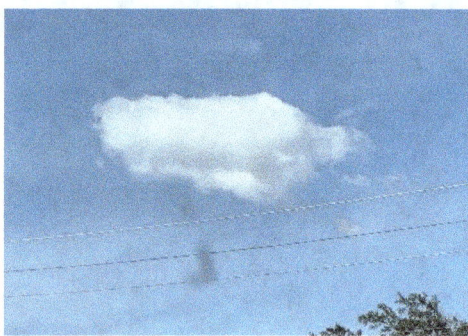 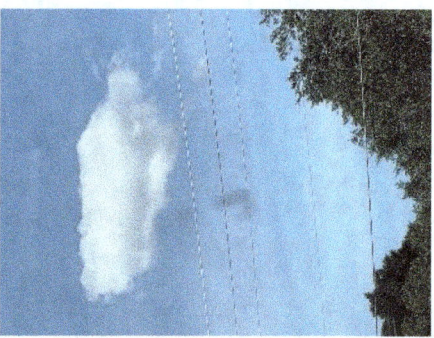

4/17: On this Easter Sunday, The Father's chatter filled the sky at dawn. Keep looking up and use the clues to decide what His message to this troubled world is. What's bugging you? "I C" it in the clouds. Have no fear because Jesus is the "V"ictor over evil.

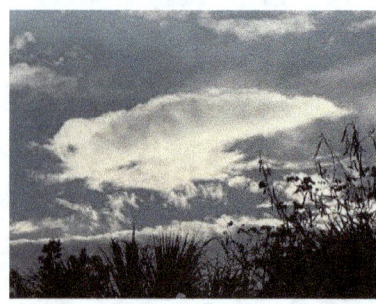 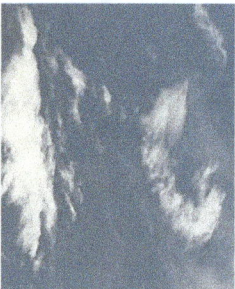 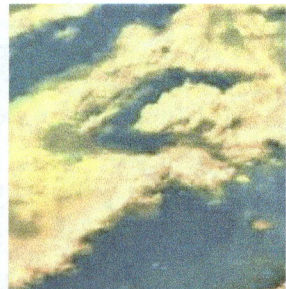 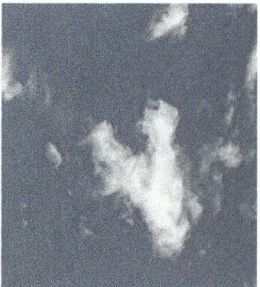

All you need is Love similar to The Anointed One that reopened Heaven and resides, there. Are you troubled by The Easter Bunny seemingly replacing The Lord in this world? Jesus is The Prince of Peace; Just like The Easter Bunny, which is a rare animal because it is mostly passive instead of vengeful.

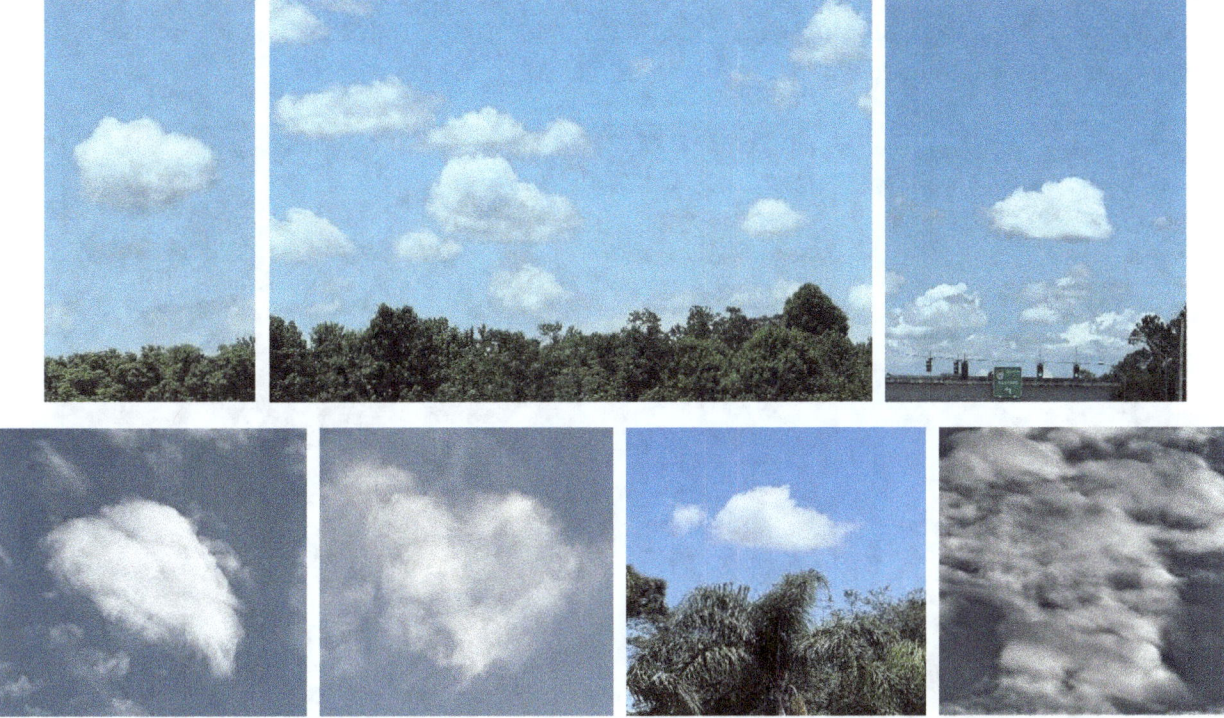

Follow The guidance of The Holy Spirit; He brings good things to Light. Also, keep looking up especially if you are being bugged by evil of this secular world run by busts of idols and self-proclaimed icons.

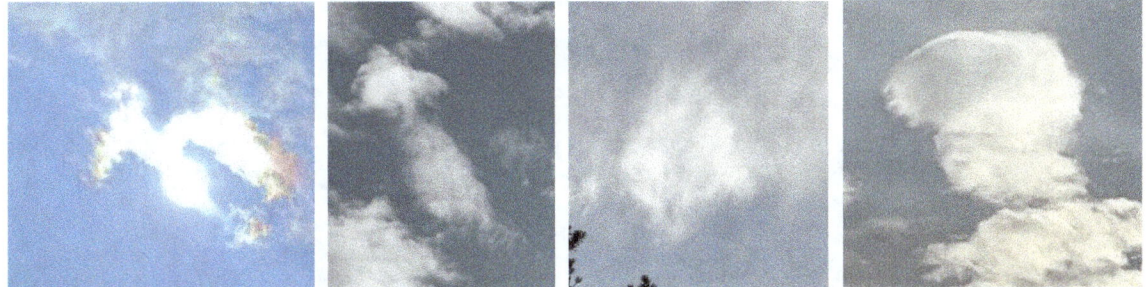

Enjoy the beauty of The Supreme Being's designs.

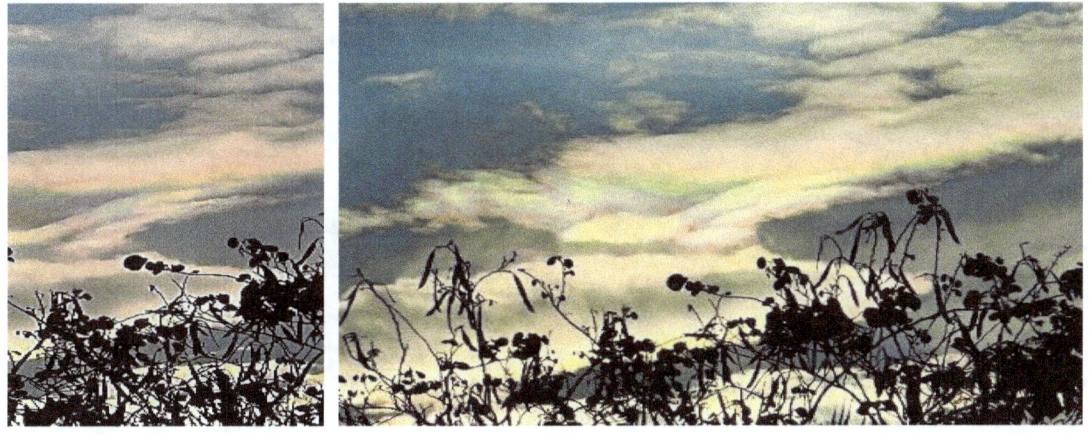

4/24: Divine Mercy Sunday falls on the 8th day of celebrating Salvation History or the opening of The Pearly Gates by Jesus The Christ after His Crucifixion. Once again, there was a colorful show in the sky. Is the messenger cloud implying The Heavens see rays of hope during these uncertain times of war, famine, and growing fascism? That was a rhetorical question. Keep the faith while reflecting on the promise of God to Noah and Jesus to this troubled world.

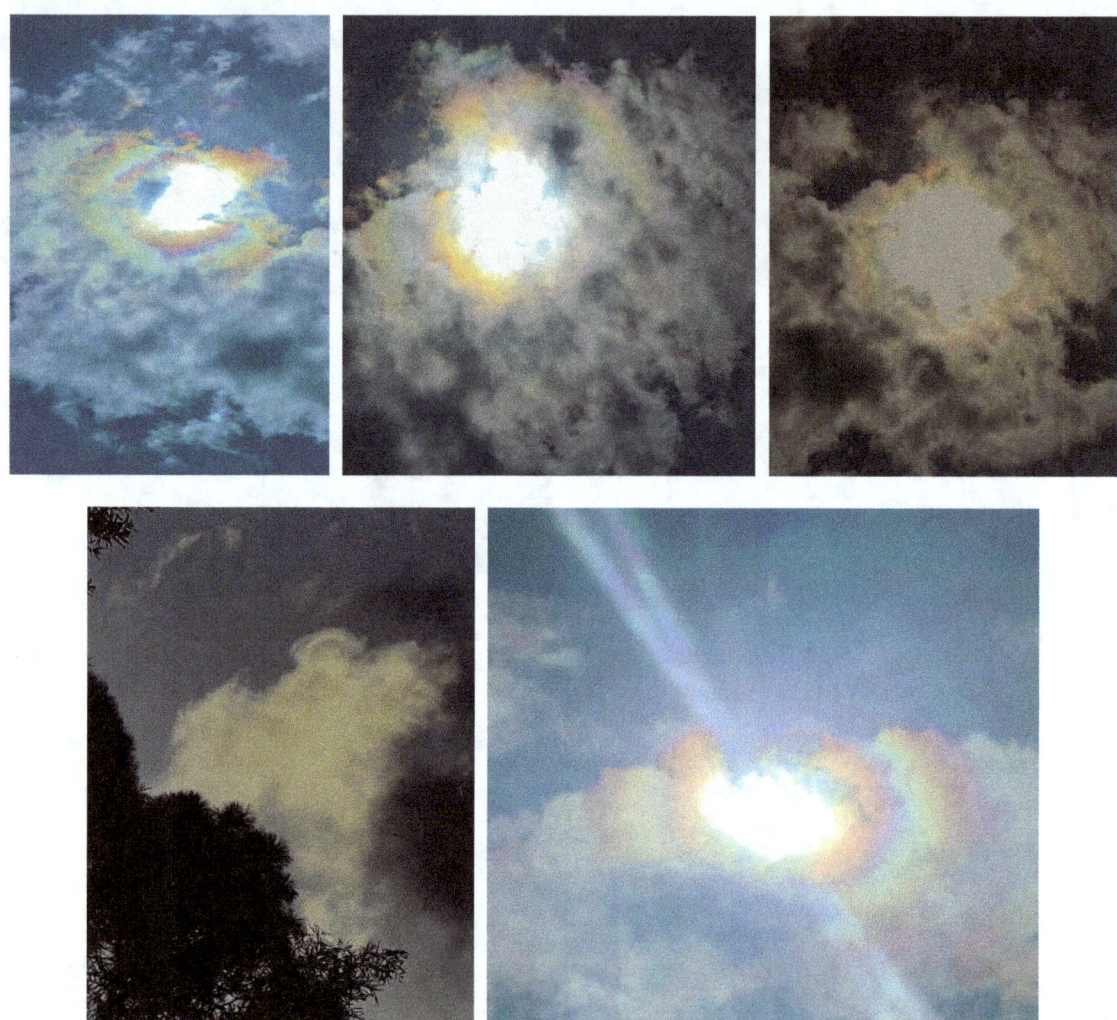

Chapter 4: After Years of Looking Up at The 7th Heaven

Surely, God guided my photo sessions and my scribing journey aka pseudo-diaries all these years.

10/20: Clouds can change the way things appear; the picture of the moon's surface at dawn demonstrates that thought. By the afternoon, while walking on my covered, back porch- my eyes noticed that the grayish sky was unveiling a sun halo or heavenly royalty. Immediately, I recognized a Circumzenithal Arc was developing. The sky lit up as I walked down to the yard and then looked up. While enjoying the view including sundogs and sunbows (or halos) sharing The Heavens at the same time, the unveiling of the unexpected colorful, upturned bow above the sun felt amazing. An earlier in the day exclamation point drawn in the clouds punctuated God's interactions; He is still The Light. Sometimes, I make light of that grammar, sentence ender intentionally calling it an explanation point giving the "!" heightened meaning. The phenomenon lasted quite a while before waning; the light kept returning in various formats and all over the Western point of view as shown in the pictures. The vision was so amazing that I kept snapping photos for posterity.

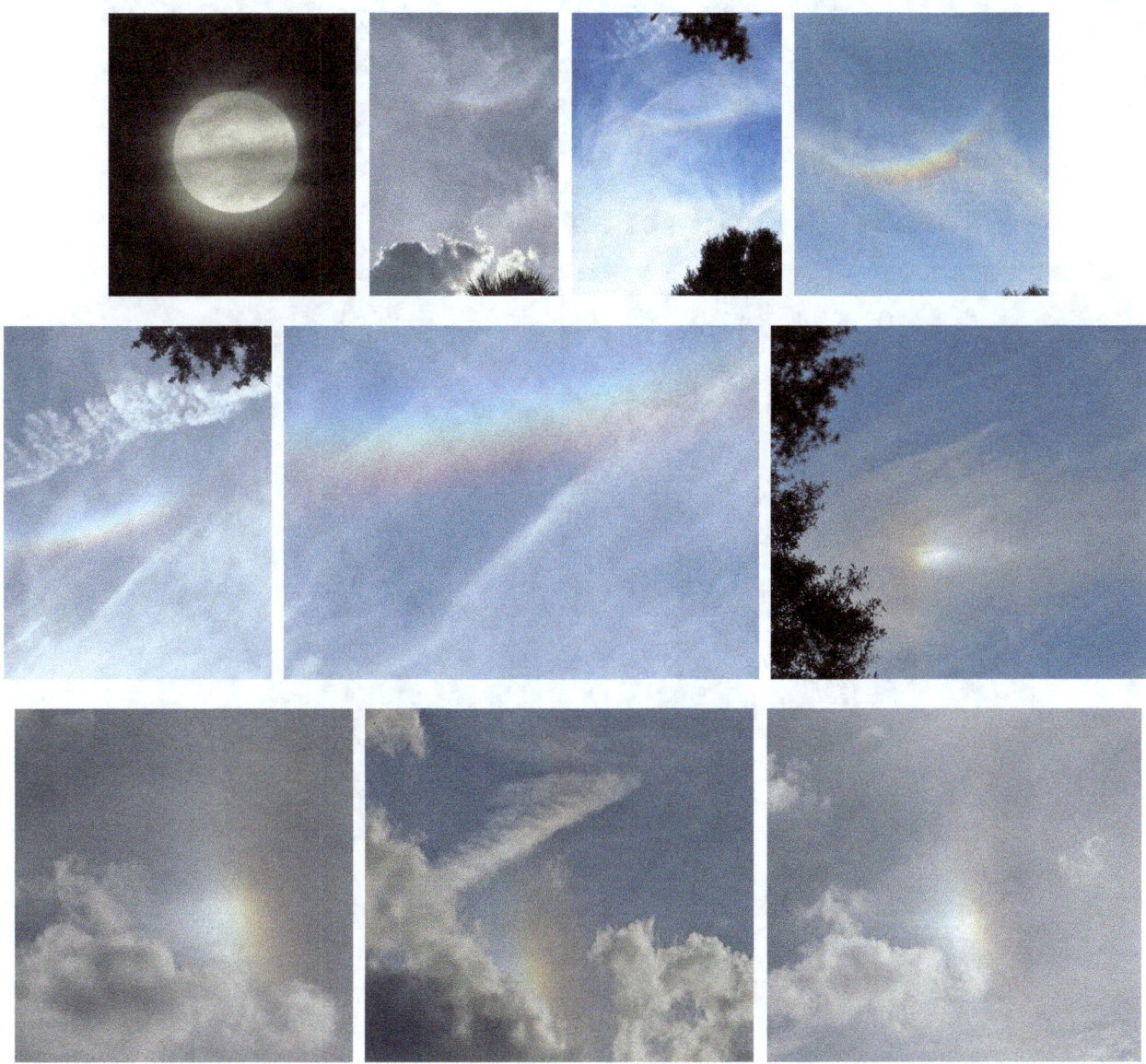

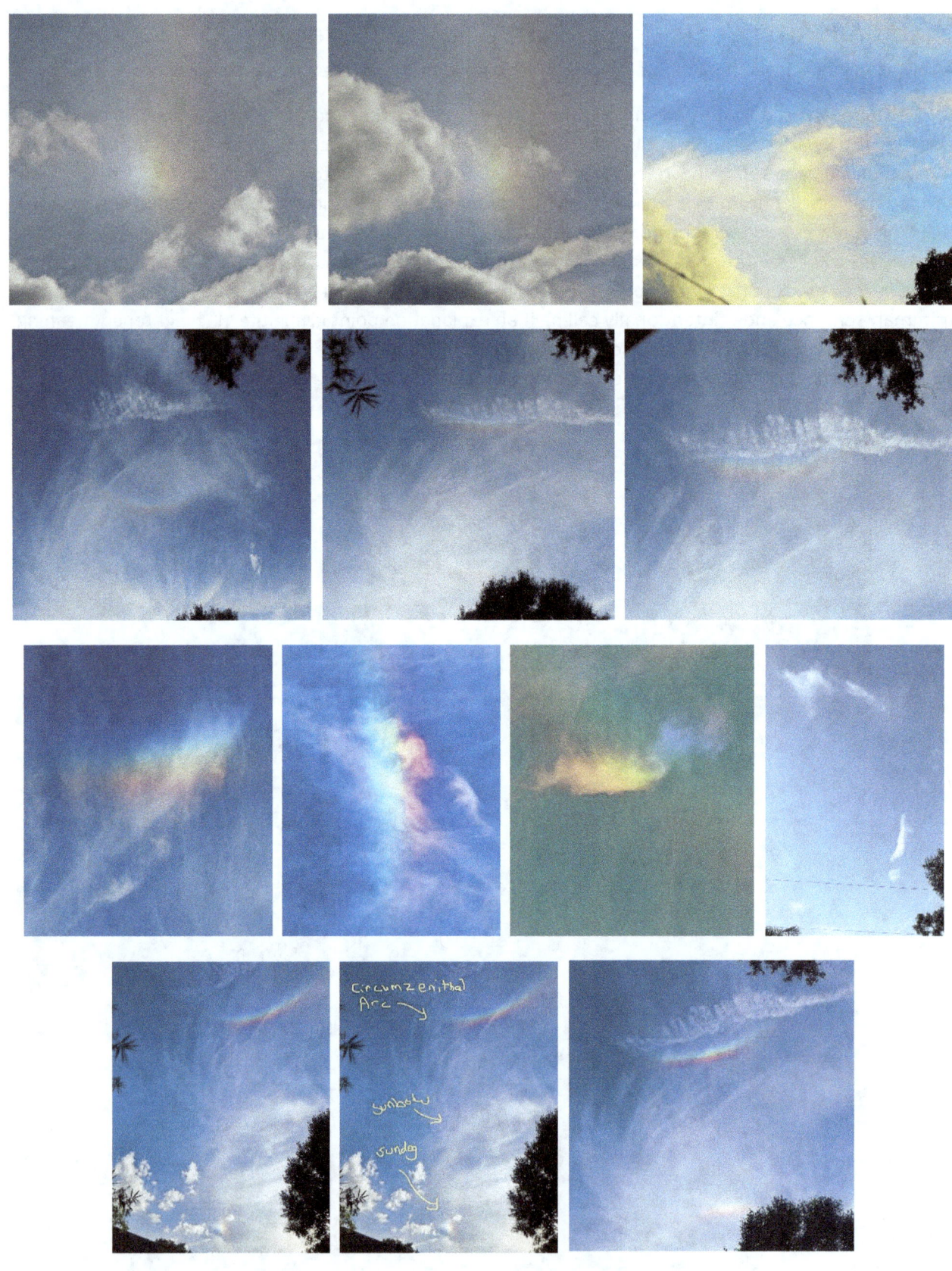

11/27: Frequently, a vision appears through a window; by time I race outside, it is gone or converted. Sometimes, it's better; often, it's gone because the revelation was meant for my eyes only. As a friend and I discussed the malice and unrest or lack of humanity in this world, signs of hope arrived in the sky; in other words, The Almighty painted the last three visions before our eyes. I told her that when people vote hate as many in the USA did in 2020 that they live with the consequences of those actions. Luckily, there is always hope for change via God's plan. It's never too late to see things through the window of opportunity The Creator provides.

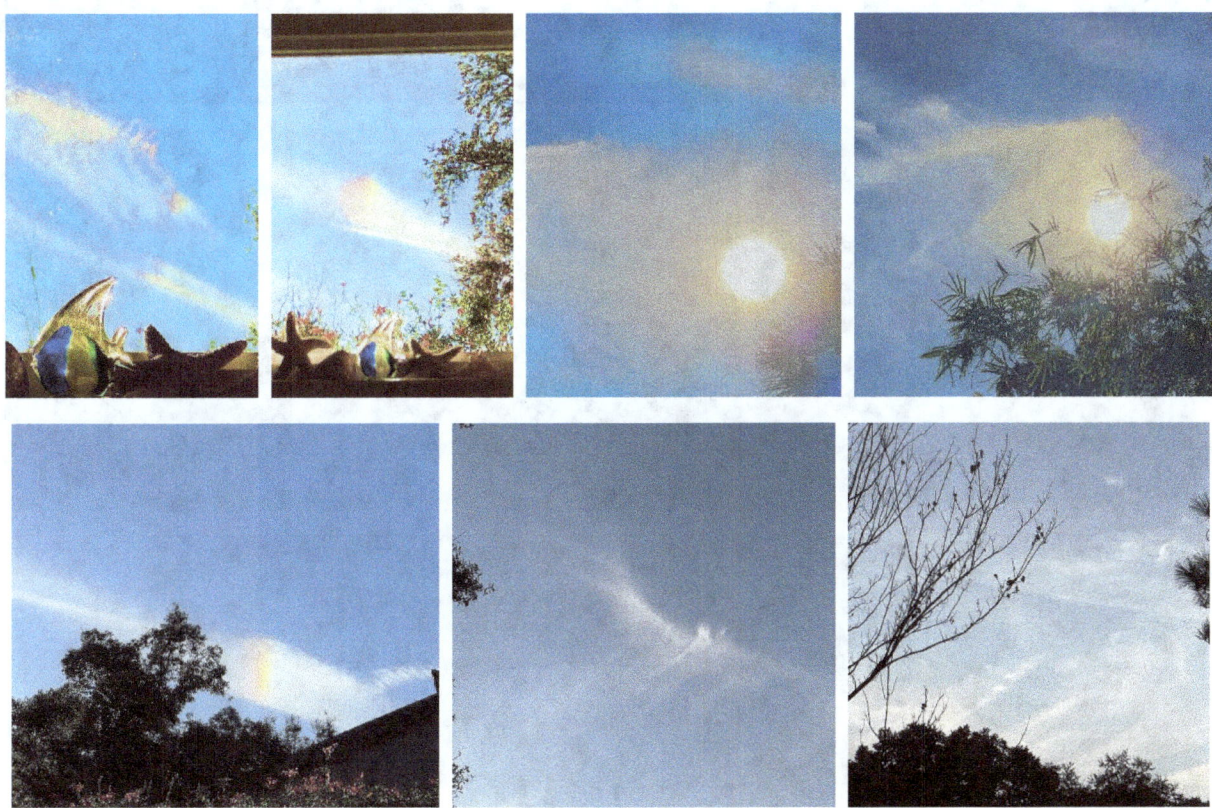

1/31: Near dawn, I heard a voice calling my name; this type of awakening has happened to me- before. Thus, my expectations for a sunny day led me outside and to mystical but mist free horizons. After days of dark cloud covered views and the colors above my head blending black to gray, out of the clear blue sky, near sundown, the following scenes lit the pathway from my back to front yard via a Western and well-worn route. It started with a flash of light and a few Southern sunbows; the brightness was mimicked to the Northwest but mostly hidden by trees. The visions were so grand and large that the viewer would have to be looking down to miss the evolving scenes.

As my thoughts wondered if a sun halo or a sign of royalty in the area would happen, it did. In the midst of it all, The Holy Spirit depicted as a Dove as well as angel figures arrived in the sky. As I turned West, while meandering into my backyard, a face appeared that grew into a familiar sight in a portion of the sky. Immediately, I thought; "She's back and accompanied by The Third Entity of the Trinity." Meanwhile, over the waterway, clouds appeared to be festive including white-light fireworks. Evidently, there's a celebration going on in The Heavens. In short, no matter how dreary or hopeless the day feels, keep looking up.

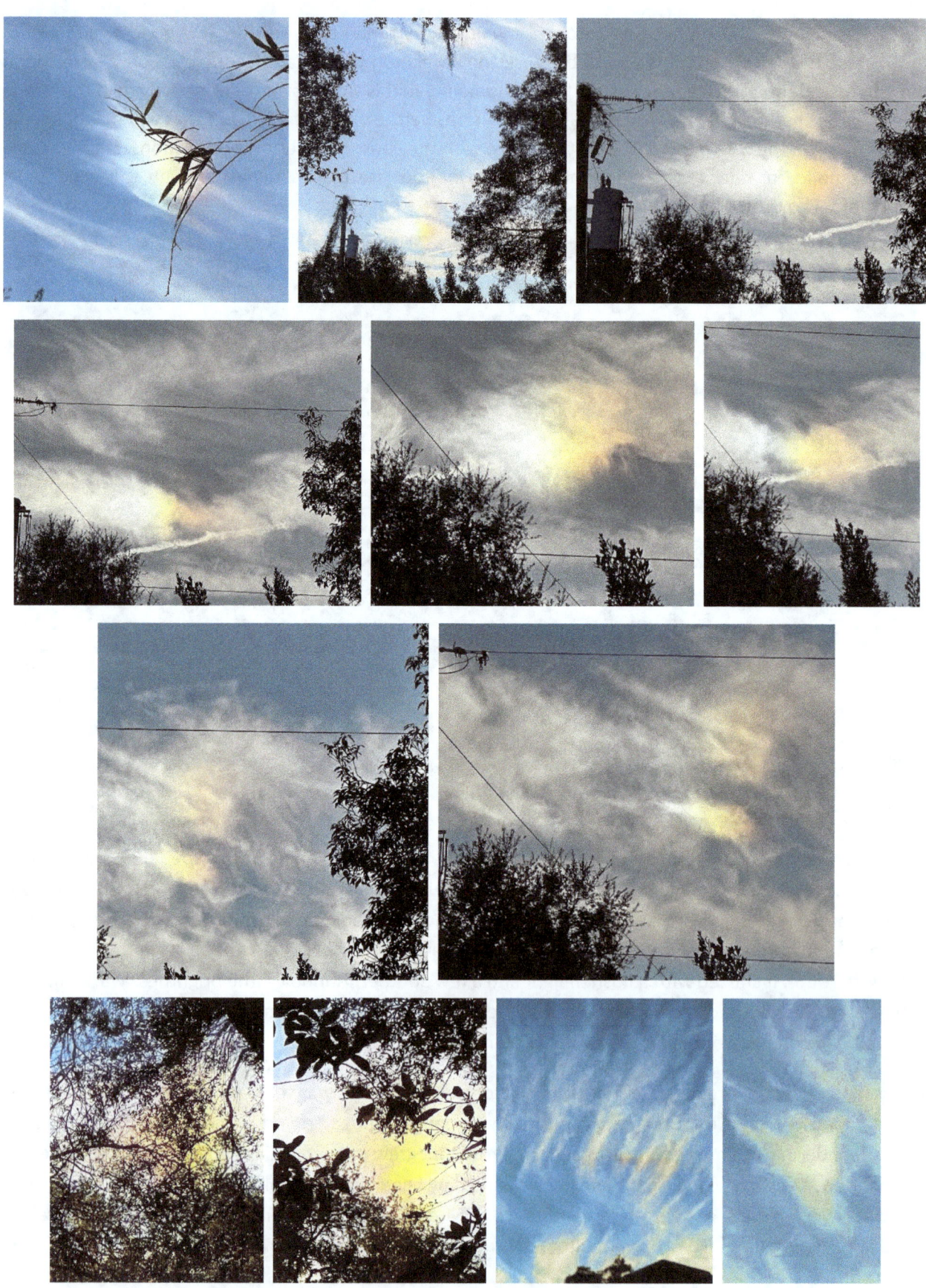

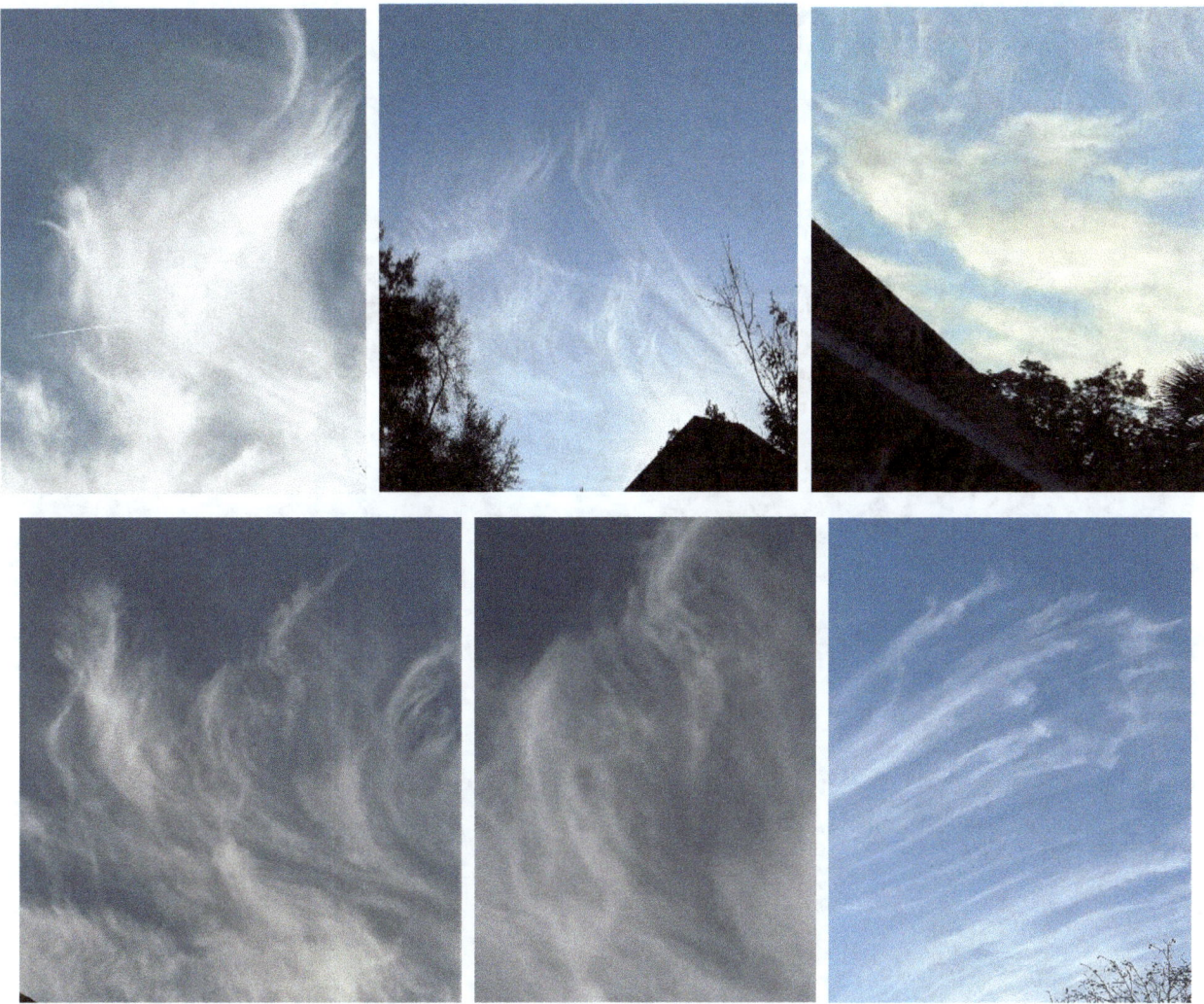

2/11: To understand The Alpha and Omega's goals of peace and love on The Earth, people can read and follow His signs and symbols using The Bible as the key reference. In my picture stories, The Natural Order of The Light reacting with things such as clouds can be awesome as well as deliver messages from The Maker of all things. More often than not, the spaces in between The Heavens and the land or the seas paint a concise and vivid picture of The Best Artist-Ever's temperament, personality, and His Will for this planet. On this day, everything captured in photos for posterity should remind a viewer of God; His rays of hope should make faith and true love easier to keep alive. The sunbow aka halo is a symbol of royalty; it circles The Main Light of The Universe aka The Supreme Being. Upturned rainbows or Circumzenithal Arc are one of many colorful signs of God's promise to Noah; multihued wonders in the sky confirm that The Creator is for mankind's success while The Devil works against humanity. A sun-dog symbolizes man's best friend or The Trinity, which includes The King of kings, The Prince of Peace, and The Spirit of The Comforter. In case there is any doubt, in a snapshot, a misty vision provided clues as to The Director that controls the scenes in the sky. Hint: one of the misty images was the "Al"mighty. More than likely, He controlled the messengers depicted and communication in the visions.

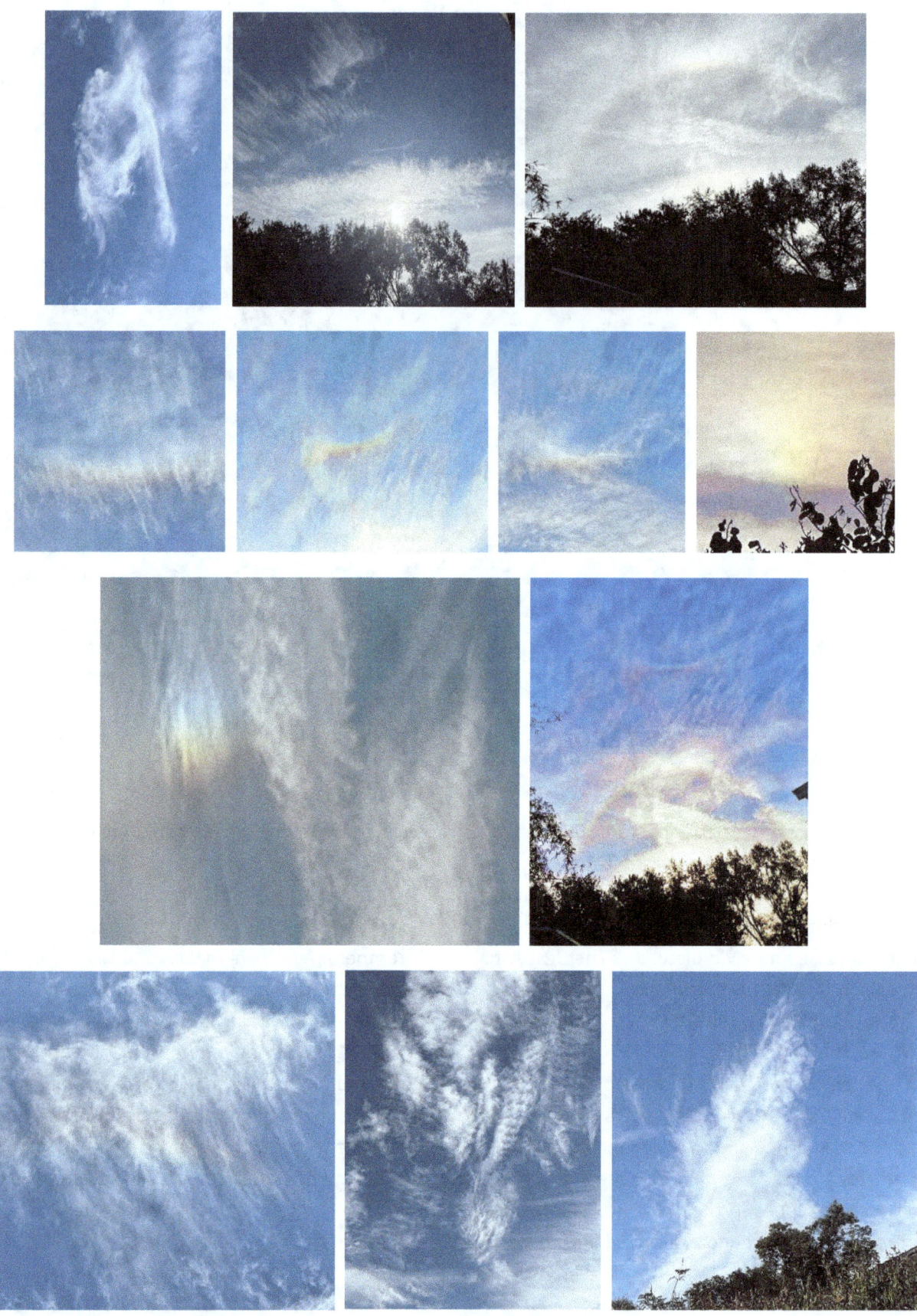

2/13: This date was a very lucky day filled with an explosion of color via (son) sunrays of hope. Coronas appeared so brilliant they became Fire Bows. While viewing these photographic scenes, a couple of cloudbanks seem to say, "Go figure; keep looking up!" Some of the misty visions may cause other thoughts to come to mind. "Face it; got to love it." Translating The Heavens, more than likely the overall message is; "My Holy Spirit symbolized as a bird brings hope. Things are looking up; It's time to celebrate instead of howling at the moon."

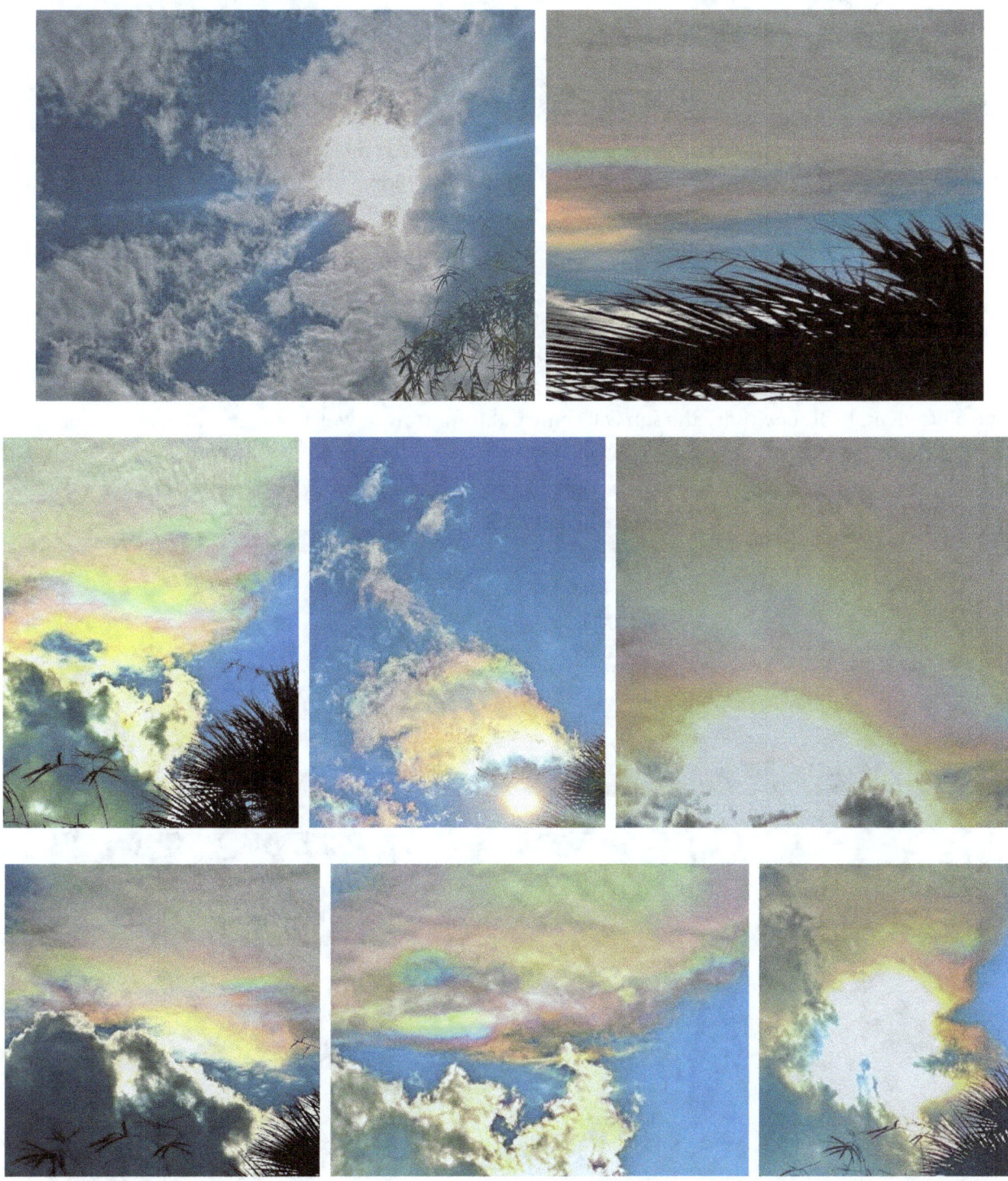

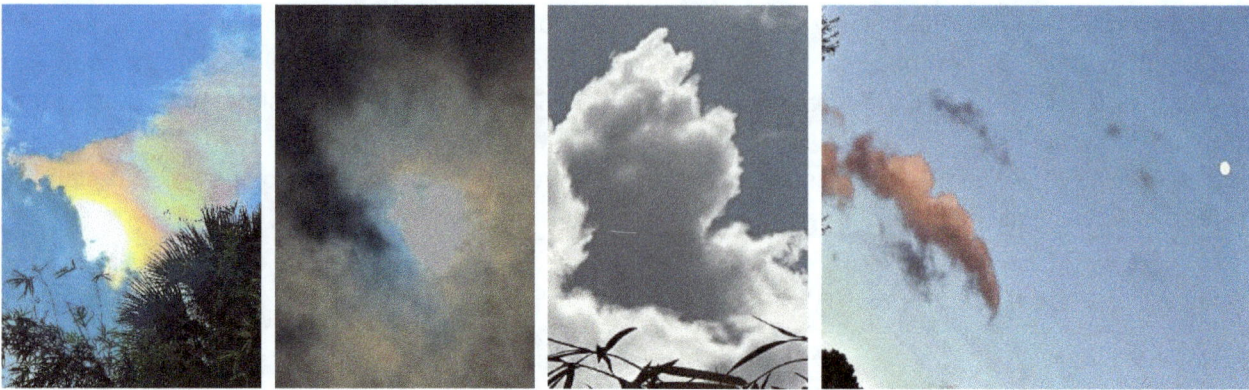

2/17: The clock showed it was an hour before moonset. My camera captured rarely visible sunrays reflected as shafts of light reaching out from the moon; my IPhone, also, snapped a moonbow or halo, which had hints of a corona. Was it my luck or God's providence helping my lens capture these visions for posterity?

Before sundown, there were signs of love, figures to the rescue, and rays of hope. By the way, one of the cloudbanks reminds me of The Tortoise and The Hare. Just as it appears that a speedier force is winning, the turtle, often, meanders to first place because victory is in The Almighty's control. Even as it seems darkness is unconquerable; The Alpha and Omega shows that the shadowy imagery of nightfall is not in control- forever. In other words, the sun will come out tomorrow as well as today and every day until the end of this universe arrives. Thus, keep looking up because all things are possible with God. (Mark 10:12)

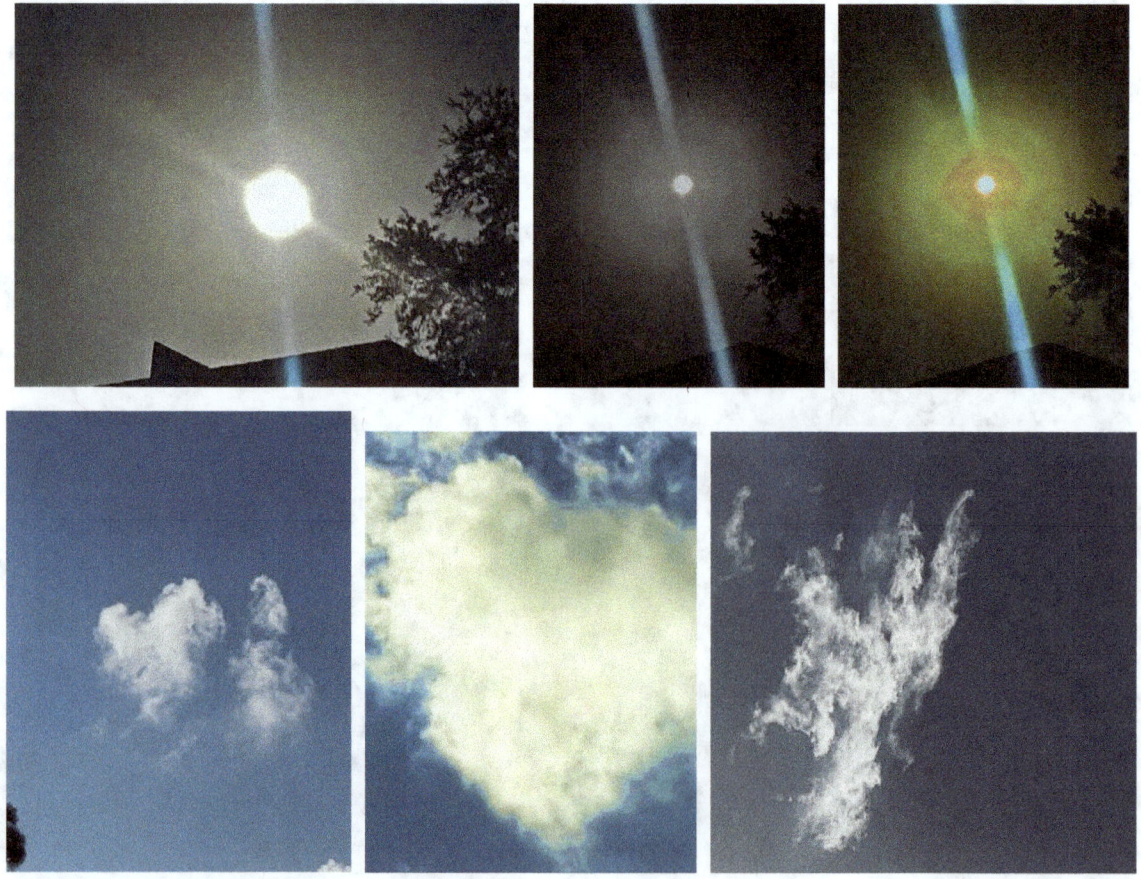

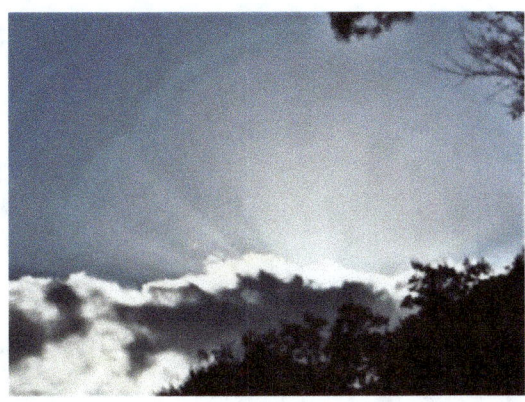 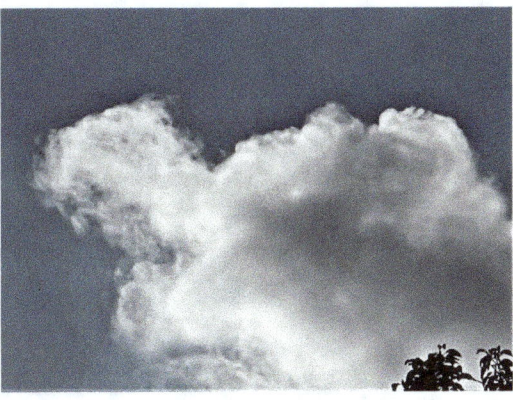

4/29: During this photo session, one cloud looked like the once endangered species called a Manatee. Another water creature caught my eye in the reflection on a pond. Was something fishy going on? While further surveying the sky, I snapped many heart-shaped clouds; God is Love; man's Creator is, also, The Light. Furthermore, His Son or Jesus The Christ used water to describe His own nature; He is the spiritual life healing H2O. Together The Two Entities paint beautiful, iridescent, cloudy scenes in the sky as well as on The Earth.

It appears that The Trinity did some skywriting on the date listed. What could that mean? Everyone sees the vision through their eyes and concepts; take some time to reflect on that thought.

After His crucifixion on The Cross, The Savior left behind The Holy Spirit, depicted as a bird or Dove in The Bible. That Third Entity of The Creator is here to guide souls to the right answers. Just like an elephant, keep in mind that The King of kings or Maker never forgets His own. Yahweh really wants humans to enjoy His Eternal Paradise; therefore, trust His heavenly guidance to lead your soul to Eternal Peace.

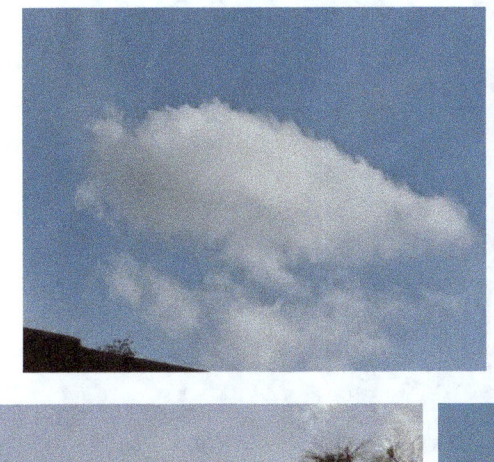 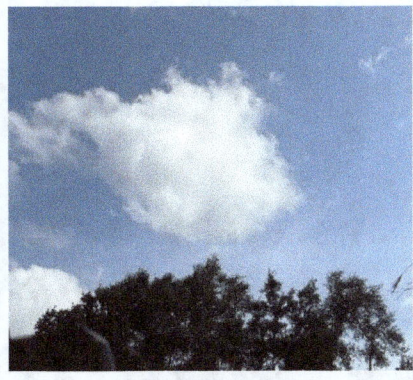 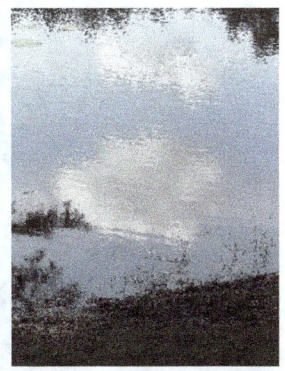

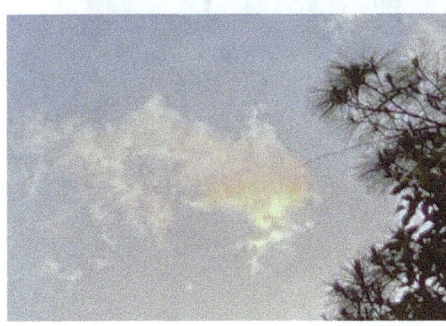  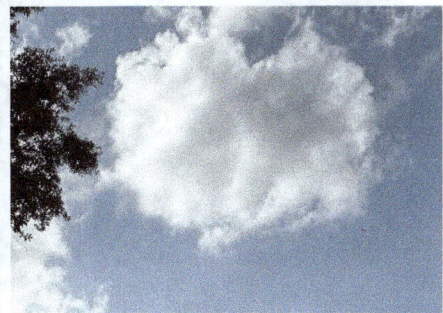

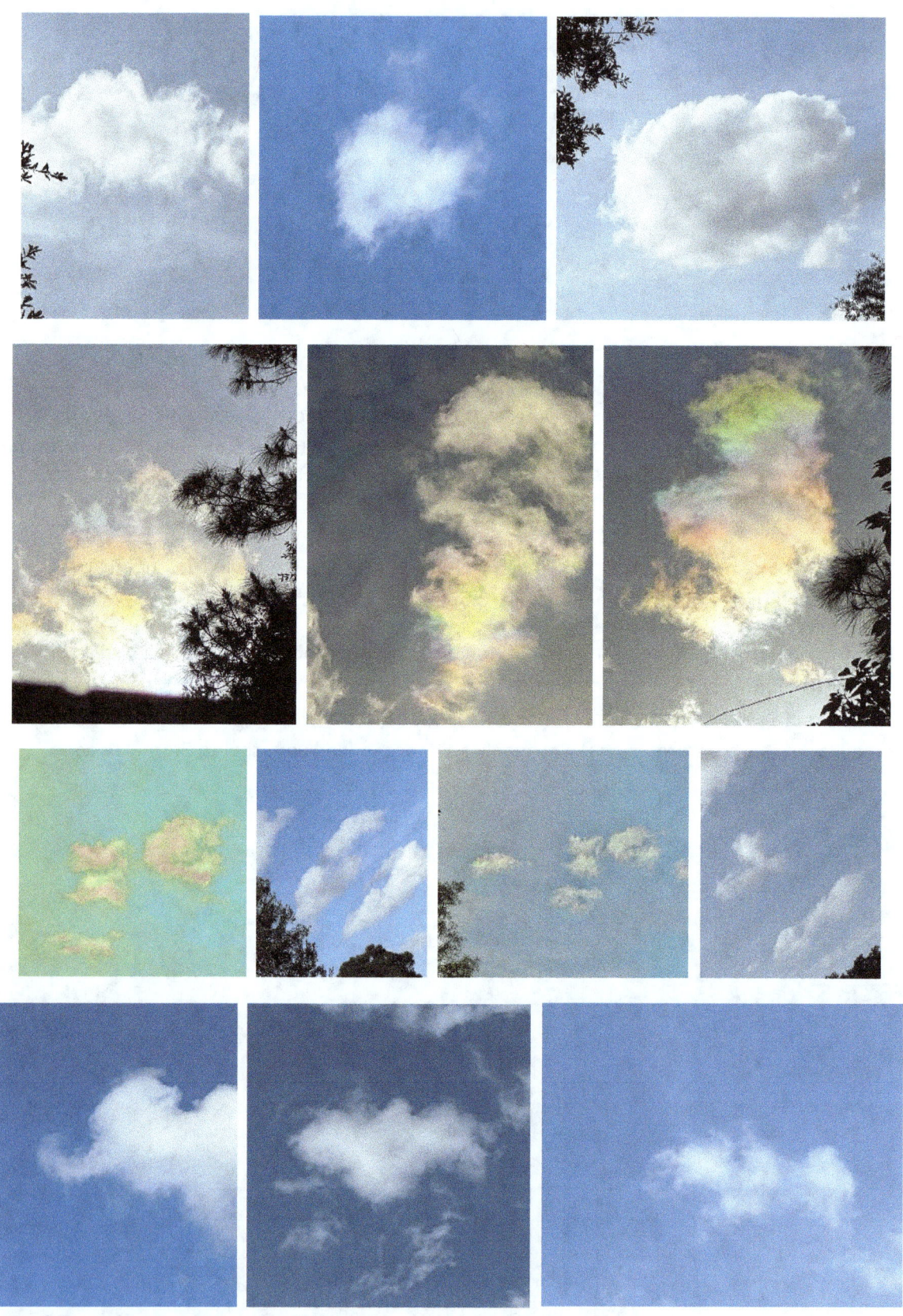

54

5/13 or Friday the 13th: God is "1" Being with "3" Entities; thus, "13" can be accepted as a good instead of as a superstitious or bad number. Look at all the good signs in the sky especially the promise of the two rainbows appearing with about an hour break between each sighting. By the way, the last photo shows that the double rainbow was near dusk and near the time of a full moon; that celestial body is present in the last picture.

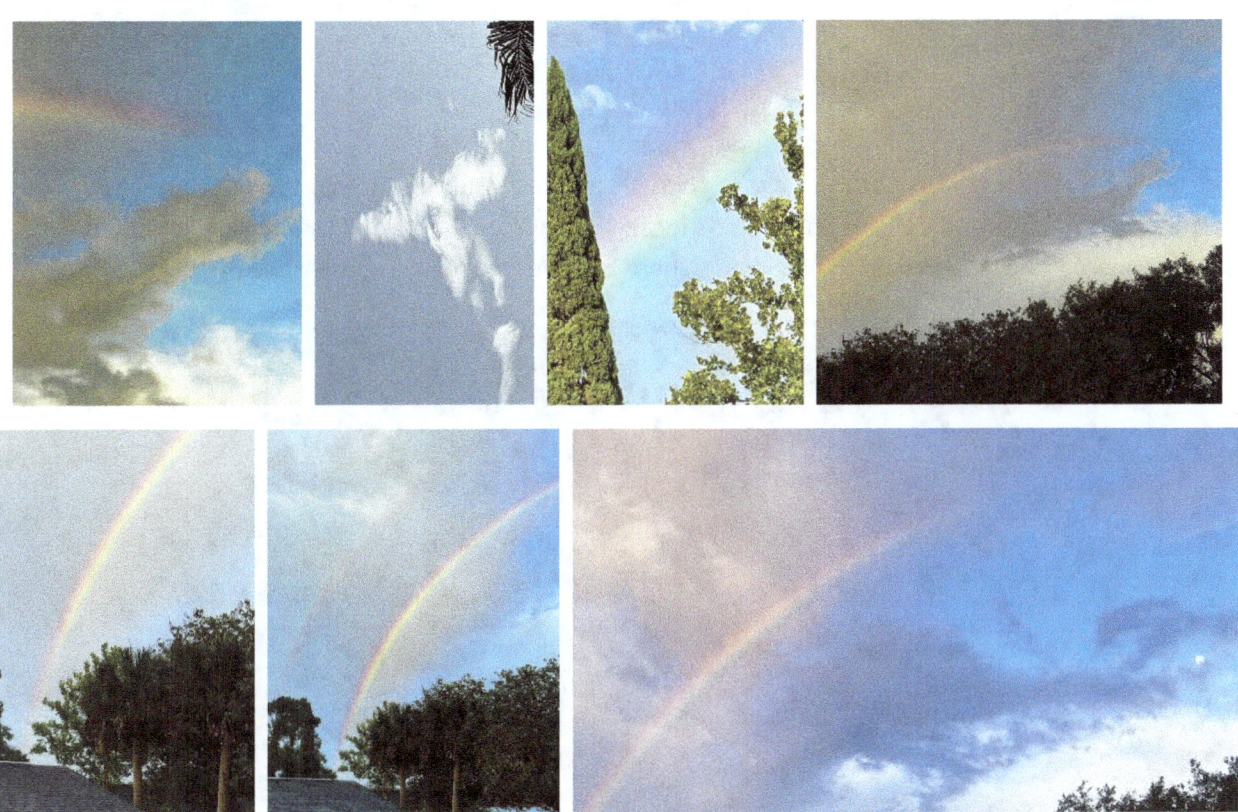

6/3: As described in my series of nonfiction books, my photographic journey started "7" perfect years ago, in June. Since the start of these pseudo diaries full of awe-inspiring scenes with explanations of those snapshots, The Supreme Being still seems to be moving my spirit to the right places to capture visions for posterity. This day started with a burst of color in the sky as well as various signs of The Holy Spirit.

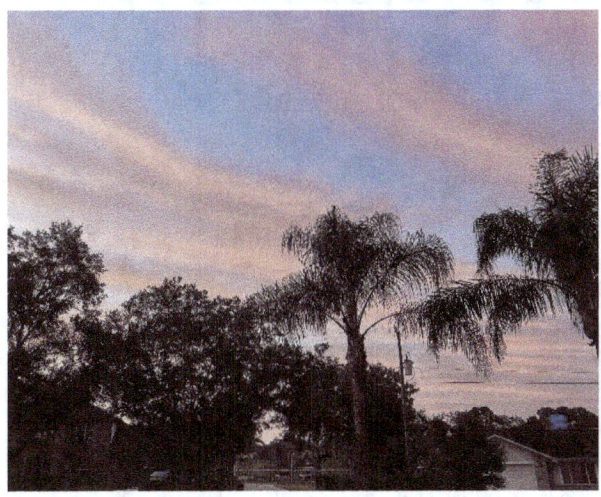 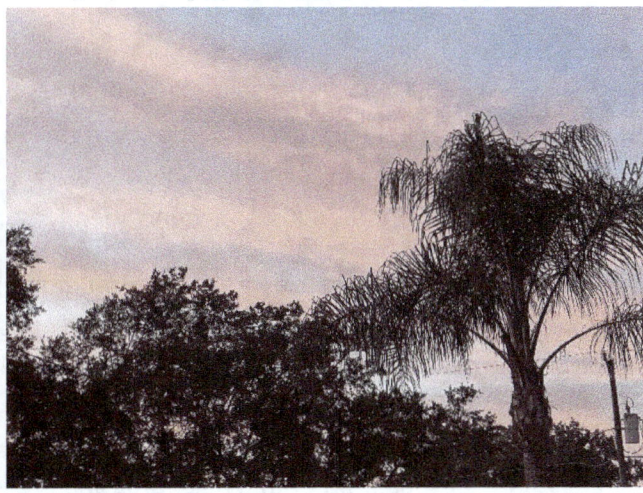

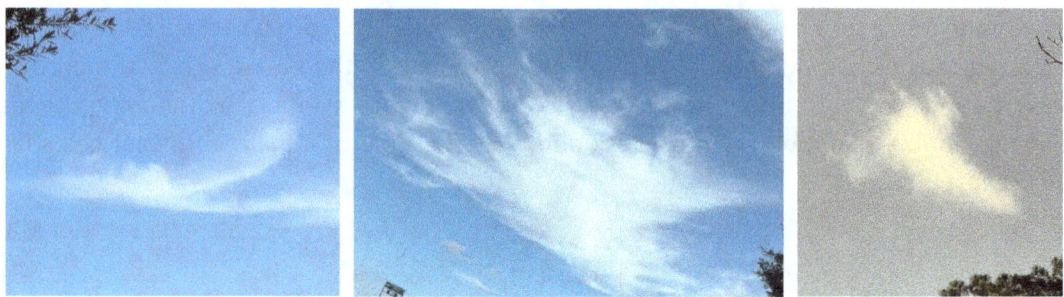

Before the end of the day, many lovely and wonderous clouds came and went. However, once a rainbow appeared without local rain, God's glory really began to shine. Is there a message in the visions? FYI, I have learned that precipitation does not have to be local or visible for the colorful semicircles to appear in the sky; however, it does have to be raining somewhere between the sun and the opposite horizon.

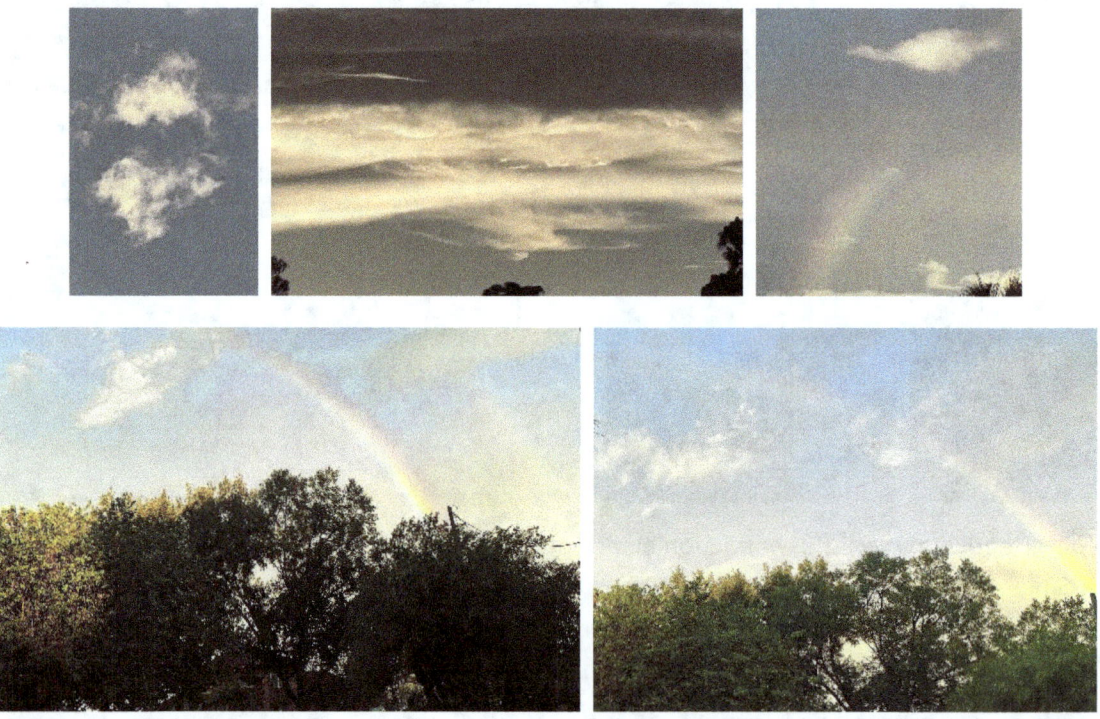

How do I sense a phenomenon is unveiling in The Heavens? Does God guide my footsteps and camera? The Spirit moves me. On 6/3/2022, at around 8PM; through a window, a weird glow outside caught my attention. With my iPhone, I raced outdoors to the back, covered patio. Most of the sky was blue but in one corner I saw a stunning and vivid scene. Colorful archways and glowing clouds were a part of what captured my attention. My sunset view included "3" or more rainbows in the sky at once.

The two overlapping semicircles are called a Twin Rainbow. That bright, fat, colorful curve was on my radar as I leaned over the rail of my covered back porch. It's a rare situation where "2" bows sit almost directly on top of each other; and it is caused by "2" different size rain drops in the sky- simultaneously. I'd seen the phenomenon before while in Colorado. In June of 2022, I didn't see the overlap area until my camera lens zoomed in on a huge, multihued arc. Near the purple area, faintly but most definitely, the dueling rainbows fought for dominance. Amazingly, a double bow developed as a part of the twins.

Then, oddly, weirdly, or miraculously- misty visions included an angel-like cloud. That vision was shocking pink and captured my attention while leading my footsteps to the front of my house, which faces mostly South. Surprisingly, a rainbow was in that part of The Heavens. Its right side shined at 152 degrees on a compass or mostly South; the left side was just a tad East. I'd seen that vision once before in the nearly fifteen years that I've lived in this part of Florida.

In fact, on 6/14/2021, a scientist and I chatted online in a photo group after I posted that other skewed rainbow; he said that it may be that sunrays were bouncing off the surrounding lakes and waterways causing the phenomenon. I live on a narrow peninsula; so, that could be the explanation. Or, are the "5" planets lining up in June causing weird scenes above my head? Maybe, a Mighty Wind is in control and blowing the curve due West!? Note that the first photo shows that rainbow planted in the Southern Sky in June of 2021. That picture is, also, in an earlier dated and different nonfiction or pseudo diary.

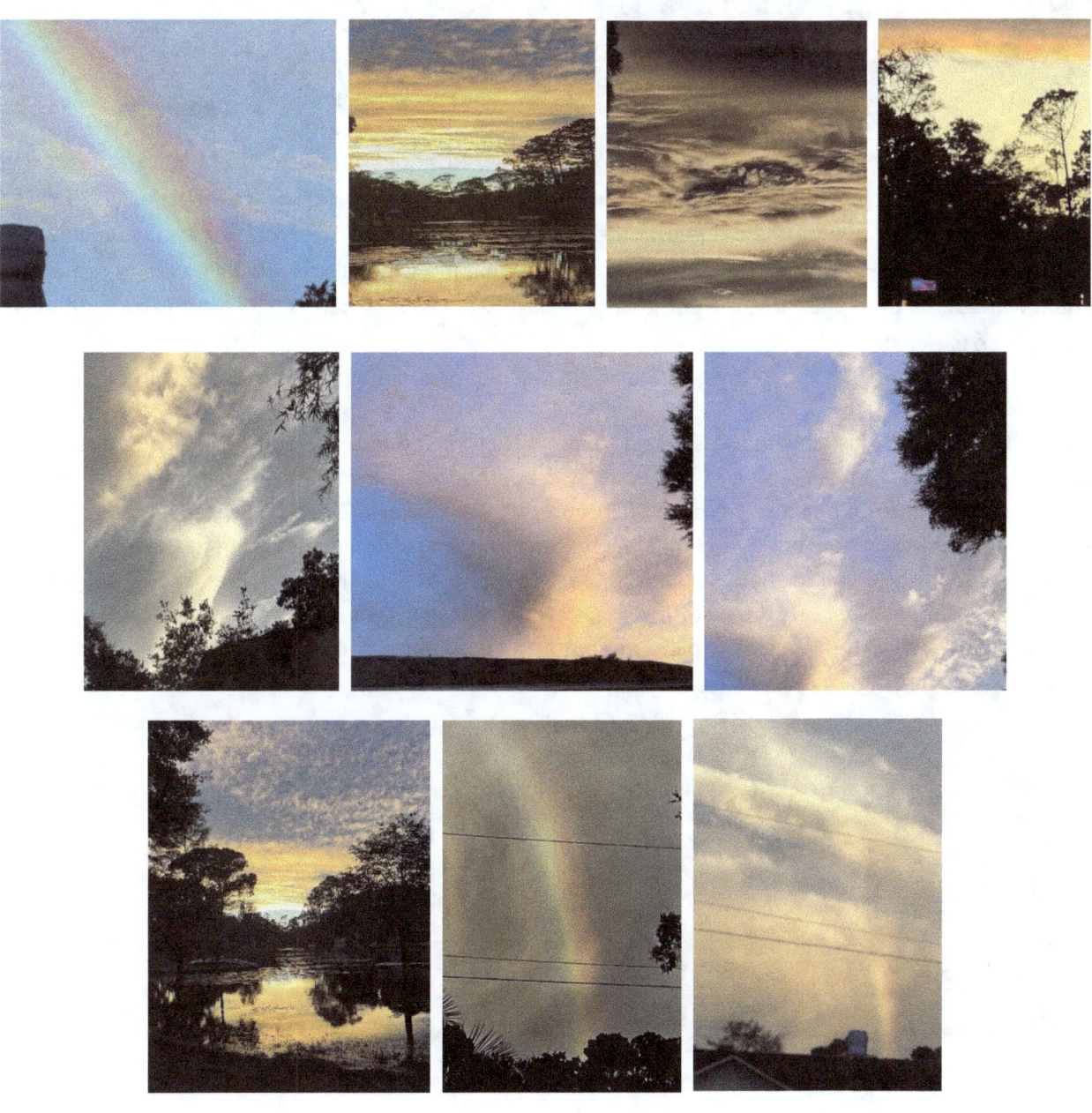

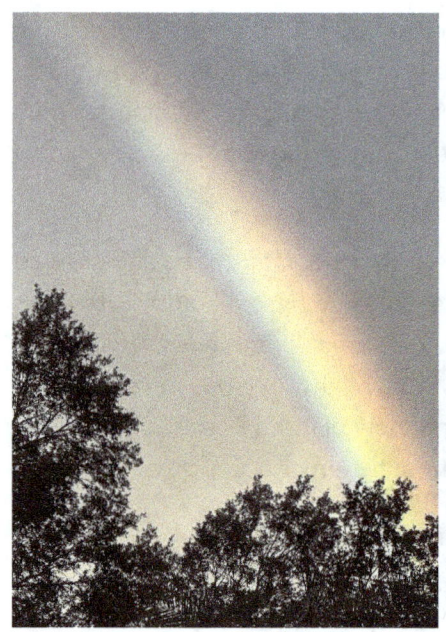 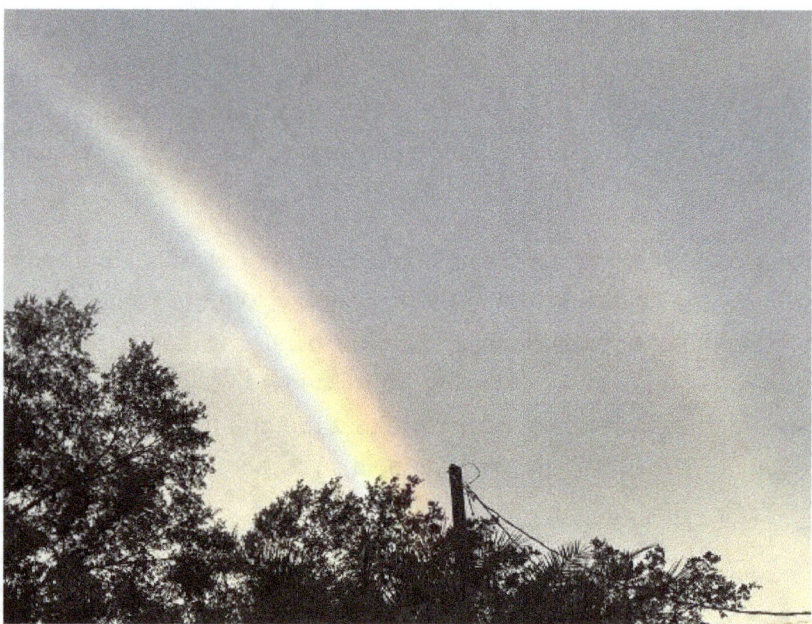

In short, On 6/3, the skyborne message from God may be about promises that He keeps. The Old Testament contains The Almighty Father's pledge to Noah and the world. Meanwhile, in The New Testament, there are two prominent guarantees by Jesus. He said that The Holy Spirit's guidance would remain behind after His Crucifixion. The Son of The Alpha and Omega told His followers that mankind would witness His triumphant return- someday. The last two vows are part of The New Testament in The Bible. Three is a charm.

Antisolar Sunrays

This next discussion may explain the skewed rainbow that moved into the Southern Sky. Shafts of light pass The Earth to the opposite side of The Heavens from the sun. Sometimes, they are visible at dawn or dusk. This phenomenon happens because The Center of The Universe is a huge, three-dimensional ball. At certain times, its rays passing this planet can be seen as illuminated beams racing to the other side. On 10/6/2018, the sunset included antisolar rays; these two photos are, also, explained in <u>God's Present in Photos</u>. Snapshot number one is the setting sun; the adjacent snapshot is the Eastern Sky; and the scenes happened nearly simultaneously. The pictures captured for posterity follow.

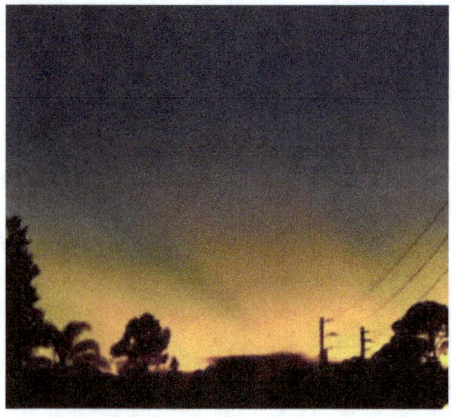 

6/4: The first photo of a rainbow was from a transient beam of light; my iPhone helped capture it in a grocery store's, parking lot. About an hour later, the view was from my lawn. Almost twenty-three hours passed before a repeat performance of the visions from yesterday occurred. This time, it dawned on me that the moving rainbow might be a result of where the dark clouds opened and the way the sunrays escaped to form the imagery. Near the end of the photo session, a colorful arc sat at about 152 degrees or Southwest. Since I began my photo journey of The Heavens "7" perfect years ago; this is the third time that I've stood by my garage wondering how a rainbow was sitting more South and West than normal. What is really going on? I believe that antisolar sunrays are moving the rainbow as they break through dark clouds in the West Sky. Those light beams may be bending and moving the appearance of the rainbow's location. God does amazing things in The Heavens.

The sky visions got even more incredible that day. As I filmed that 6/4/2022 bow, the curve appeared fatter; thus, I zoomed in. My lens captured a rare phenomenon, again. Another, uncommon, Twin Rainbow was skewed on the horizon. An up-close picture shows the two semicircles fighting for dominance. Each time that these unusual, dual archways battled for supremacy- it happened after "High Noon." It was the third time that my lens captured an uncommon, Twin Rainbow. Luckily, in some of the next photos, the viewer can sort of see the second semicircles jockeying for attention; oddly, two of those three occasions were yesterday and today or in June. The other time was during my first visit to Colorado to see my new grandson or on 9/14/2021; that Twin Rainbow is in this book, too. No matter what caused the visions, God is The Artist of these mystical scenes.

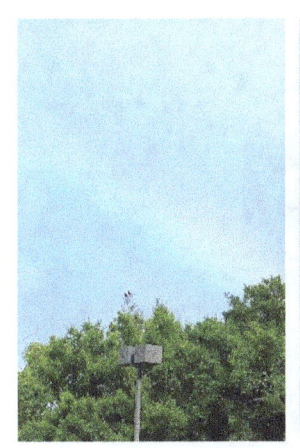
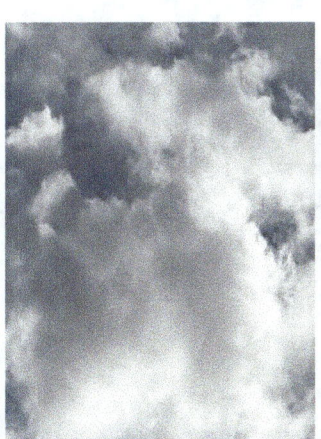
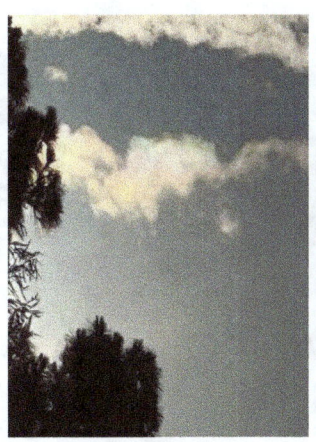

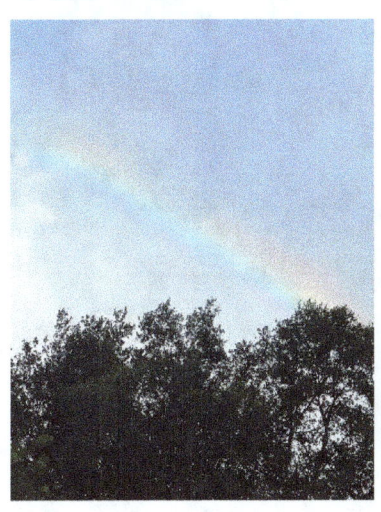
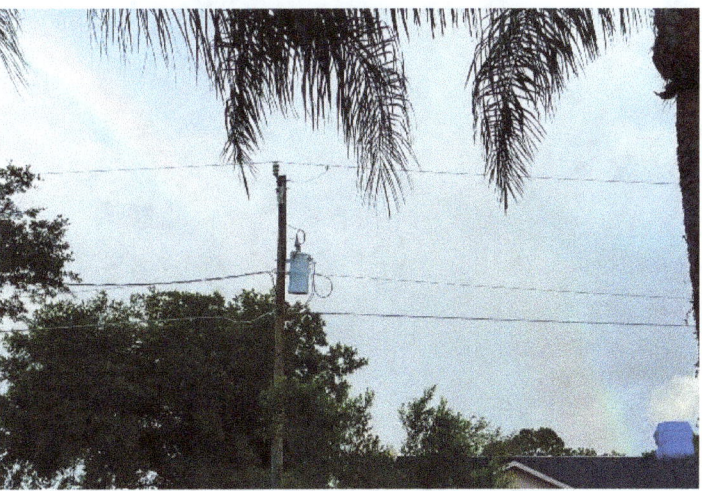

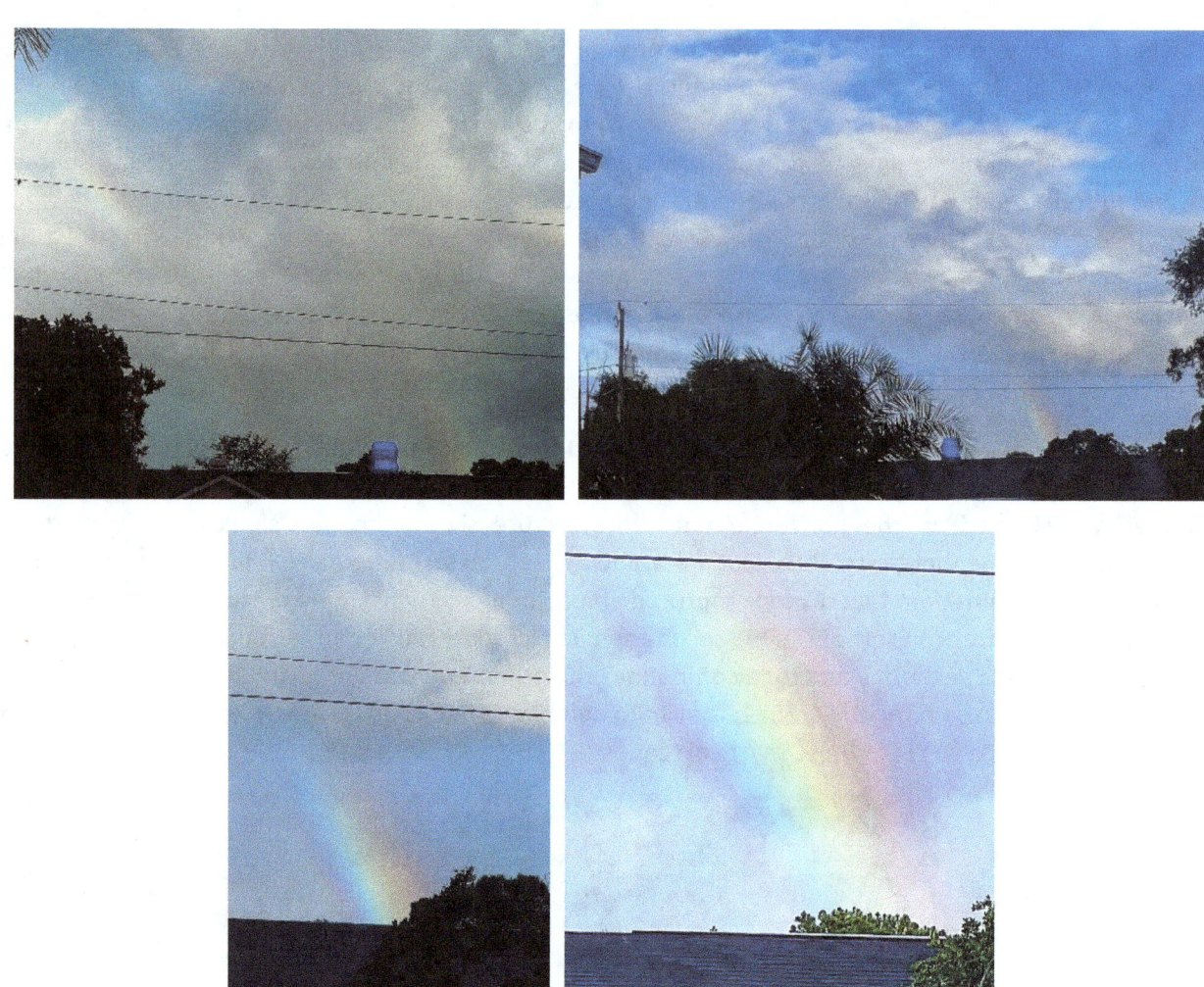

Chapter 5: Vacations before Heaven's Paradise

8/12:While at the beach, I wondered. 'Are there messages in the sky?' FYI, during this excursion, my grandson was born premature in order to save my daughter's life; she was diagnosed with HELLP. They both survived the over a week stay due to my child's condition; the baby was released from neonatal care within two days. The first photo kept me sane because The Artist painted light, happy rather than shocking scenes.

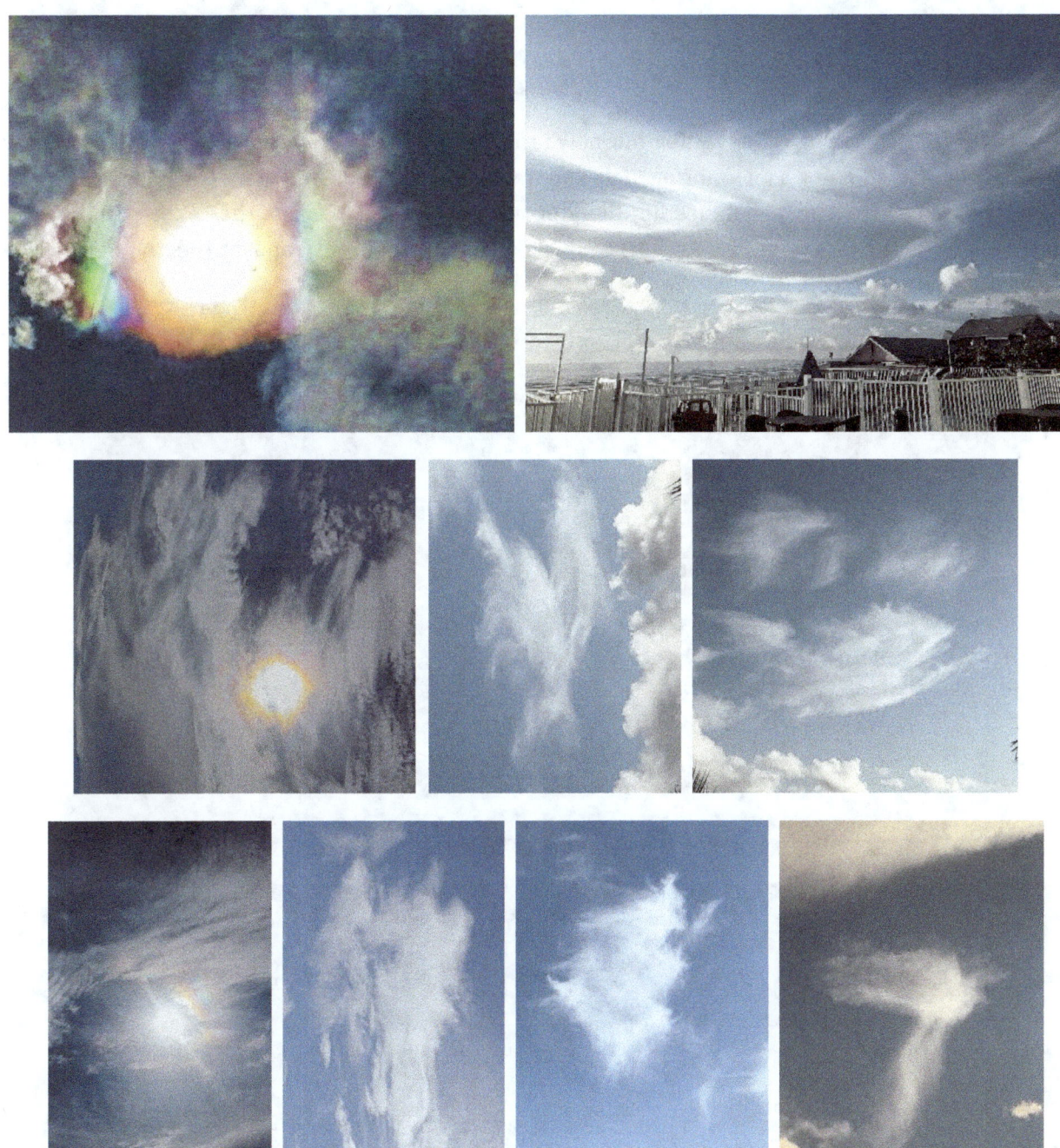

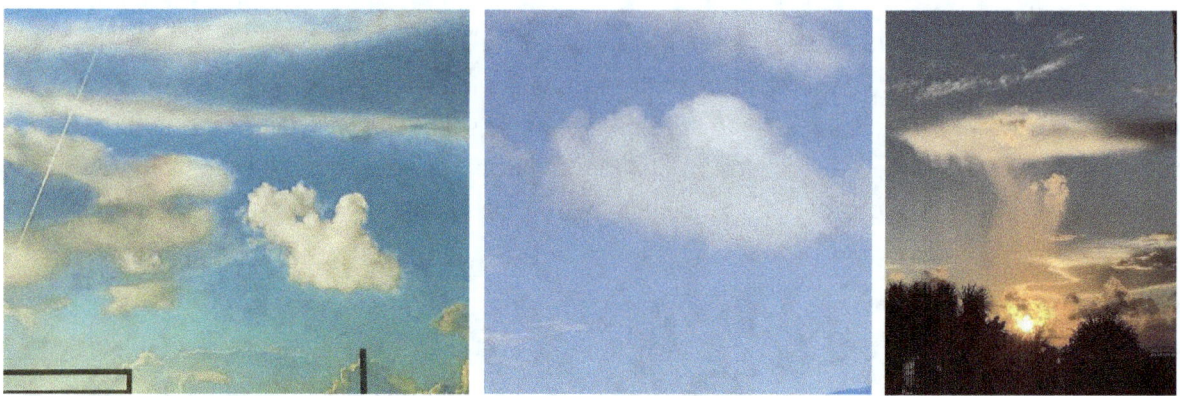

10/11: We were sightseeing while visiting our newborn grandson. This day was windy as we passed by Castle Rock in Colorado. At a soul's mortal, life's end- the goal is to reside in or near God's castle. Jesus is The Rock as well as The Christian Redeemer that opened The Pearly Gates due to His acceptance of His Father's Will and plan. (Psalm 118:22, Acts 4:11 …) Enjoy the next snapshots, and let The Holy Spirit guide you towards Eternal Peace.

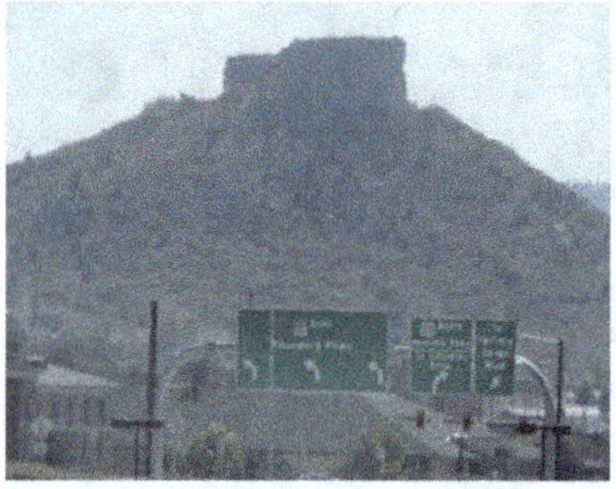

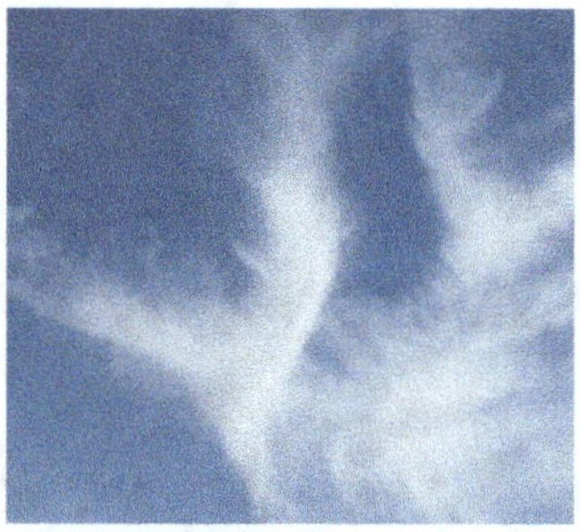

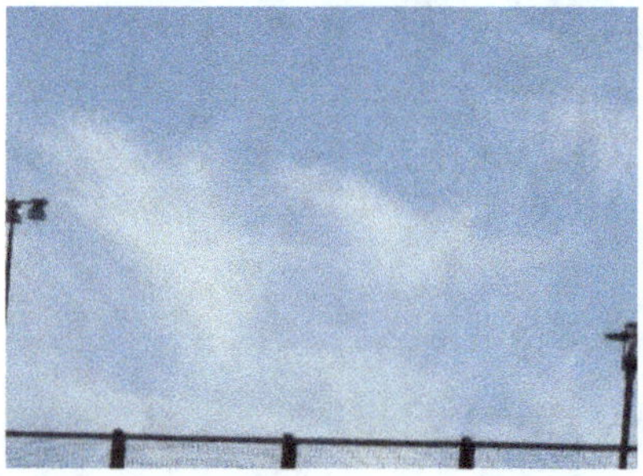

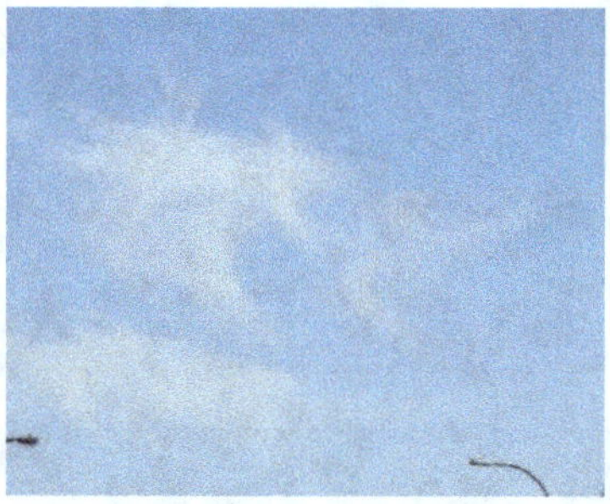

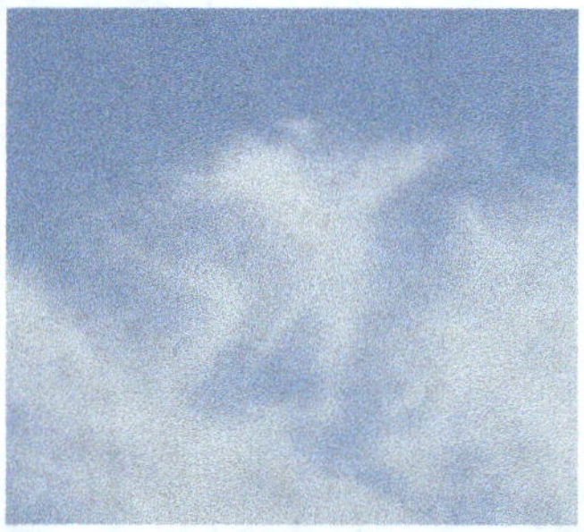

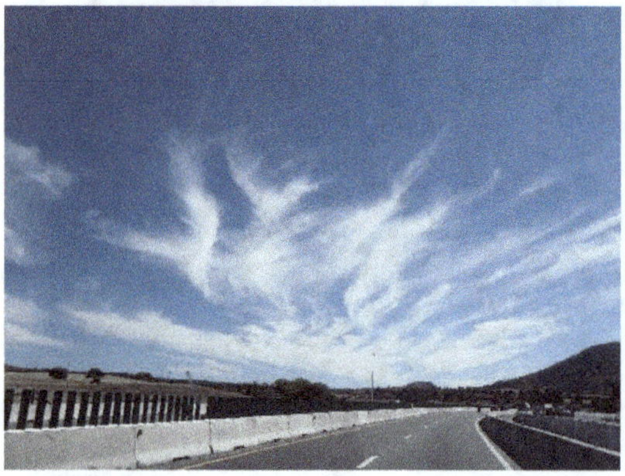

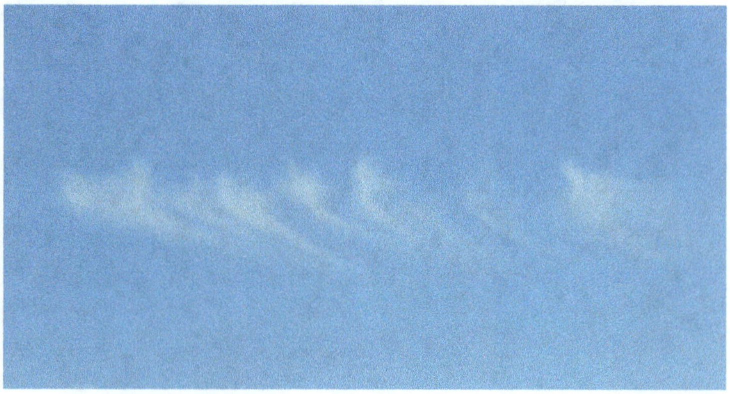

2/22: When Mike and I eloped in our twenties, it was not for immature reasons. Both of our sets of parents were in bad transitions in life. My husband's mother and father were divorcing. My folks were in a sad period based on Dad's, ongoing, mental illness. Everyone said our marriage would not last a year. For our 43rd anniversary, we decided to go to my first church and school on the way to South Beach. Life changed even in Miami. Why did I want to go back to my old stomping grounds? The Presence talked to my soul for the first time during my kindergarten year; back then we were in portables awaiting the school house's completion. I'm missed my ride home. As I sat on my classroom's steps, at age 4, the message was that I was in the most selfish generation, yet.

Some things changed in sixty plus years and not always for the better. When I was a child, my family went to Miami Beach after mass on most Sundays because dad was an avid surfer. While at the shore, Jewish, old folks gave kids quarters for reminding them of their grandchildren in the Northeast. South Beach is not that kind of a neighborhood, today. Meanwhile, my brother, sisters, and I played with green lizards or chameleons; they were native reptiles not Iguanas. In a world of turmoil, my soul wonders what transitions are good and what adversity should be converted or completely avoided.

Day one of our trip, while we were driving South, in the sky, a bird as well as heart-like clouds raced past. Later, a ray of hope appeared. The Holy Spirit whispered; "I'm still present. Look up at the well-lit sky; my Son is The Ray of Hope; it's still about My Love in The Heavens."

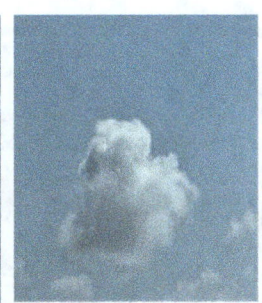
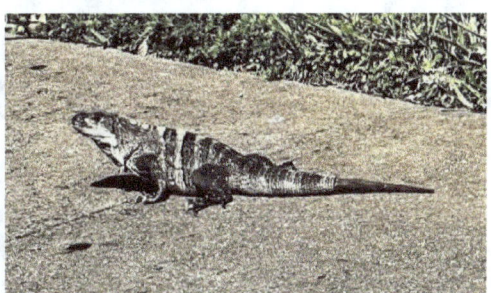
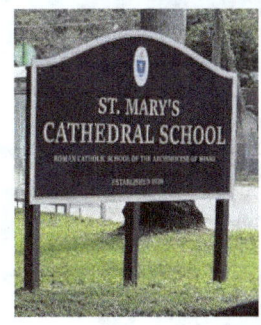
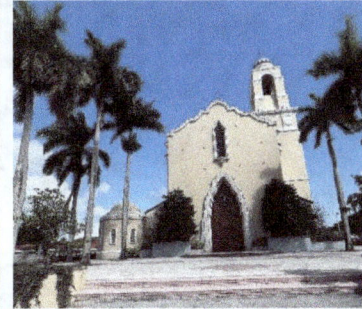
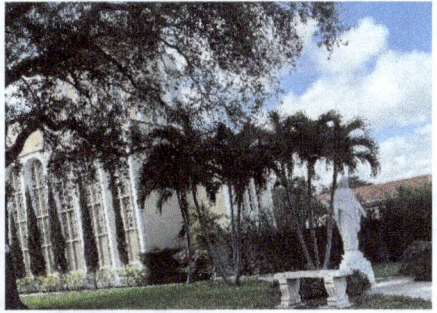
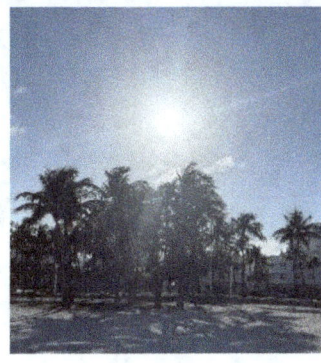

2/23: This day was my husband and my anniversary; it was our day at the beach. Once back to our hotel room, we discovered that this selfish generation made the news. Did the Third World War start while we were enjoying life? Surprisingly, a happy face filled The Heavens. It seems that God is still okay with some people, places, or things in this world. In Revelations in The Bible, The Almighty warned of The Evil One's goal to decay and root out The Supreme Being's goodness planted on The Earth by Jesus The Christ or The Living example of The Law of Love aka The Golden Rule. The King of kings warned of wars and rumors of wars during uncertain times. Our Father in Heaven, also, said; "Don't worry; be happy because My Son will claim the final victory."

Is Yahweh's writing, also, on the wall? By the way, the white hieroglyphics or symbols are reflected sunlight from dawn. On the building there is a glowing angel-like area with a downward arrow indicating that His Story or communication is ongoing on this planet even during uncertain times. Keep The Faith; seek rays of hope; and find Love at the end of each rainbow because that is The True Treasure in Heaven's opinion. In case you were wondering, I have hundreds of cloudy, heart-shaped images to prove that thought. Enjoy my point of view captured for posterity by the lens of my camera and IPhone.

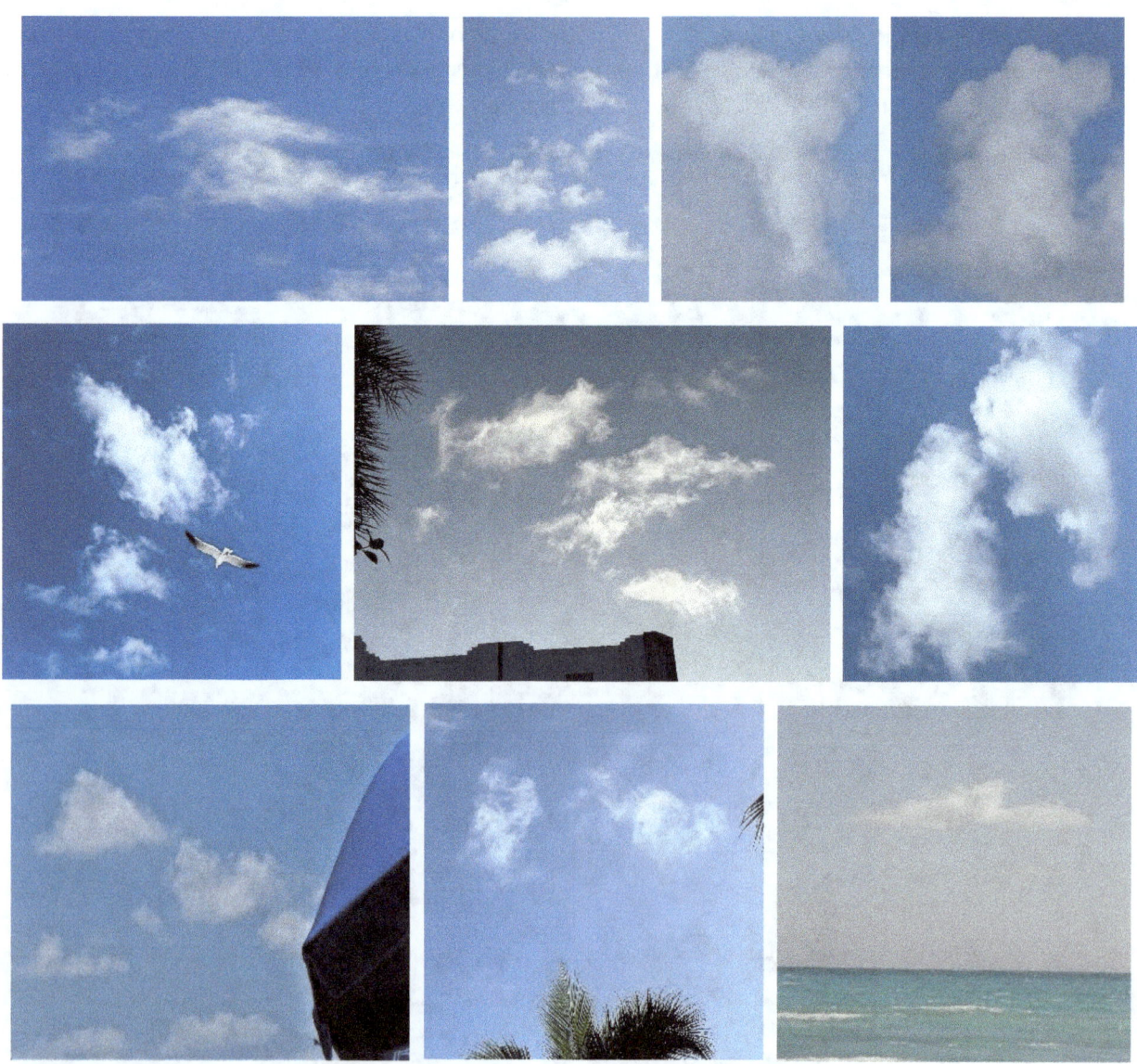

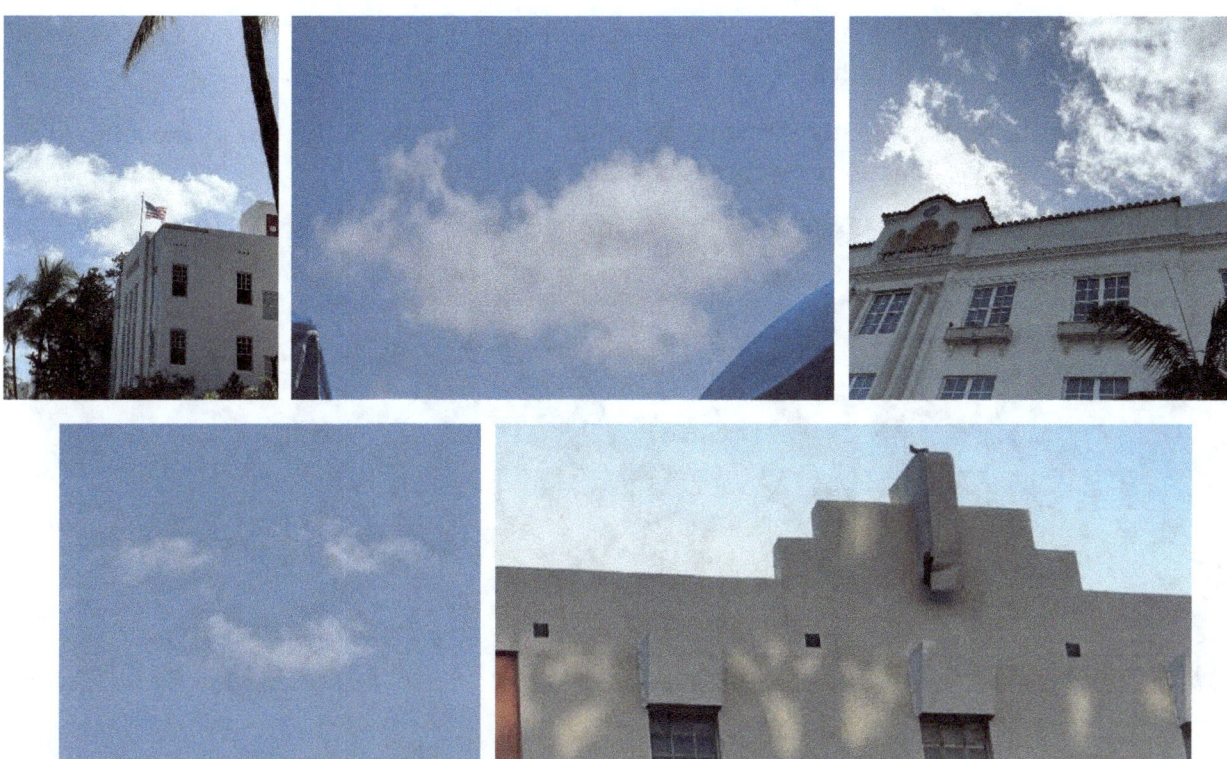

2/24: Once upon a time, while in a Bible study group, while learning about the early Christians and digesting the ramifications of their hardships and struggles, I stated. "Sometimes, innocent bystanders are affected by warring and evil humans. However, the good news is that God always rights the world; and people come out at the other end of the turmoil once they stand against The Devil's Army." While speaking, I shuddered because my psyche and soul saw this current inhumanity and destruction of morality in visions throughout my lifetime starting at age 4, which is discussed elsewhere in this narrative and other nonfictions I authored. Some of the Christians I warned scoffed at my thoughts deciding that we were not close to that situation; they thanked God.

Later that year, Covid-19 was unleashed; and then, the consequences of bowing to the wrong masters occurred. Some of the animosity converting to violence was justified; some of the antagonism was inexcusable. All along, I kept saying. "Voting based on hating one person while ignoring the evil mindset of the other candidate will hurt us all in the end."

Where do we go from here? The happy, unselfish solution is in The Heavens. Will a majority of people awaken in time to save this planet?

God asked me if I'd rather be in The Last Generation and avoid the coffin via The Rapture and The Second Coming of The Messiah or help turn this immorality around for my grandchildren's sake? As much as I try not to see my death and secular burial before reaching His Realm in The Afterlife, I'd give my grandchildren a better life over boasting that I was here when the Promised Messiah aka The New Morning Star returned. I hope to see His Triumph over The Devil but it can be from either side of life- mortal or reincarnated as in immortal as well as living forever in The Best Eternal Paradise. In the meantime, life is about enjoying the present. It's, also, about taking pleasure in the breaks from reality while on vacation or at other times in life. In addition, it should be about celebrating all the good relationships along the way to the best bond, which is with Love aka The Creator of Heaven and The Earth.

While looking at the beauty in nature around the world; can you imagine the rest of the vision of its Maker? I hope my photographic journey opened the door to His Splendor.

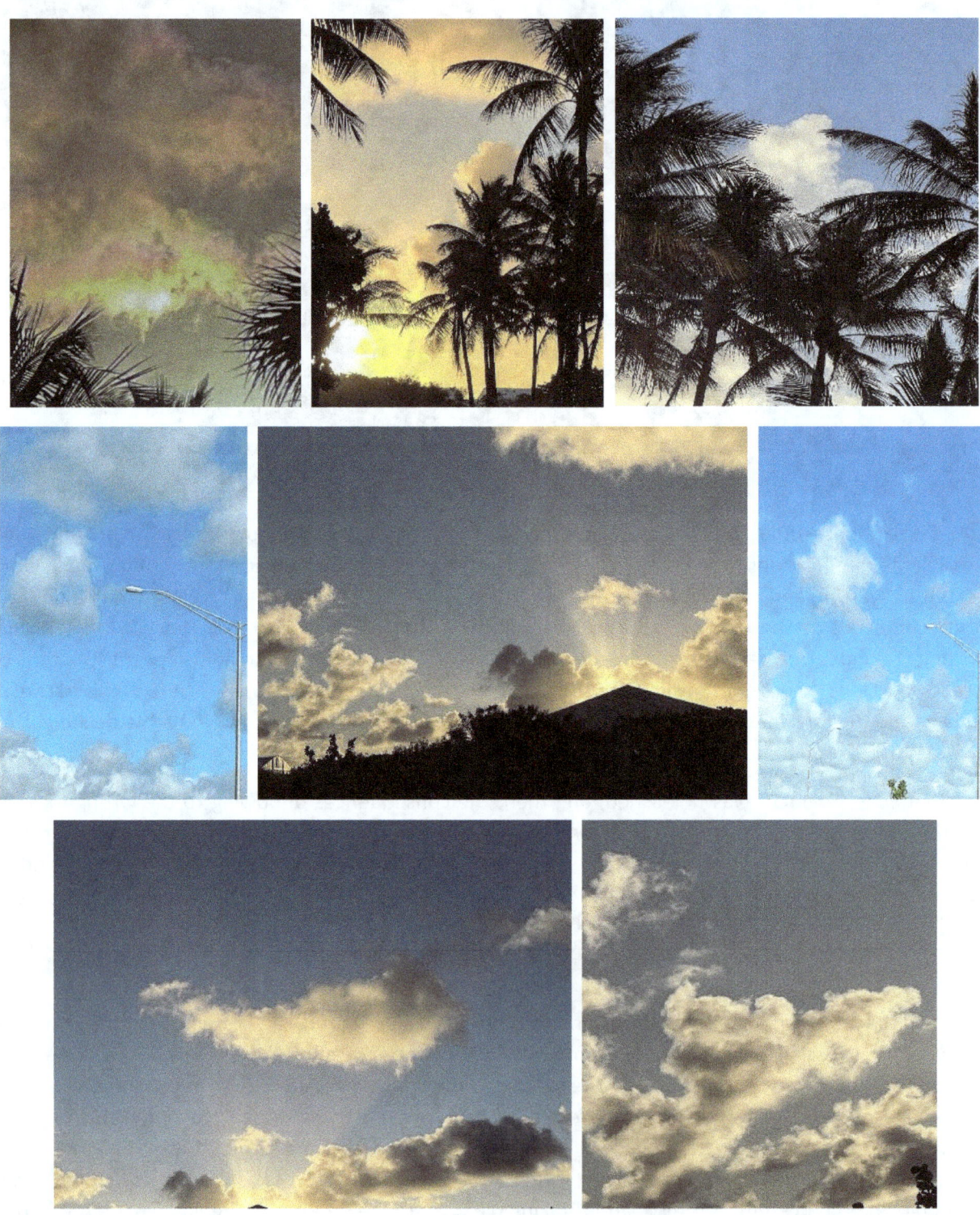

Chapter 6: The Book of Life

Don't Worry Before It's Time to Do It

Has God's heart grown dark as he watches mankind falling under The Devil's spell of evil?

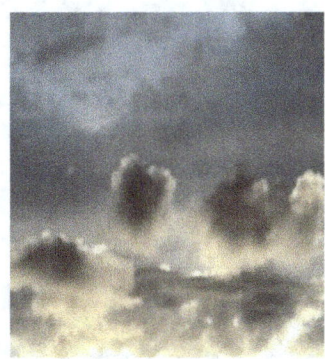 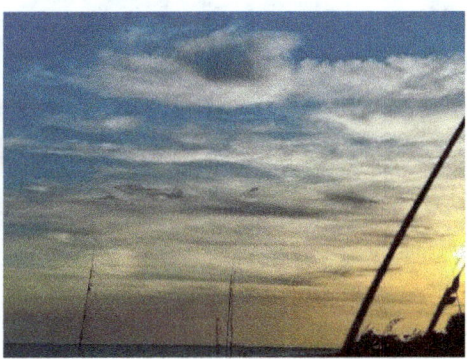

Will this generation witness a mushroom cloud (destruction) or The Tree of Life? Will The Triune God prevail?

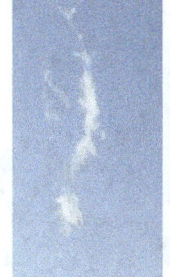 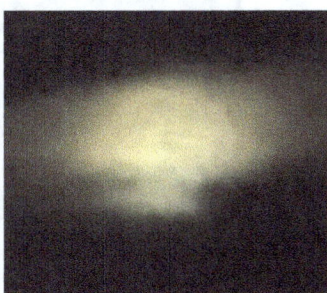 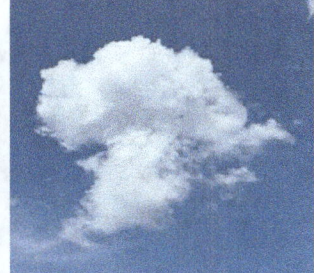 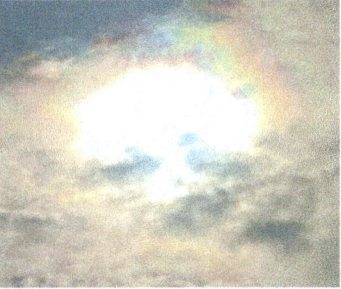

If you keep looking up, you may see that God is always there, 24/7. So, enjoy the journey of your life with Him at the realm. Remember The Holy Spirit was left behind by Jesus The Christ at The Will of His Father; that Love Bird is there to guide His people to His Eternal Paradise as well as to help promote the happiness in this world. Face it; and then, find your own Heavenly visions.

Stairway to Heaven

Can humans buy a stairway to Heaven? God, just like elephants, never forgets and knows all the figures including negative or positive influencers. In the end, He will weed out the goats from His sheep.

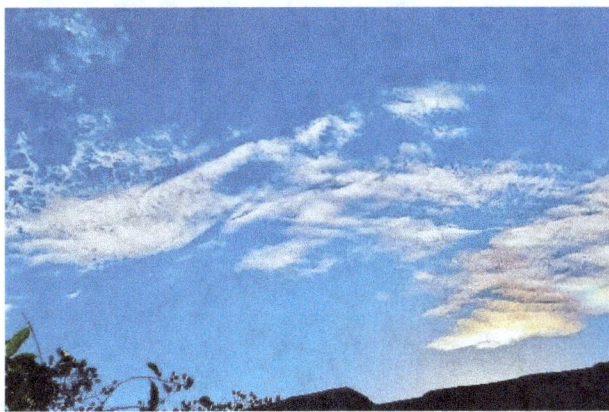 

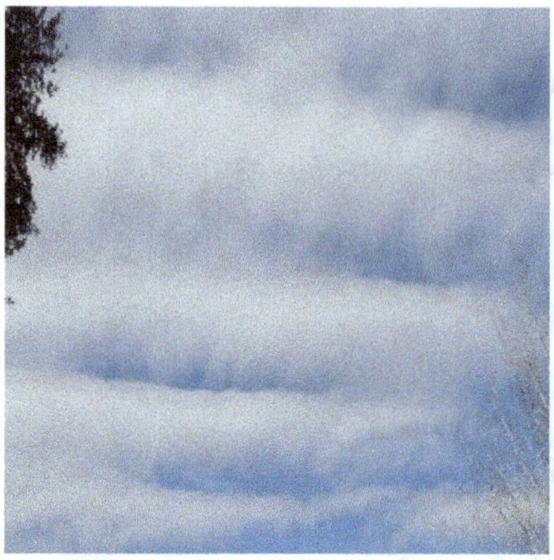

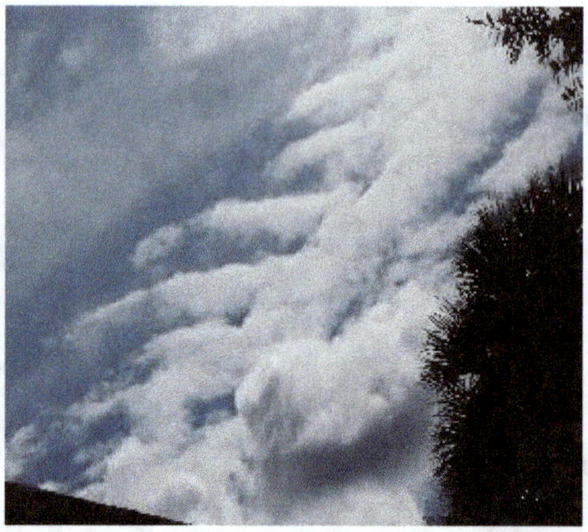

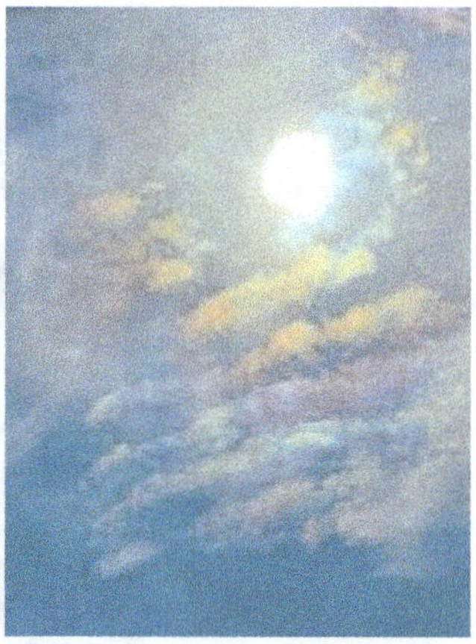

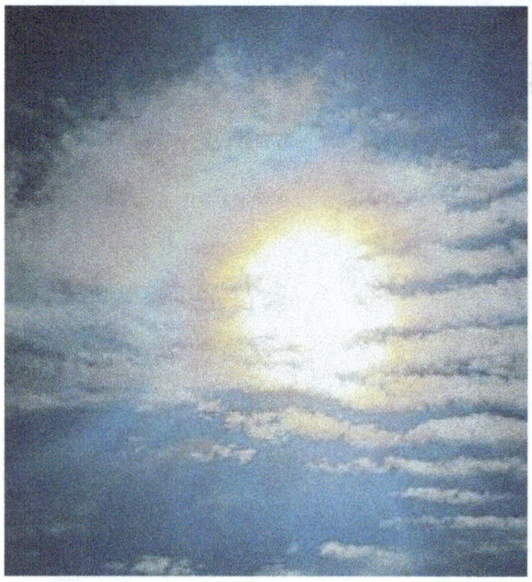

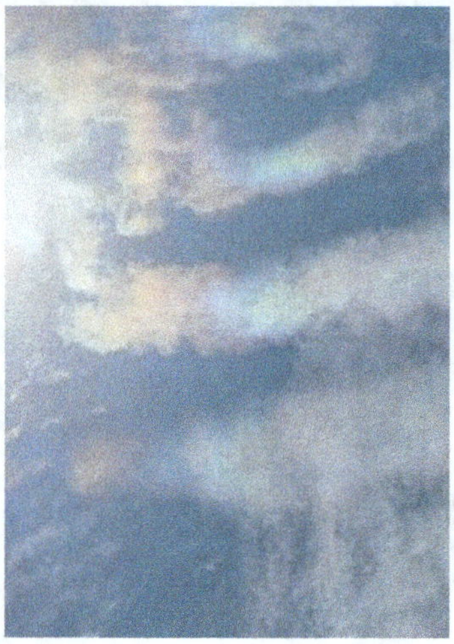

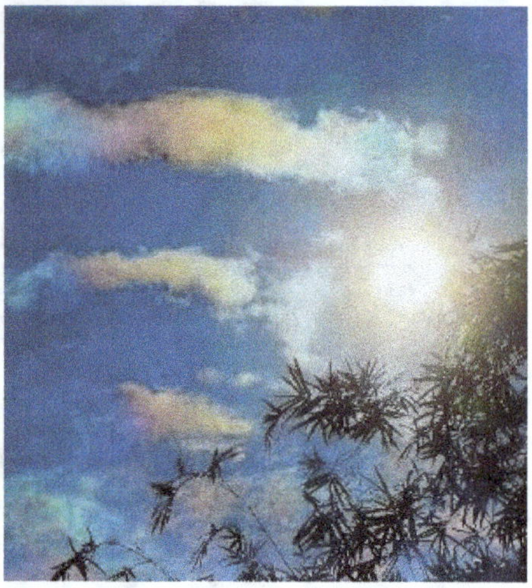

1/15: While snapping the vision, my thoughts were; "It's foggy but heavenly. Those cloudy stairs can be maneuvered with the help of The Old Man's Spirit and angelic guides; reflect on that thought. Meanwhile, the end goal of The Infinitely-Right Trinity is "L"ove aka The essence of The Creator of it all.

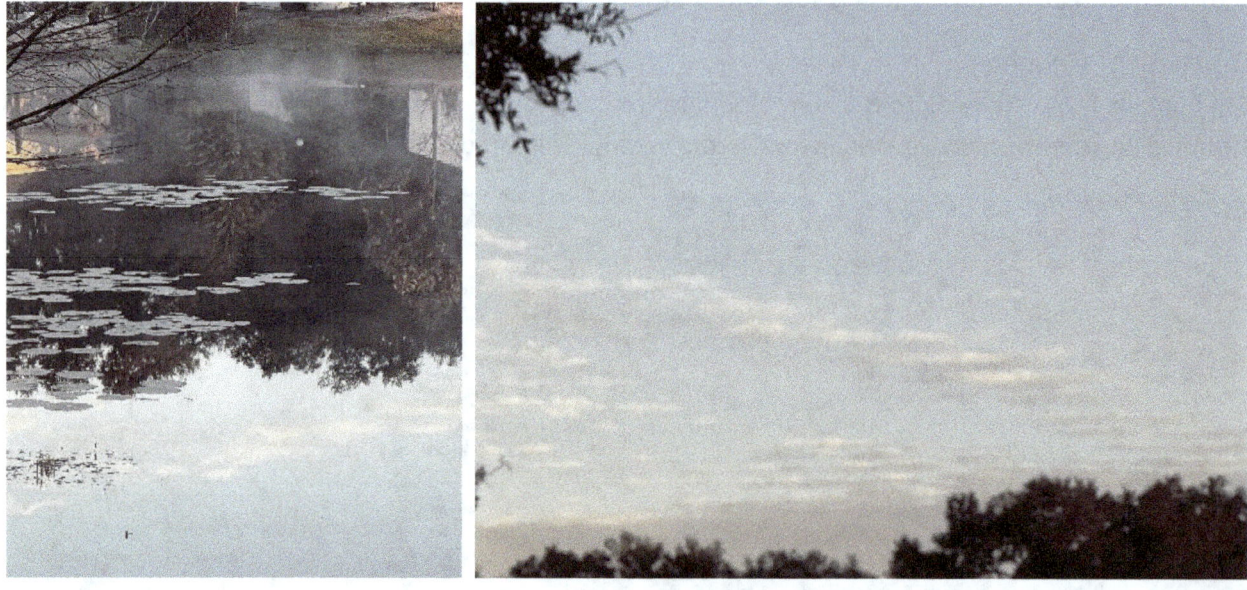

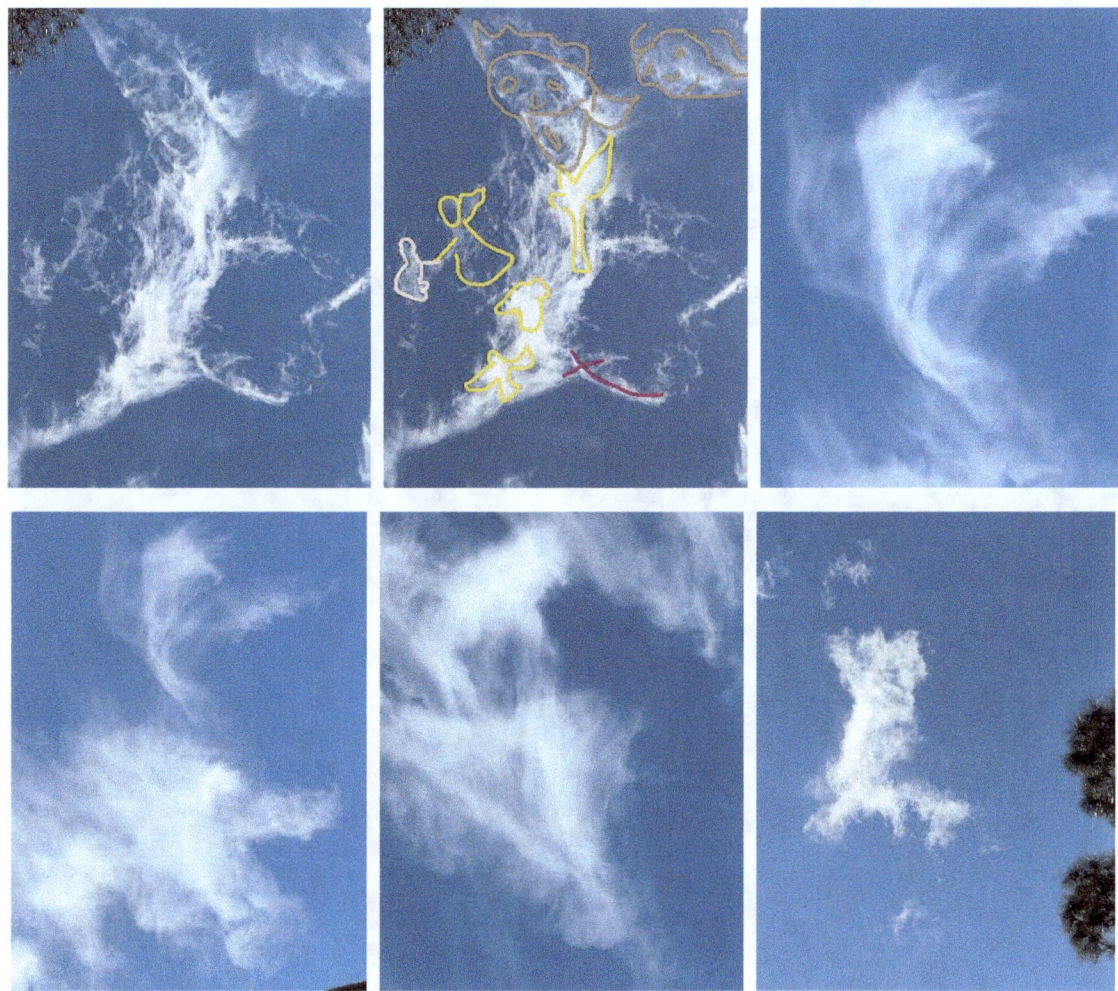

8/21: The rainbow or colorful sky bound arc in two pictures was a water spot on the camera's lens but it highlights The Almighty's promises kept. The Messiah came over 2000 years ago; dying on the cross, The Redeemer reopened the Pearly Gates reversing the sinful fall of Adam and Eve. Christ's lifestyle exemplified the perfection of living in God's Will aka The Golden Rule. On the day these snapshots were taken, a relative escaped this mortal life going over the rainbow to the other side where the true treasure resides. He's with The Father due to The lamb of God aka Jesus The Christ's noble deed. That's the good news because Jose lives on in God's Realm.

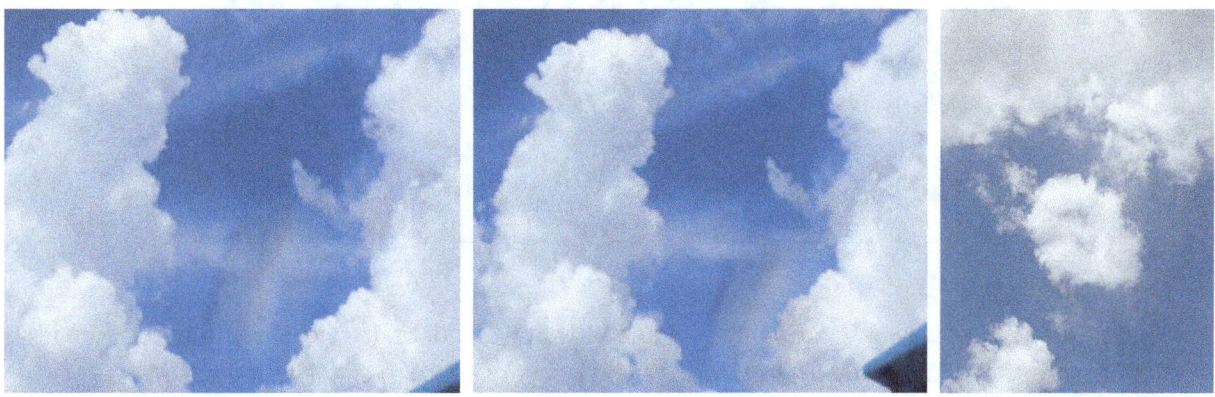

Mom's on the Roof and I Can't Get Her Down
12/29: FYI, the skywriting appears to say "ice". My mother was very demanding of that water before she left to Her vacation in Eternal Paradise. "FYI", Jesus is The Water that brings life here, there, and everywhere.

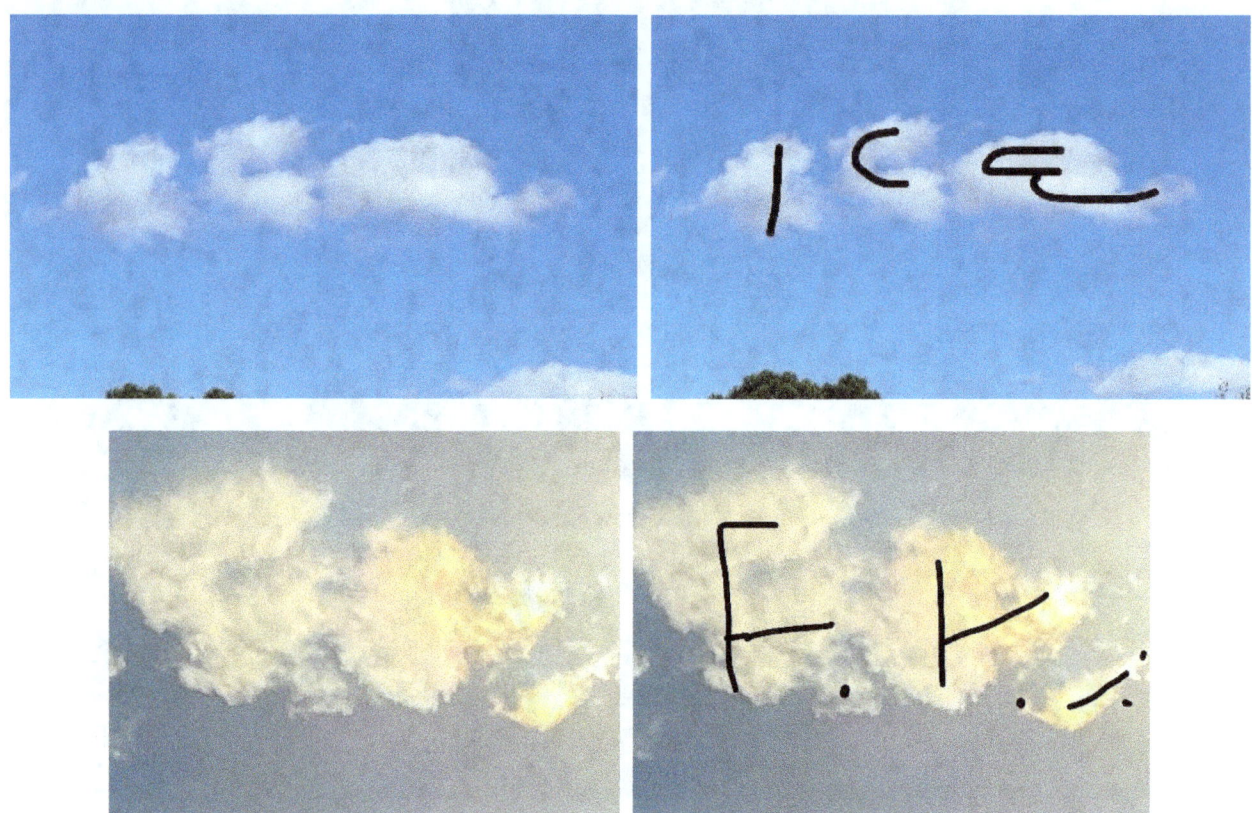

World Ends
"W"hat signals the end "?"

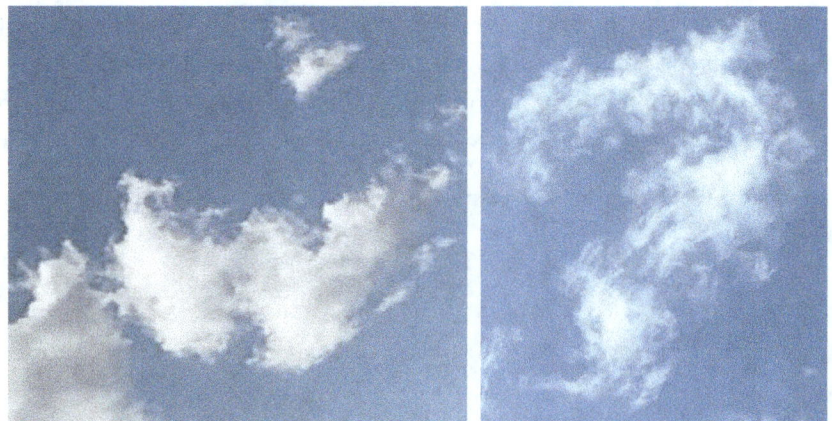

The Last Judgement
Is The End or Judgement Day at hand? Only God knows that exact date. it's His Story to tell. Is it really true that God has the whole world in His Hand(s)? The Heavens seem to speak as if it's true.

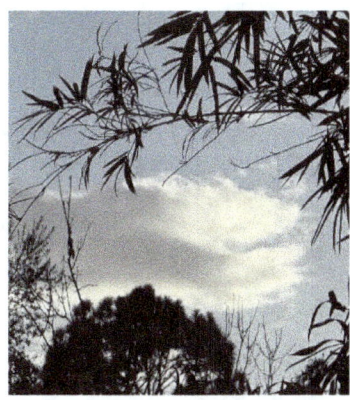 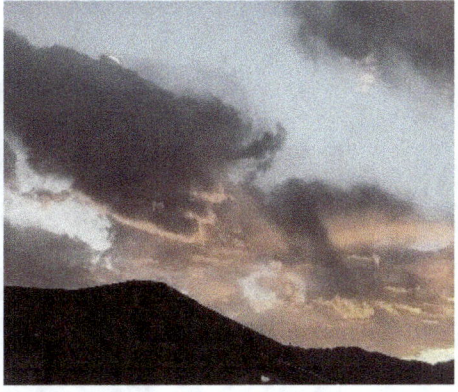 

Signs in The Heavens

Manatees are an endangered species; is mankind? Is this The End of the world as we know it? Are there clues in The Heavens?

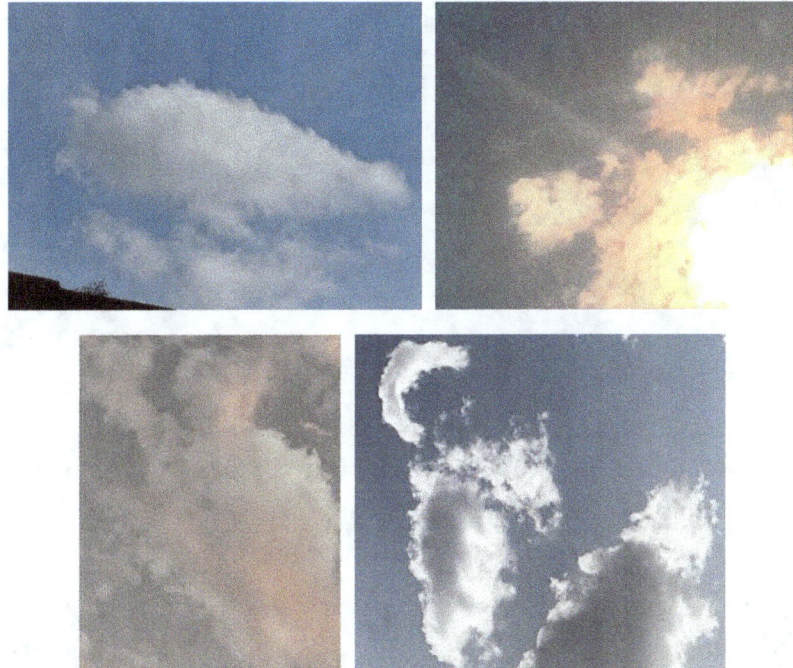

8/17: It's no "joke"; The Almighty loves His children so much that He sacrificed His Son to save the world.

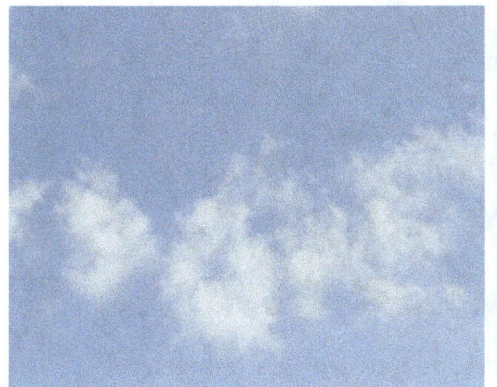  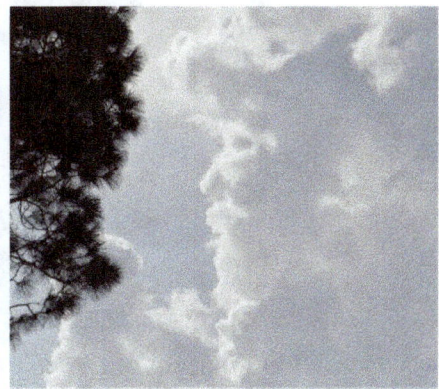

The Rescue

Are The Holy Spirit and angels coming to rescue the chosen in these uncertain times? Or, are they simply fulfilling The Signs of The Times?

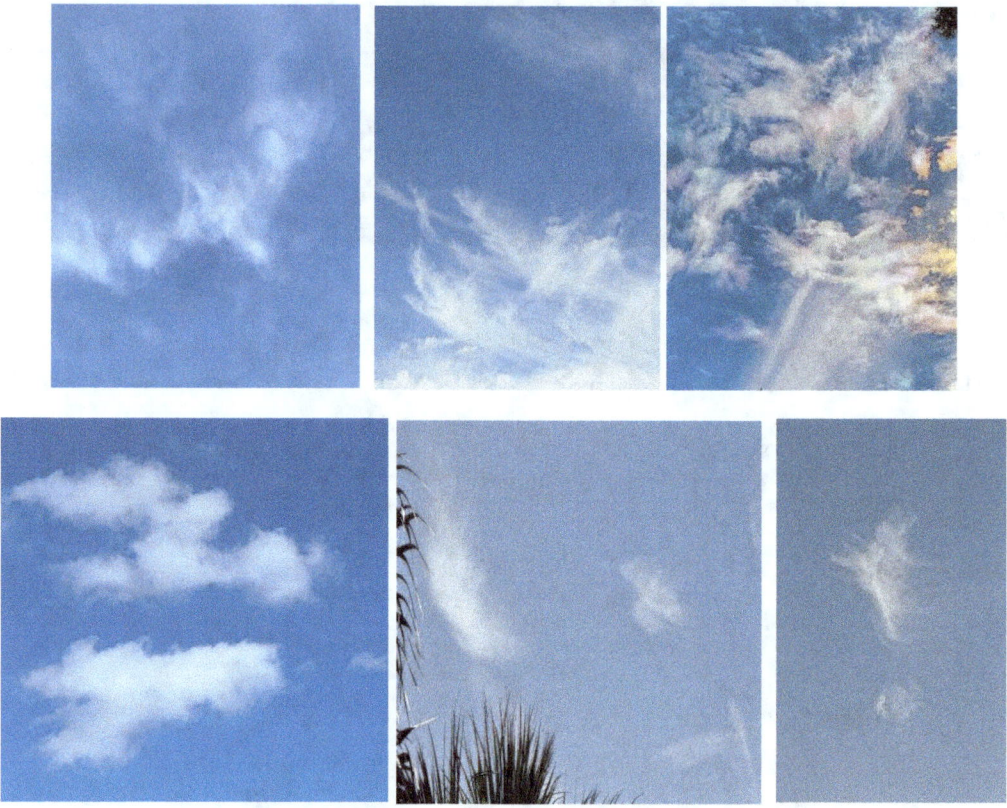

12/31: At the end of the year 2021, a bonfire appeared to have imagery. Do you see things like I do? If so, The (comical) Scarecrow's face along with its mind appears to be going up in smoke in the photo below. That's good news for those praying for the end of all scare tactics based on Covid-19 and compliance to the world-wide tyranny that grew out of the 2020, continuing-pandemic mindset.

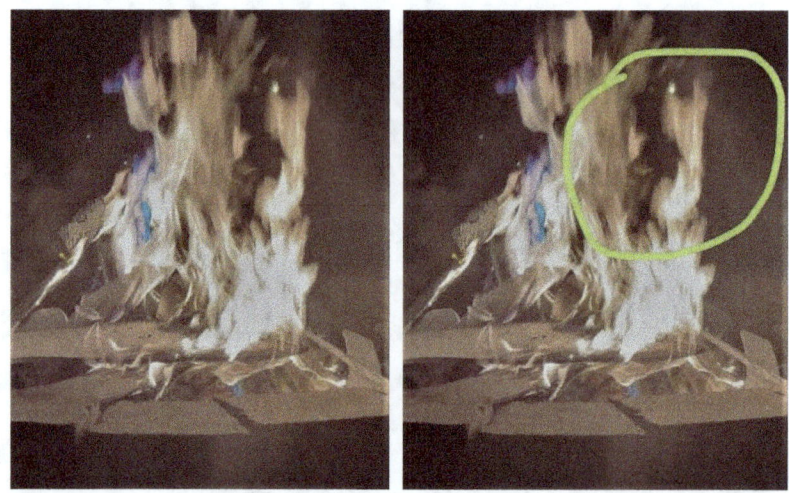

3/16: The clouds infer that Love aka The Wise Old Owl converts darkness to lightheartedness.

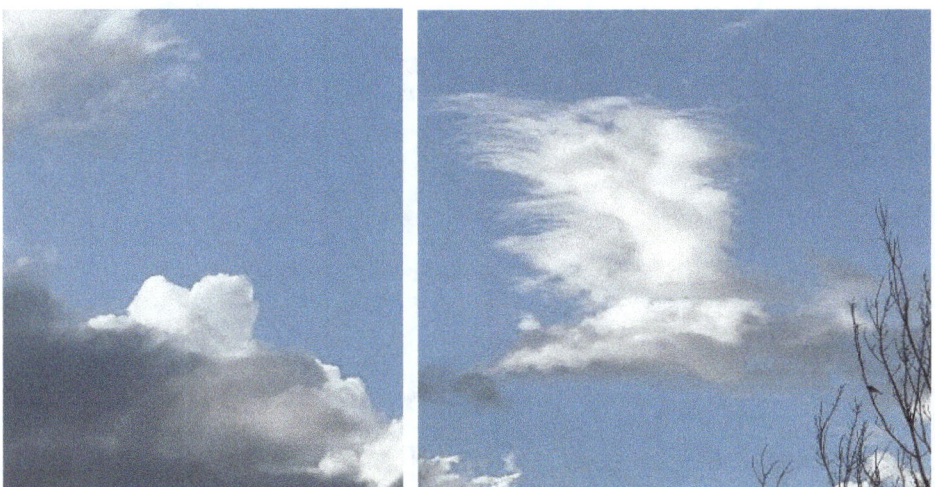

3/18: I love my new sunroom or Florida room with all glass doors leading to the outside world because no screens are in the way of my photo sessions. The lightning was flashing like a strobe light; it was so bright that the early evening seem to turn to day. FYI, the green shaft was behind the tree and reflecting its leaves colors through it.

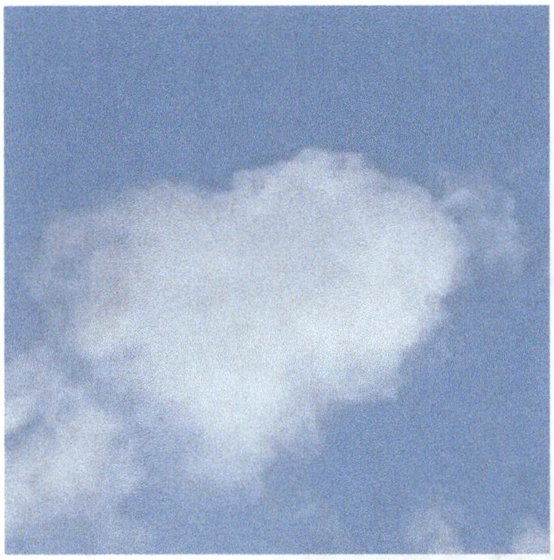

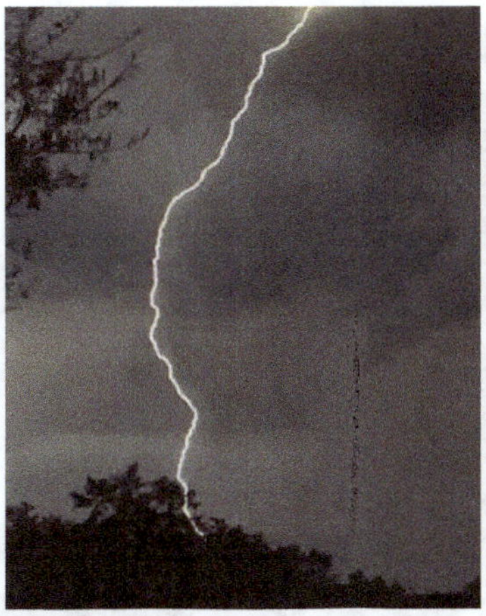

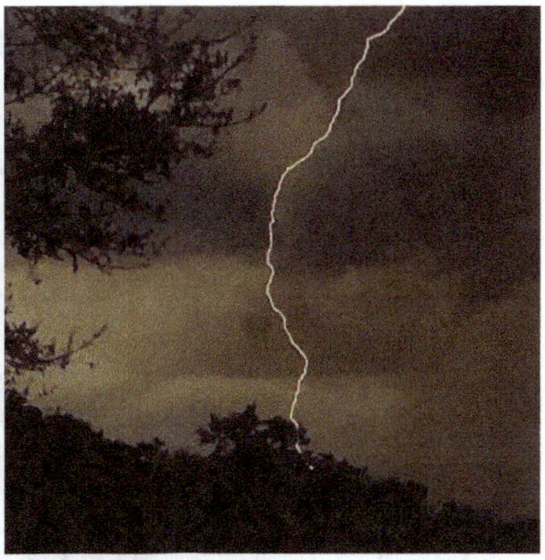

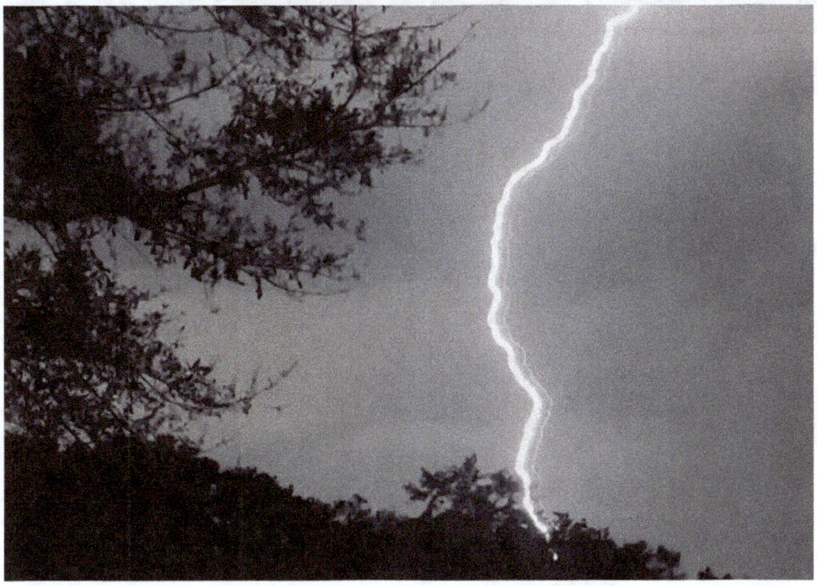

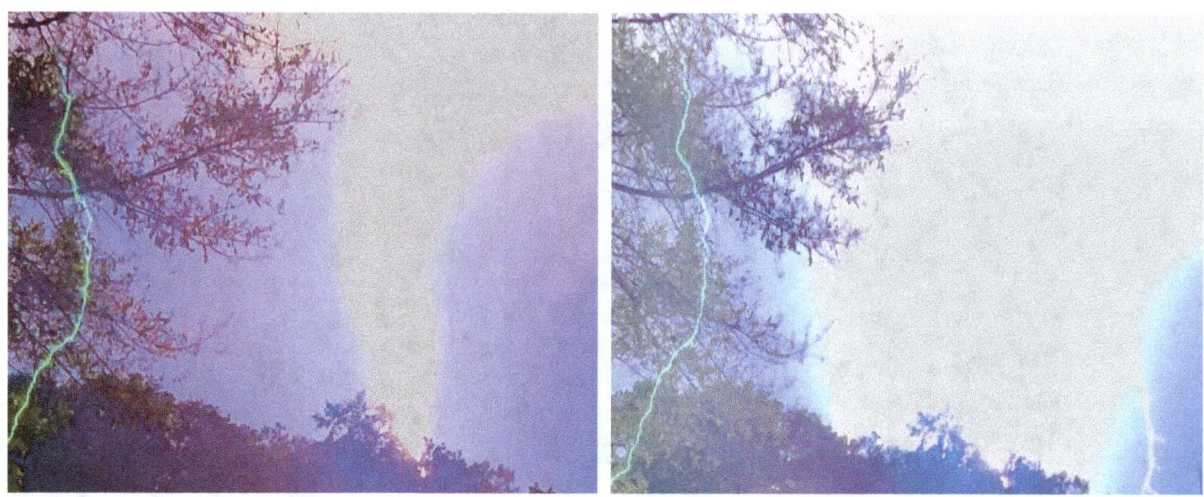

Co-authoring a Book with Wavie

3/20: It was beginning to dawn on me that <u>Through the Storms He Performs</u>. Trust God The Father to see you through. Live The law of Love as taught by His son; Jesus gave/gives His followers the keys to The Kingdom of Heaven. In these uncertain times, His Holy Spirit continues to guide individuals to The Light.

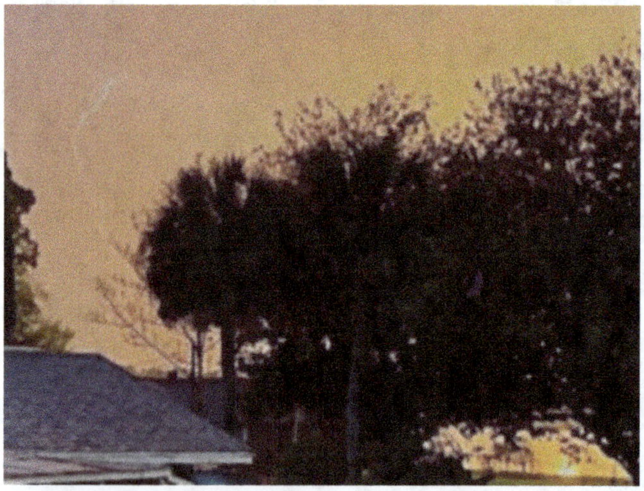

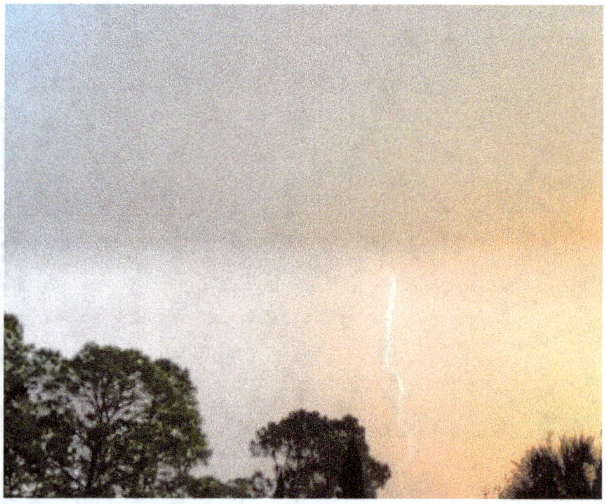

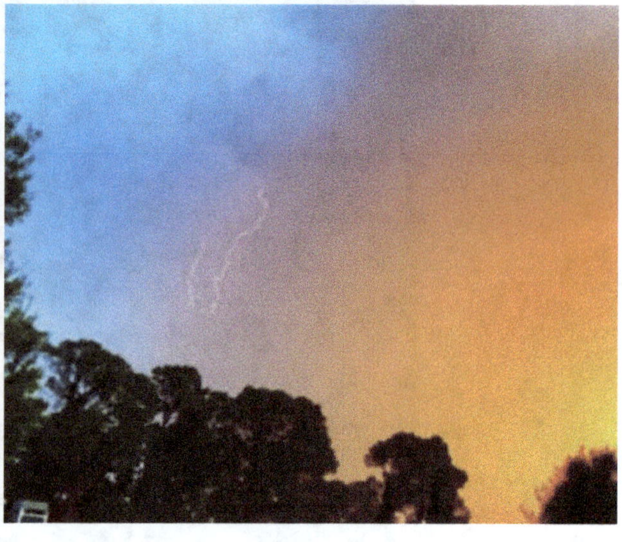

5/17: For almost seven years, I have tried to capture many lightning bolts in one shot. Just as the storm began, I hope for that vision. God provides especially when the faith is unwavering or even the size of a mustard seed (like mine).

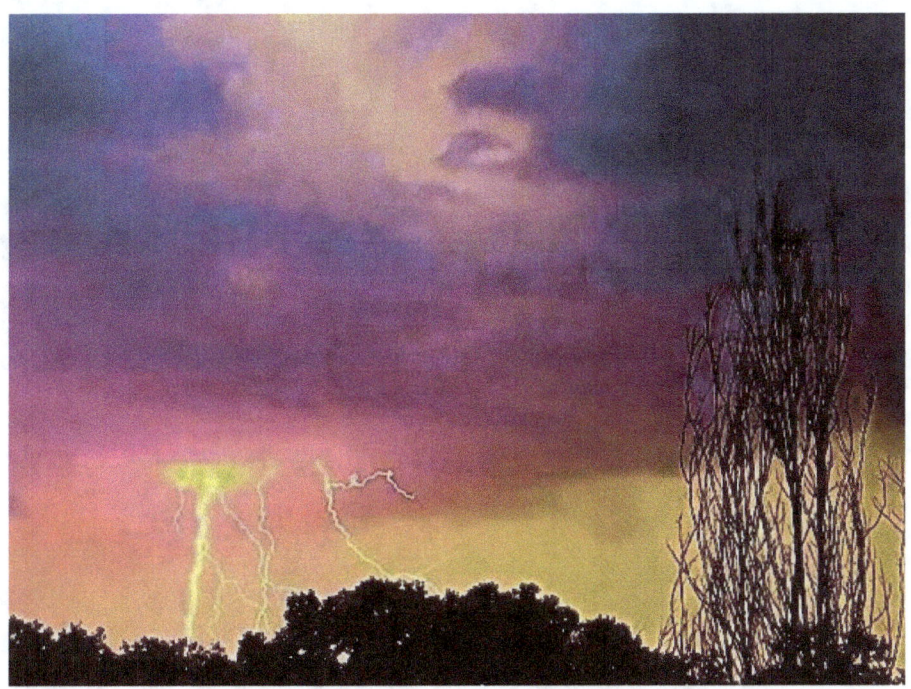

5/20: There was quite a light show; it was long lasting but hard to guess where the next strike would occur. The sky relentlessly flashed as bolts hit all over; some were invisible due to their distant locations while others hid behind trees and buildings.

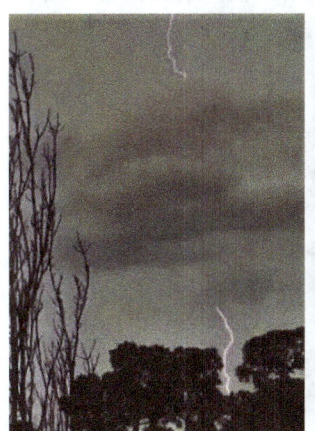 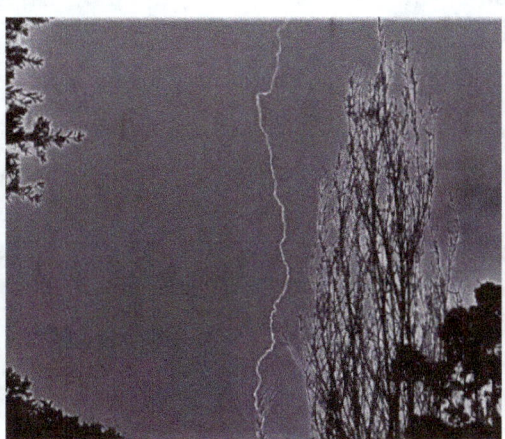 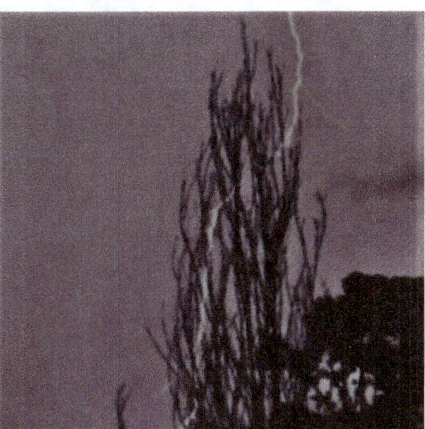

Who Wins?

The Trinity through Jesus The Christ and The Bible Revelations said/say, "In the end, Heaven wins the battle over good and evil forces!" The Son will be riding a white horse from Heaven when He comes to save His chosen from the immorality destroying mankind. Are you ready to face it? The best thing to do in troubling times is to keep looking up.

1/10: Even when the sky is shadowy and dark, it's a momentary transition. Rest assured The Light will reign supreme and color this world with hope. Keep the faith that Love will prevail through Eternity.

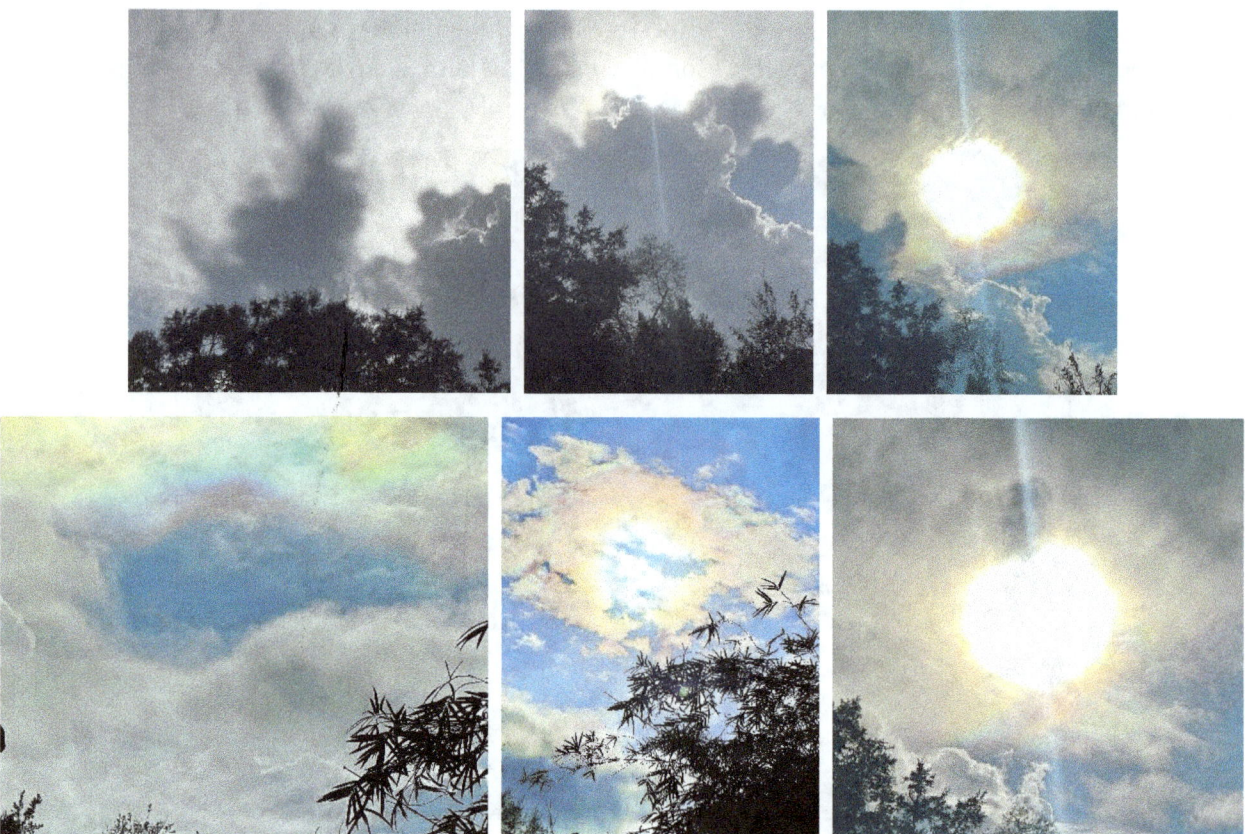

1/17: The full moon took me by surprise near sundown while driving home from dinner with my husband because it appeared to arrive in The Heavens too early in January. However, an Internet search revealed that it was right on schedule. Once home, with my camera on a tripod, I snapped a few photos revealing that celestial body's aura or halo as well as its moonbeams. My lens, also, captured its mundane, everyday likeness in the cloudless skies over my head.

During this discussion, keep in mind that the last three snapshots are the same one. The last picture is globally, color saturated. The imagery in that photograph or the "t" took me by surprise as I played with the original picture while in this Microsoft, Word document. Was a Heavenly message revealed during the darkness of night? The Cross sign suggests that Jesus The Christ due to the cross He bore conquered the evil and fearful things of this world. Hope is the overall theme. In other words, don't give up faith because The Lord continues to reflect God, His Father's Light even during the darkest hours or in these uncertain times. Be confident in His victory over The Devil and His agents. In the end, The Supreme Being prevails as in only kindness matters; God is the best key to Love.

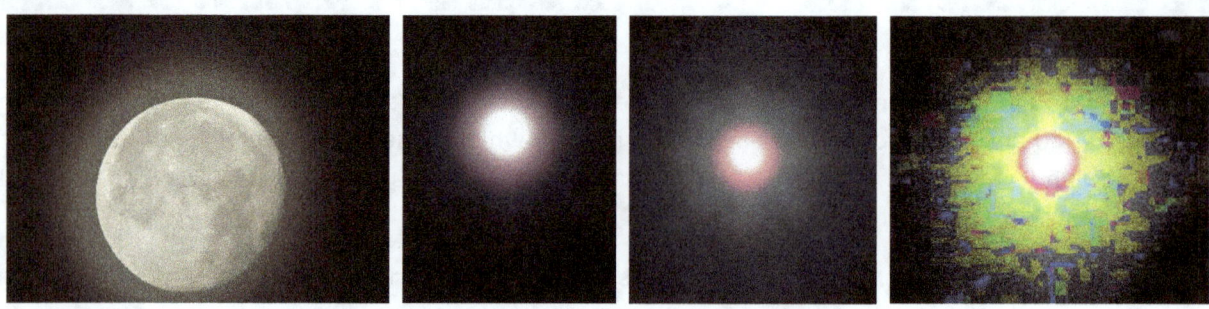

4/5: Above my head, almost daily, there are optimistic signs such as everchanging sunbeams including sunrays of hope blasting through dark clouds. Today, there were, also, misty areas anchored in the sky with symbols of God's messengers including angels and The Holy Spirit (Dove); these visions appeared to be receiving and then sending Jesus and His Father's communications to The Earth. With The Bible's guiding Word as well as The Supreme Being's celestial helpers, a soul can take life by the horns avoiding the bull of this realm. In other words, The Trinity and its spiritual envoys of peace and love can help to keep the destructive forces in nature in this world from bugging people because God's Holy Spirit has one goal, which is to guide the soul away from the damage of sin while healing this world. The Triune Master of The Universe can move a soul from the pits of despair and dark clouds ruining the scenes in life. Thus, with The Creator's help, when someone converts to goodwill it is like a caterpillar changing into a beautiful butterfly because that person finds and then more closely follows The Creator's Will. The Almighty's Spirit points the way away from the depressing ruin of this planet and towards His illuminated beauty. Furthermore, in <u>The Good Book</u>, The Supreme Being made promises to keep His chosen people from harm; seek the rainbow.

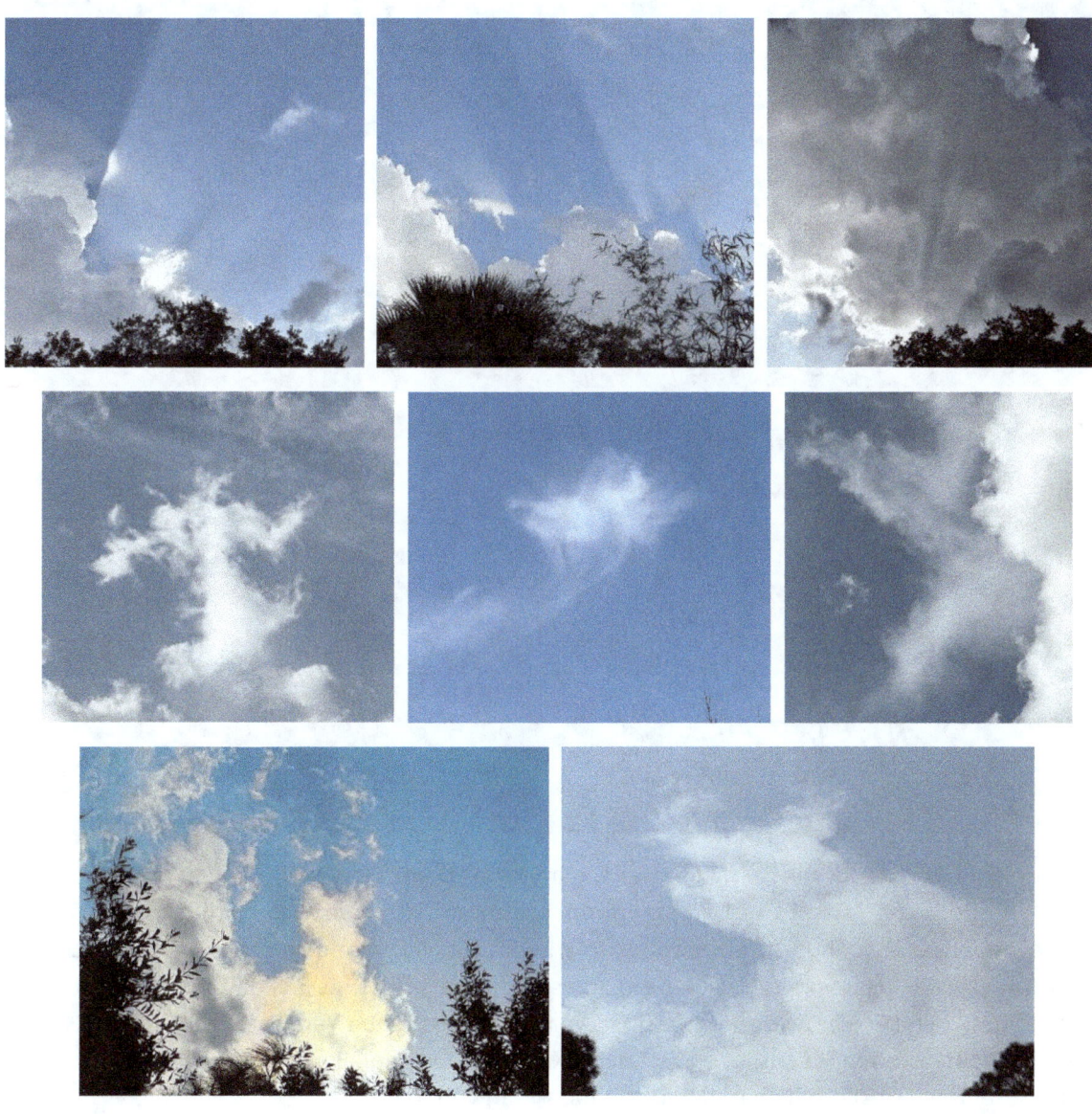

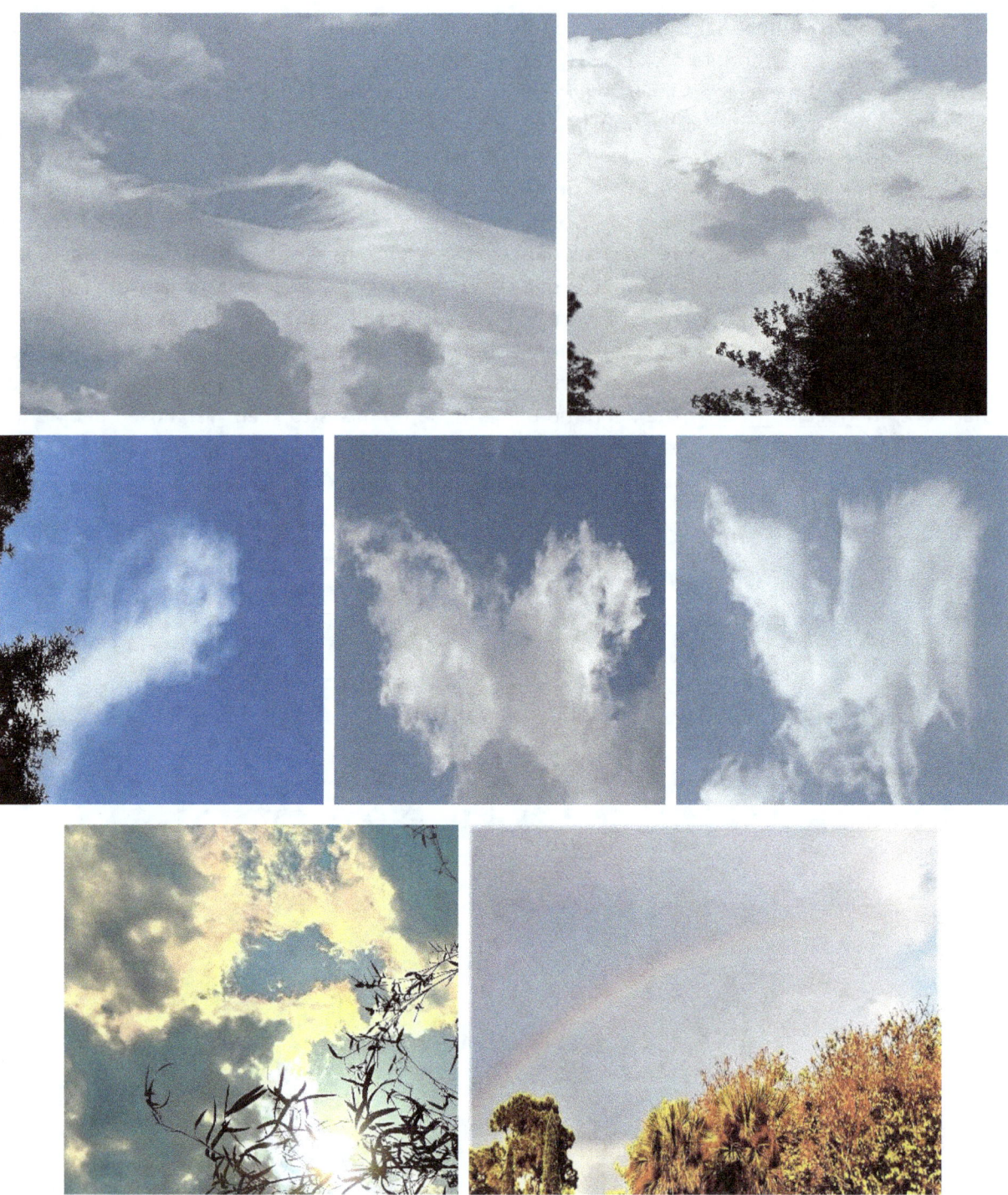

4/6: The Book of Life reminds me of my mother's, miraculous death as well as my first nonfiction entitled <u>Mom's on The Roof and I Can't Get Her Down</u>. April, also, brings memories of that parent due to her birthdate of April the 18th. Thus, it felt apropos to witness the vision of a celestial Being in a cloud; that cloudy figure was holding an open book. The vision shared the sky with signs of The Holy Spirit or Third member of The Trinity, which Jesus promised would arrive to continue Yahweh's guidance of His chosen people once Christ exited to His Father's Everlasting Kingdom. One angel mist in the sky appeared to carry a letter representing "J"esus in its hand; another has "Y"ahweh at its feet.

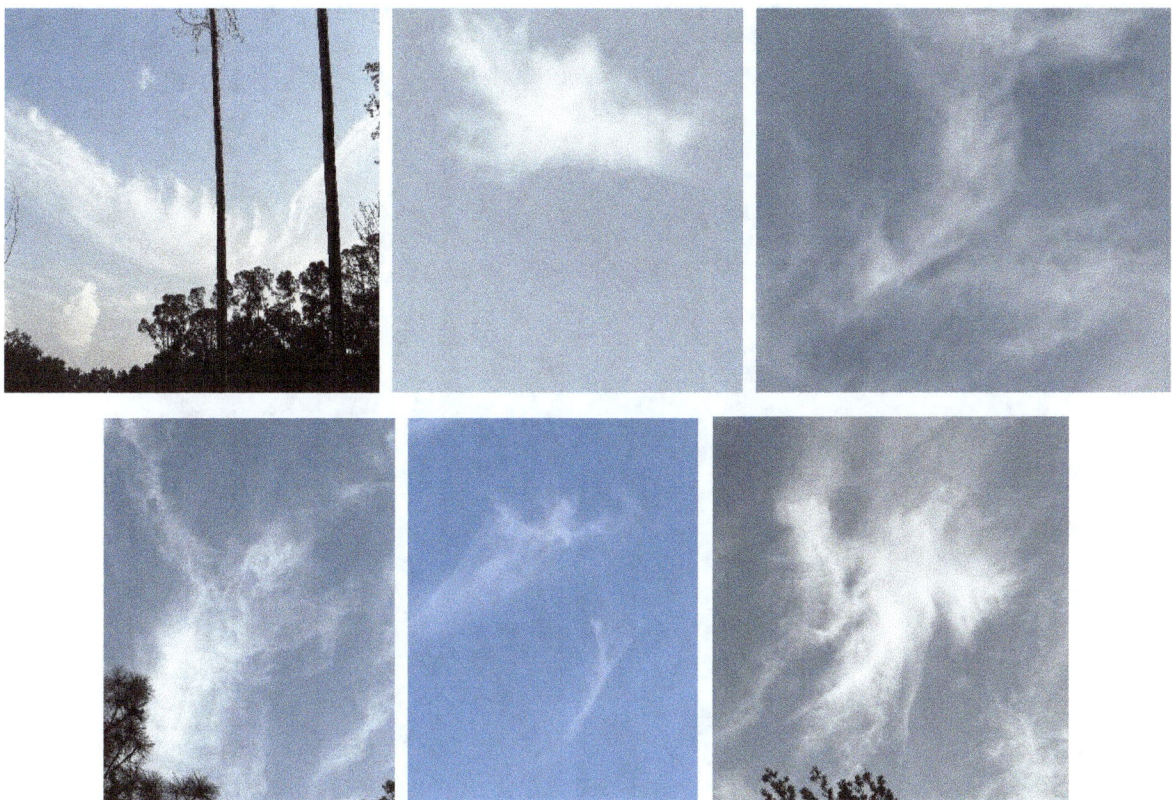

4/12: Many clouds appeared heart-shaped, which signals good relationships; the number "5" beside one of them, also, speaks to fond bonds between The Maker and His creations. These misty areas in the sky brought versions of "I love." "G"od is Love. Reflect on that.

The reign of The Most-High, Supreme Being is echoed in a sunbow or partial corona; colorful bows are part of the promise The Almighty made to Noah and mankind. Meanwhile, after that covenant, His Son, Jesus The Christ made another Heaven-sent promise while on The Cross. He said that The Holy Spirit would guide this world to its finale. "X" marks the spot where a Pine or pining tree memorializes The Crucifixion of The Lord. Furthermore, angels and Dove-like misty areas are a part of the vision during 2022's Holy Week for Christians. As mentioned many times, The Alpha and Omega is Love; the clouds remind the soul of that Biblical fact. Jesus as a human alive in The Heavens is, also, in the last picture in this depiction of these scenes capture for posterity. Enjoy the next photographic visions.

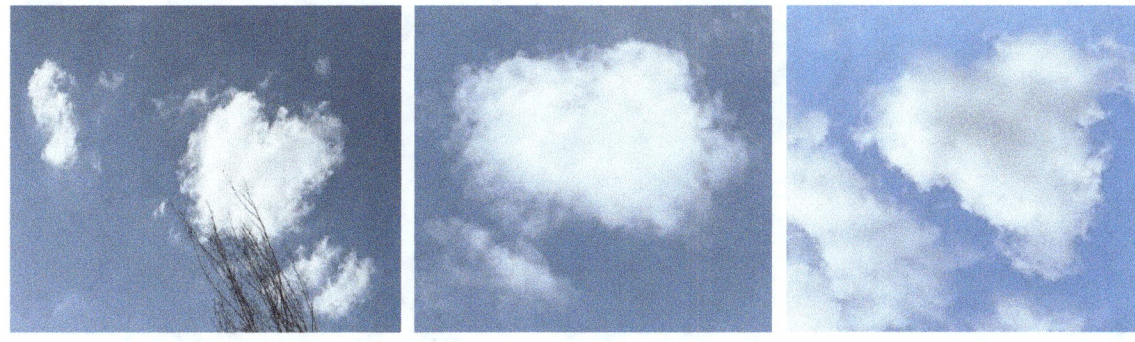

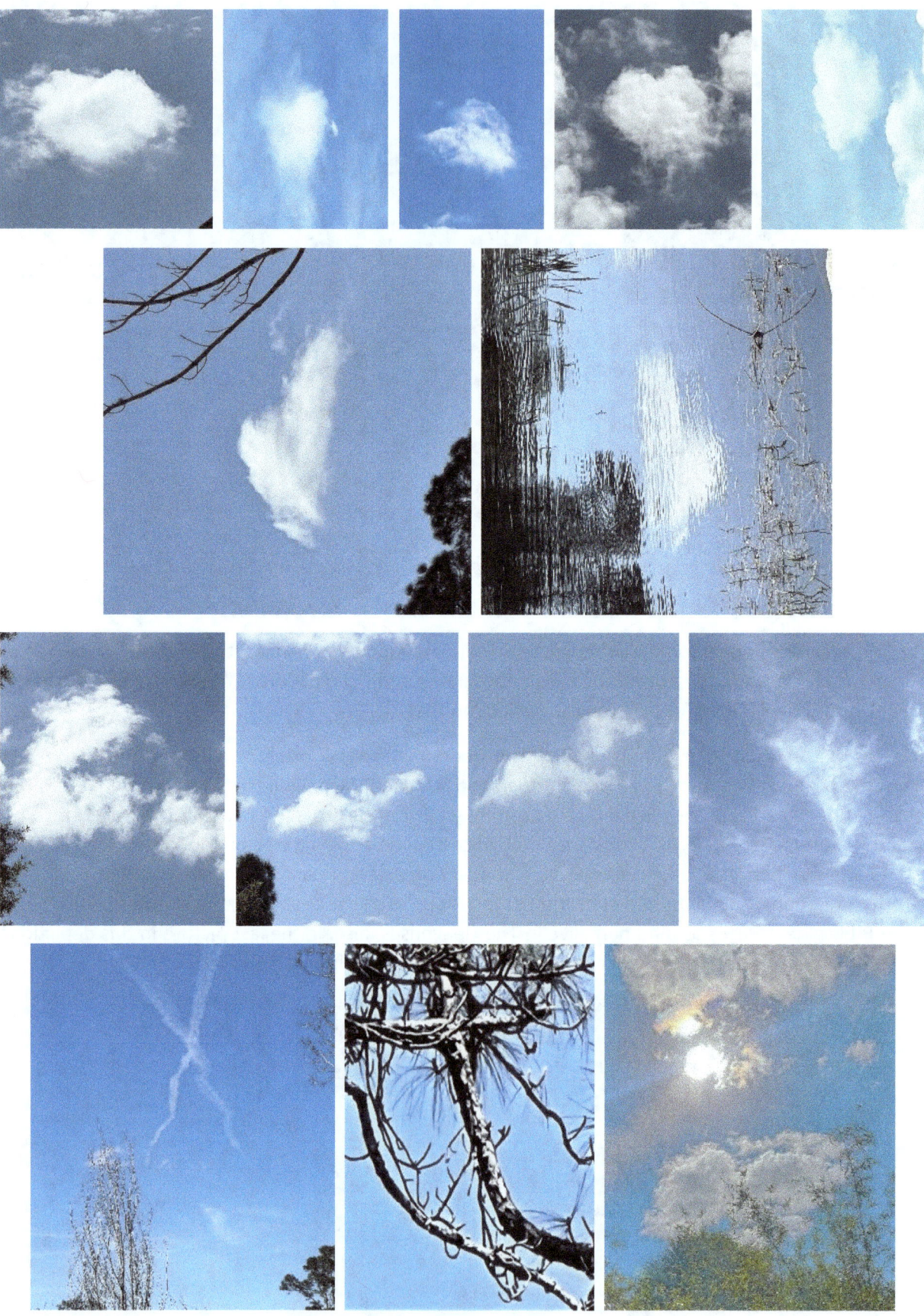

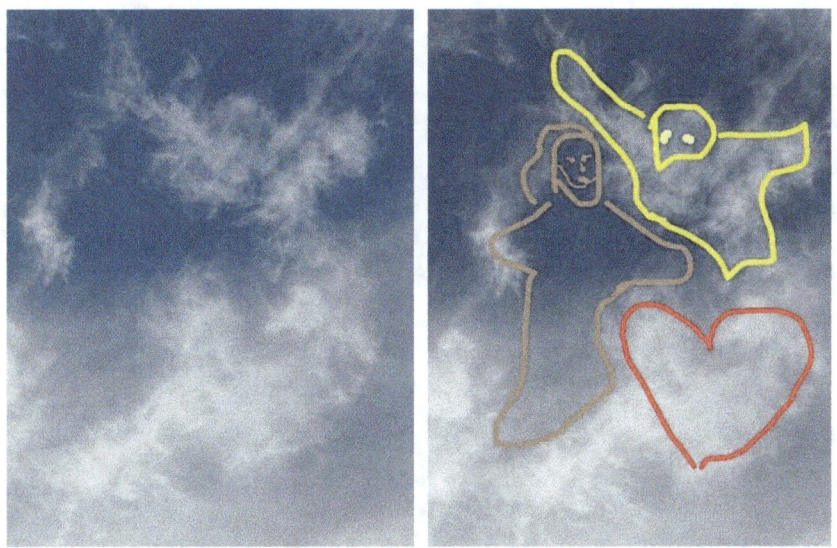

Face It
Life rarely goes as self-planned but often Hindsight is 2020. More than likely, God's vision, in action, is a more perfect plan.

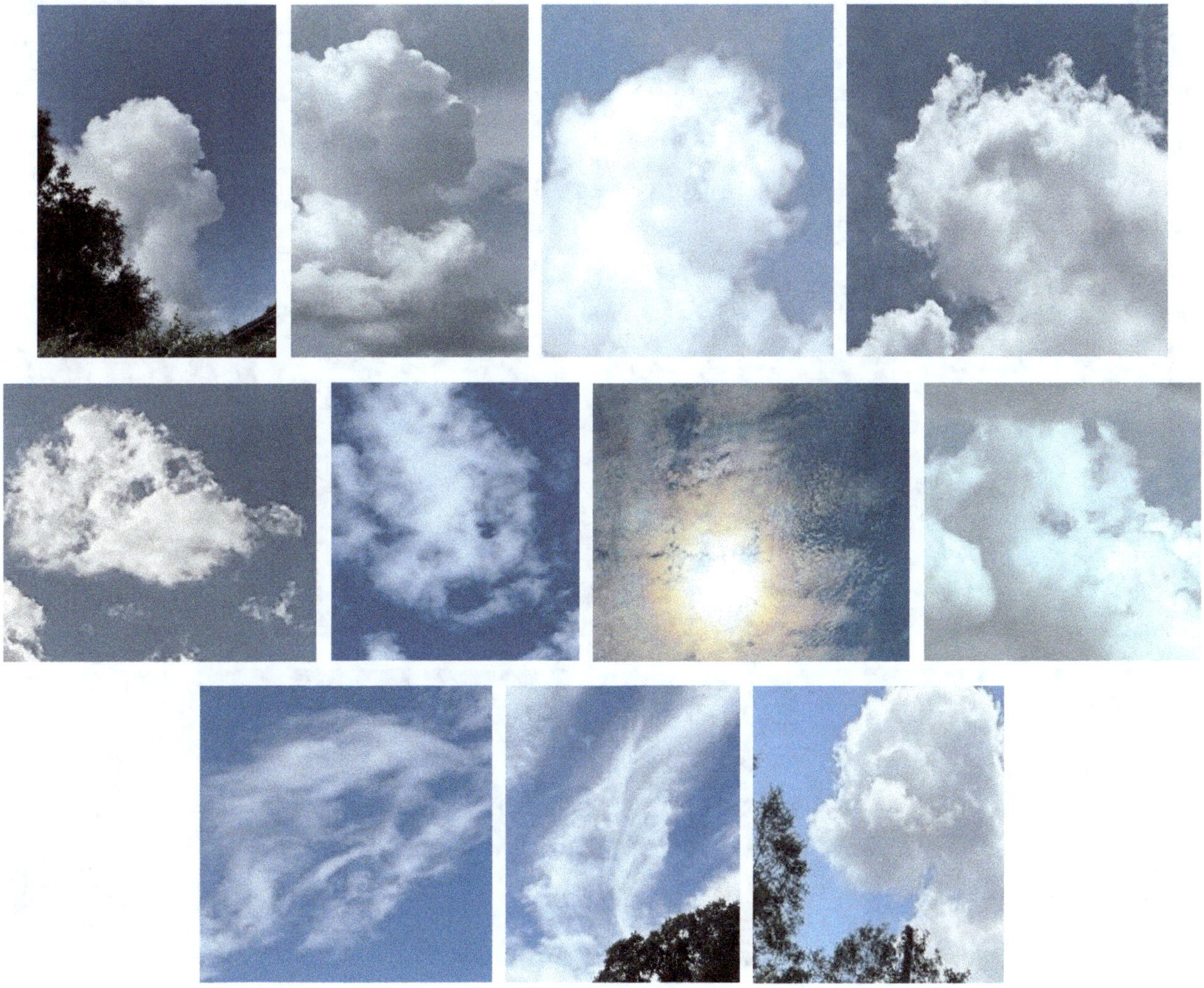

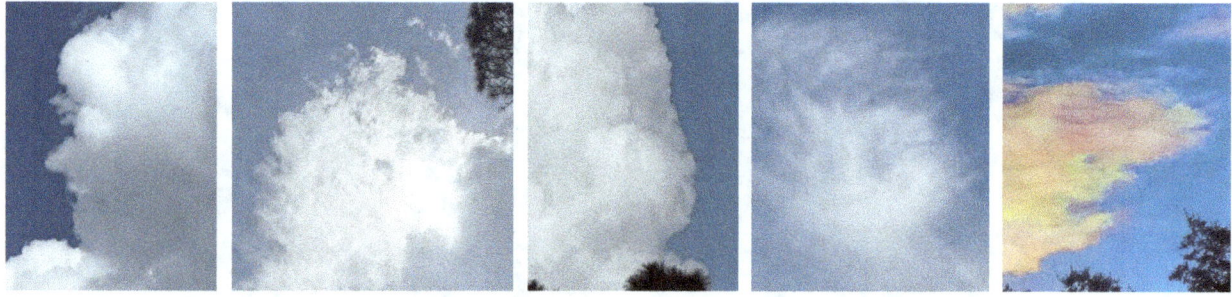

Be not Afraid
1/6: A Scary Storm may be overhead but so are rays of hope during these uncertain times.

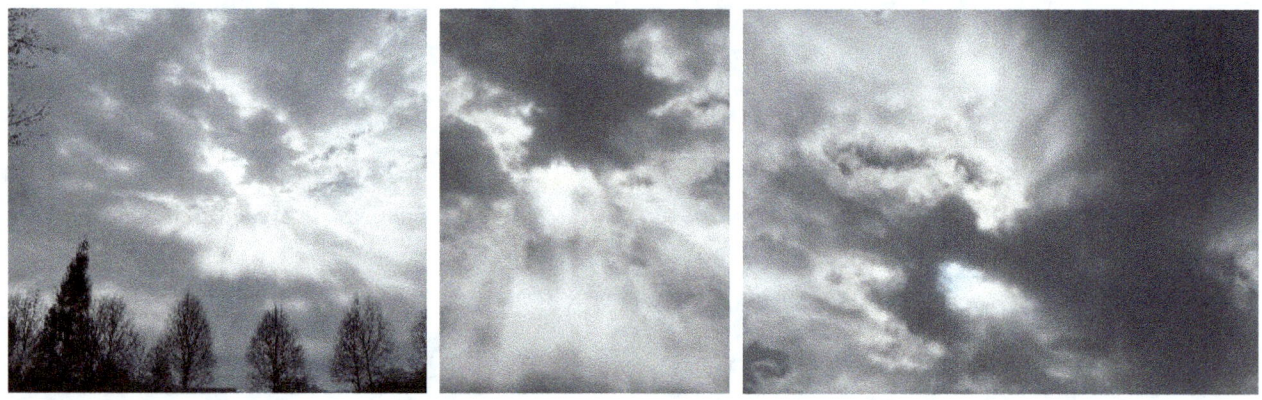

The Sun Beams
What Causes sunrays? They are shafts of light cause by The Center of The Universe; the sunny beams protrude through cloudbanks becoming visible below the mist.

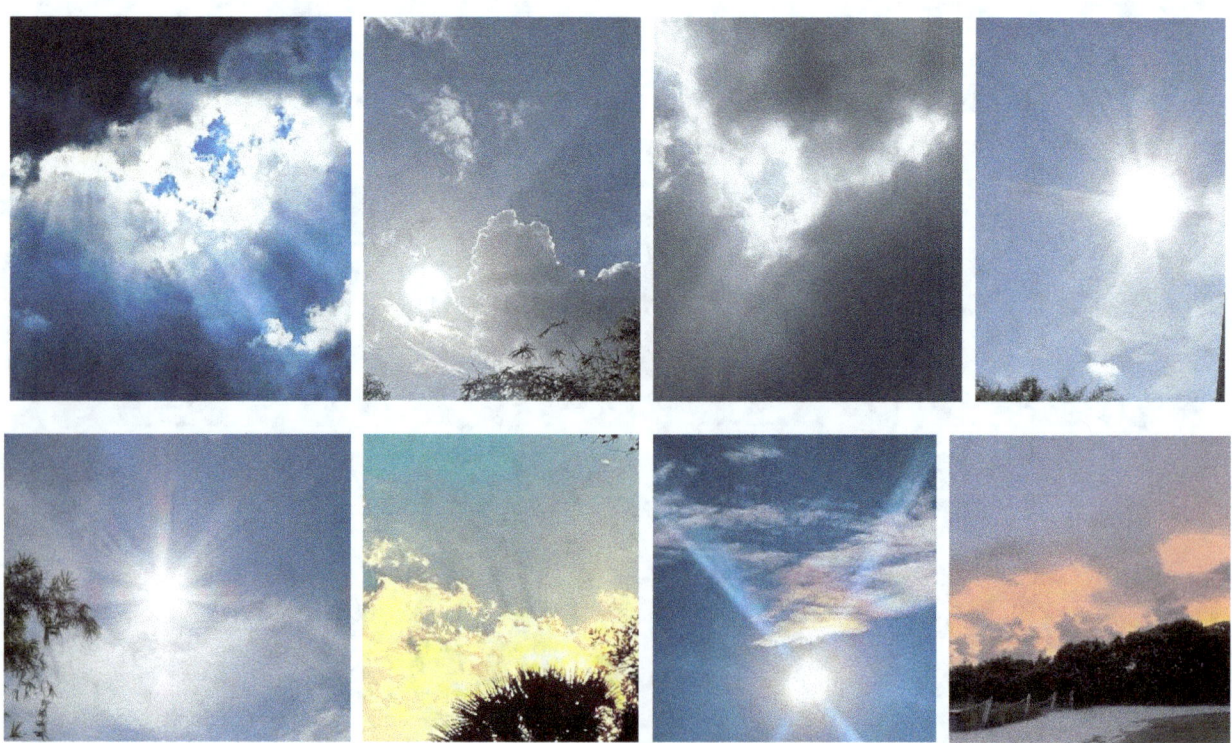

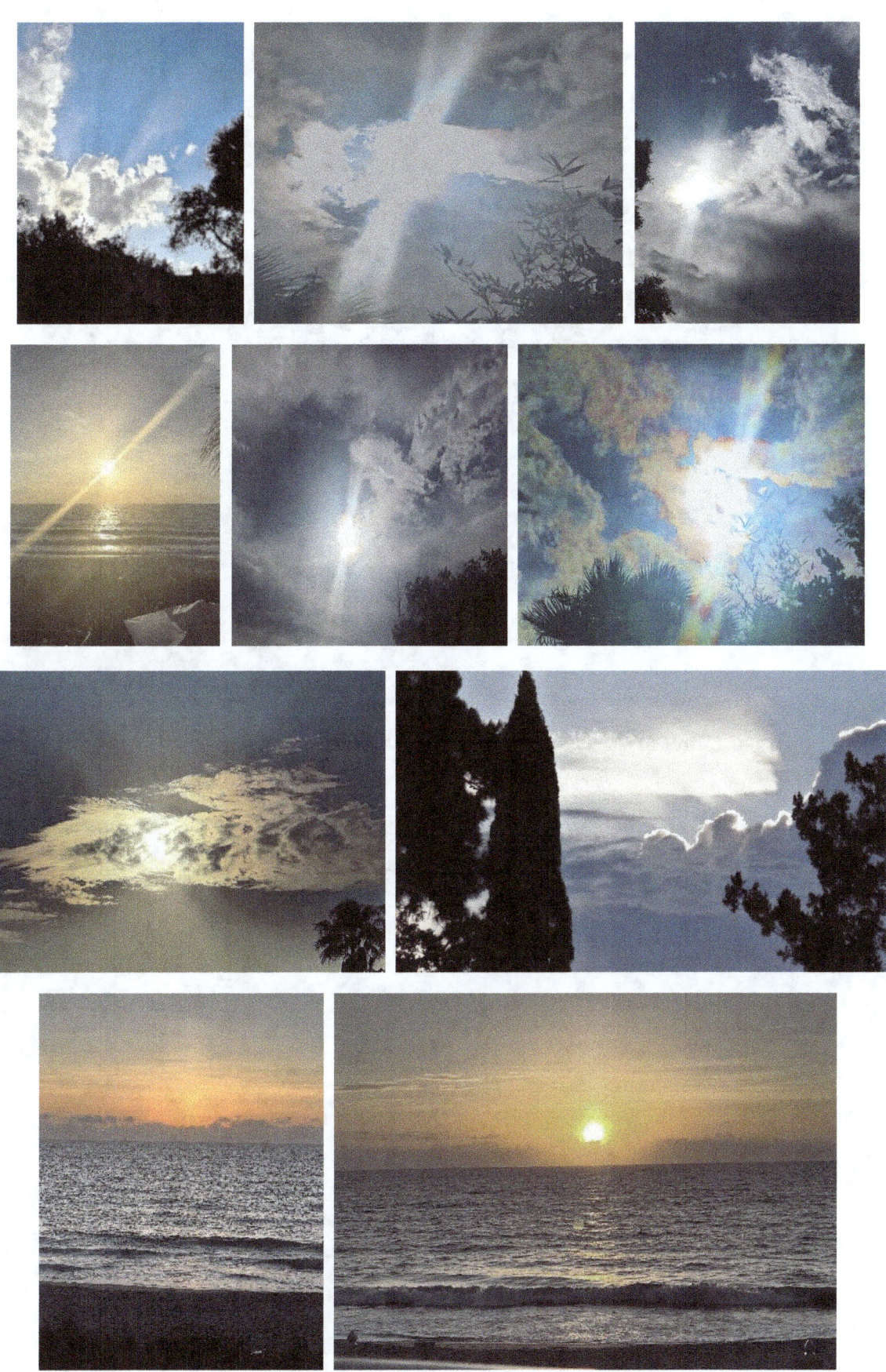

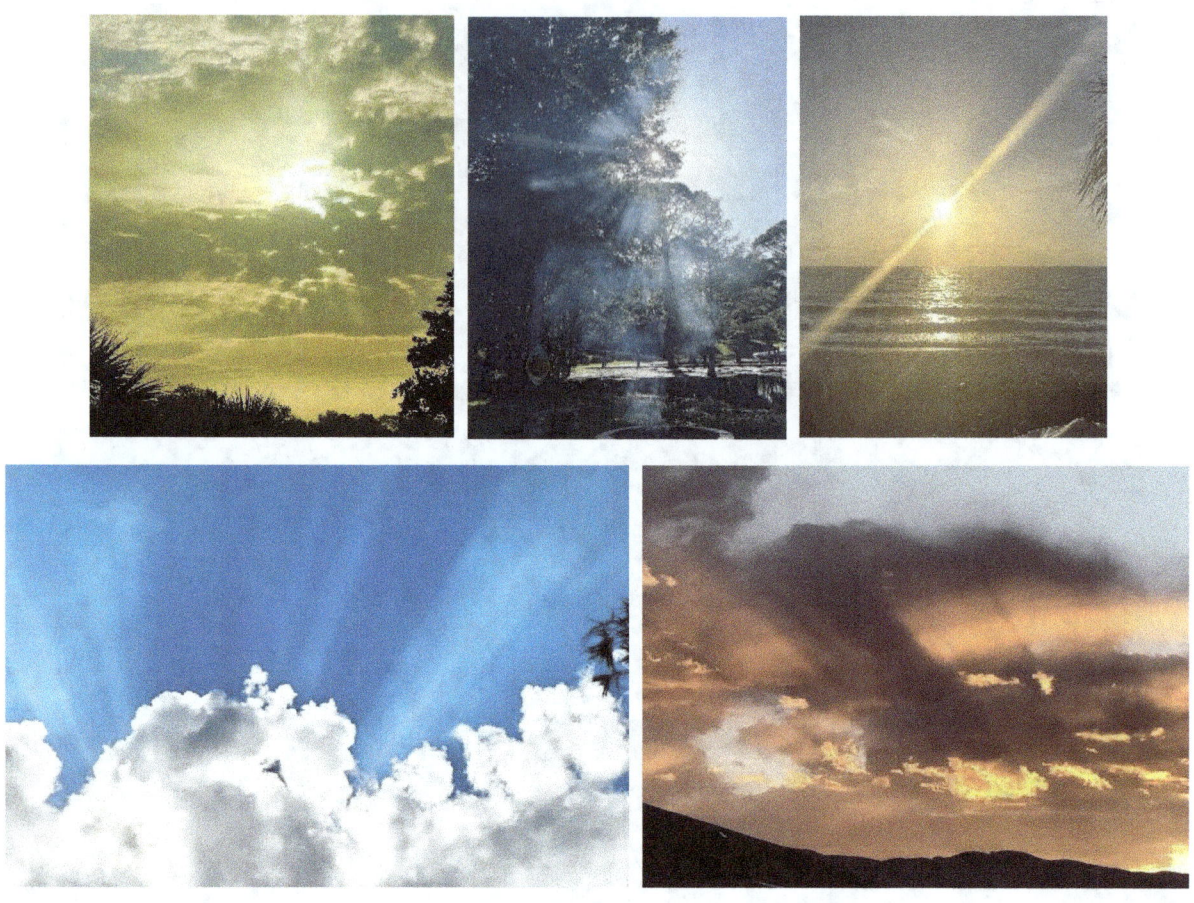

Heaven Reflects on The Earth
Reflect on The Creators purpose for your life including your cross to bear. Did you envision hope?

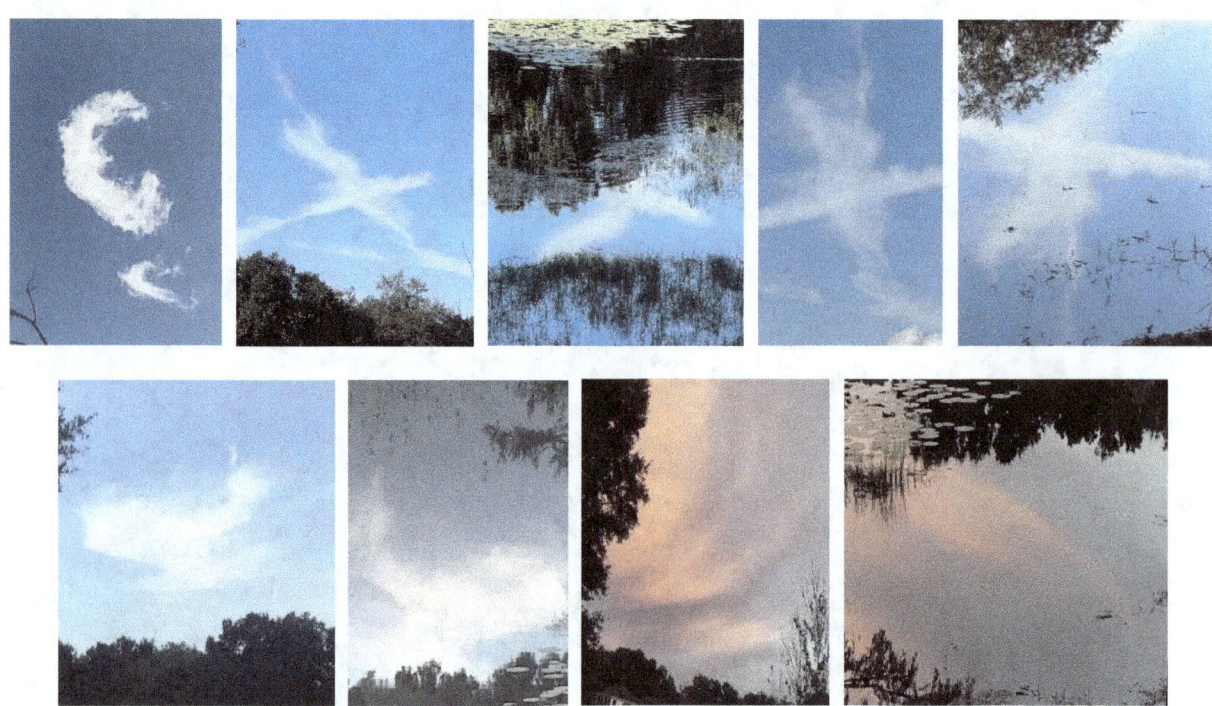

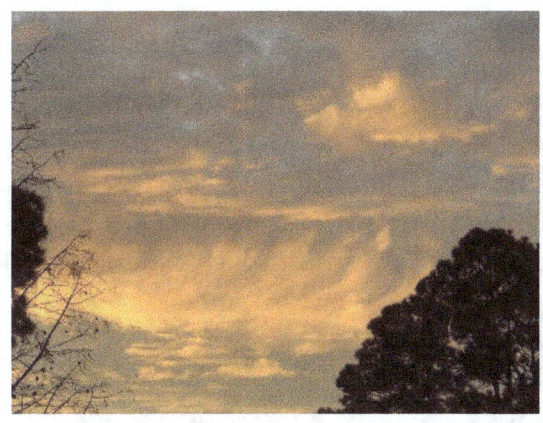 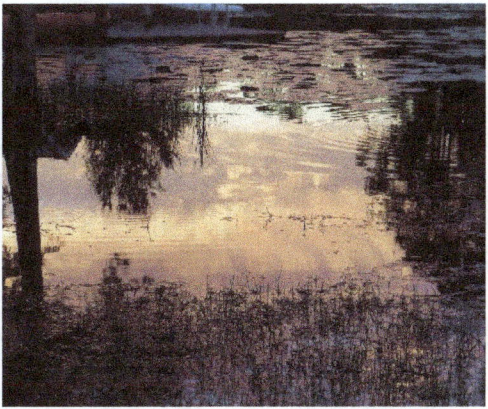

The End or New Beginning

While awaiting any last scene including the last act of your personal life or The Earth's End Times as in the end of the world as we know it, seek and you will find love and peace in communications from The Triune God. Take time to enjoy the good moments in this upside-down world including every sunrise and sunset- daily

Sunrise

When it dawns on you, the new day brings The Light.

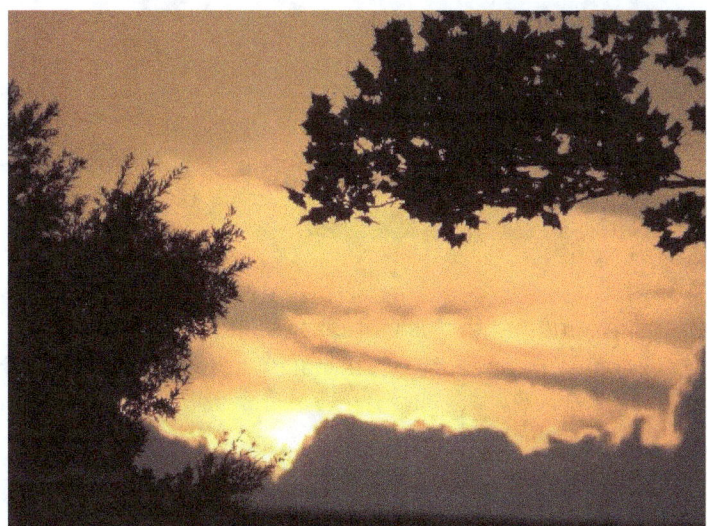 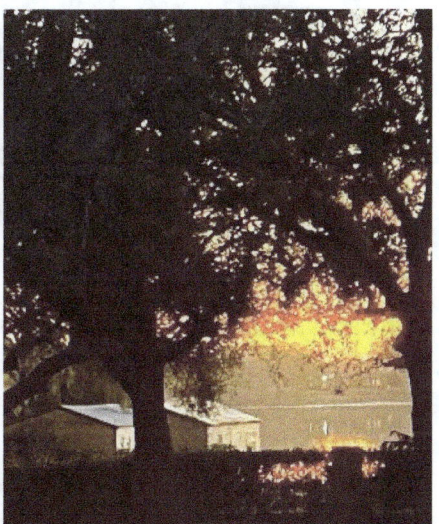

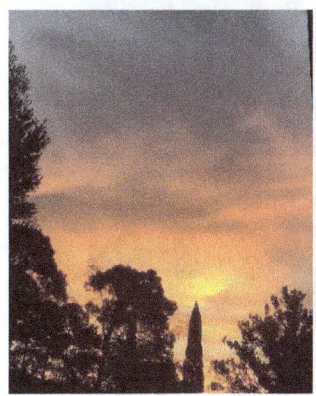 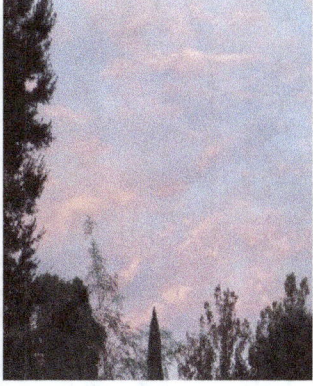 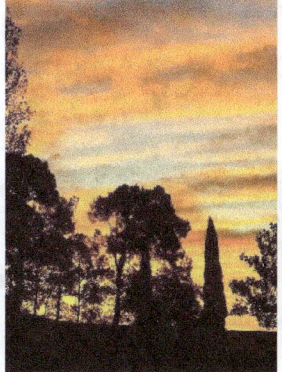 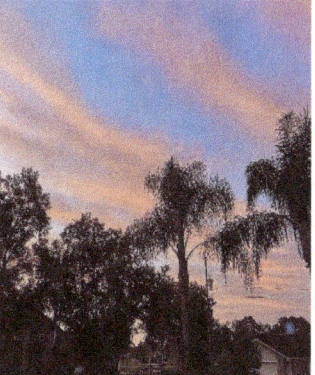

2/18: Near dawn, the sun unveiled a rainbow of color via Moon Coronas blending to iridescent, misty areas in the sky. The Alpha and Omega's imagery in The Heavens is reiterating His promises to His people. During the dark hours of these uncertain times, rest assured that He wins by the end of this cat and mouse game with The Devil's Army. While wondering about The Controller of The Earth's designs and His Will, refer to the imagery captured for posterity at around 5AM and find peace. On 2/18, we went to Leu Gardens with some grandkids to see The Dragons Exhibit. The movie "Birds" came to mind except the thousands of winged creatures did not even try to harm us; they must have been in The Holy Spirit's Airforce.

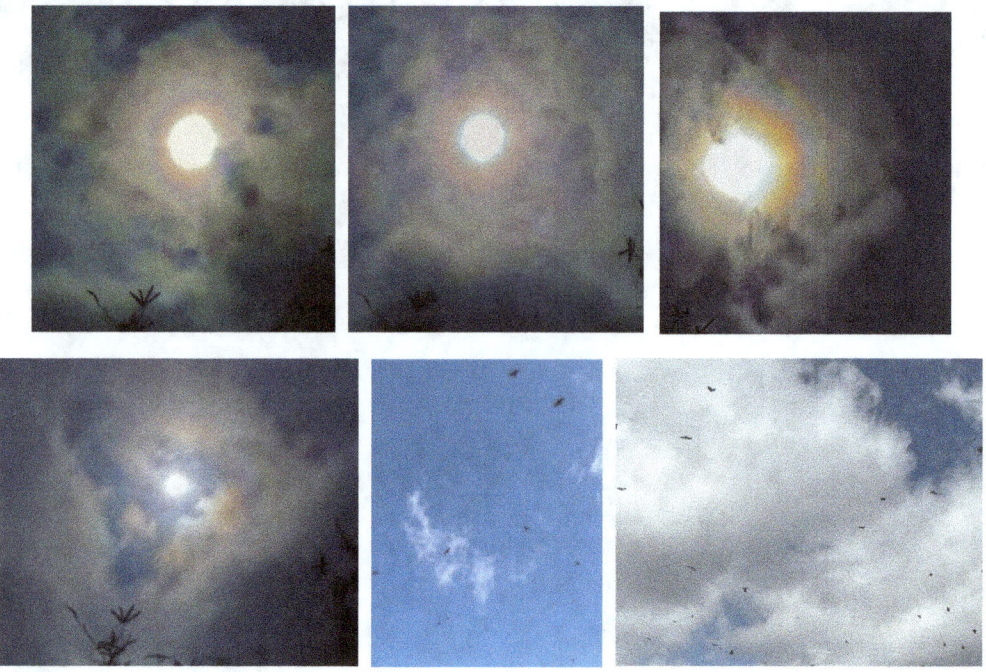

Sunset

Before the darkness God shines a light on your surroundings in this world as well as above your head. If the bottom of Heaven is so wonderful can you imagine the beauty of Eternal Paradise? The hope is that all is well that ends well.

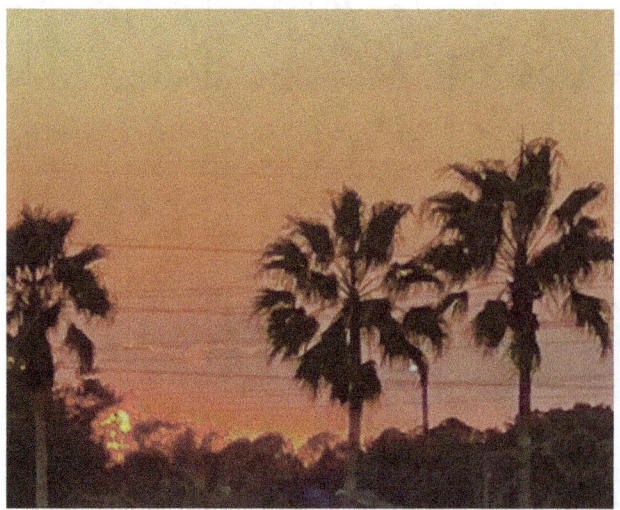
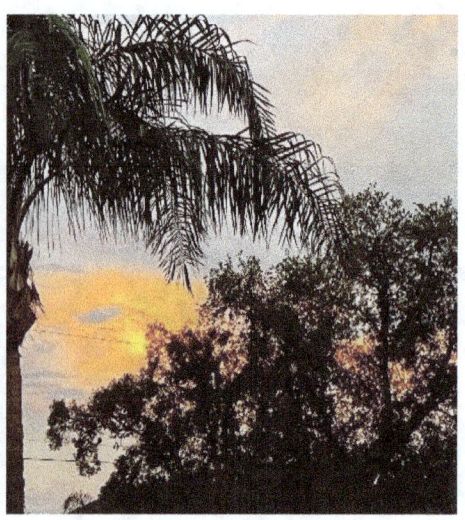

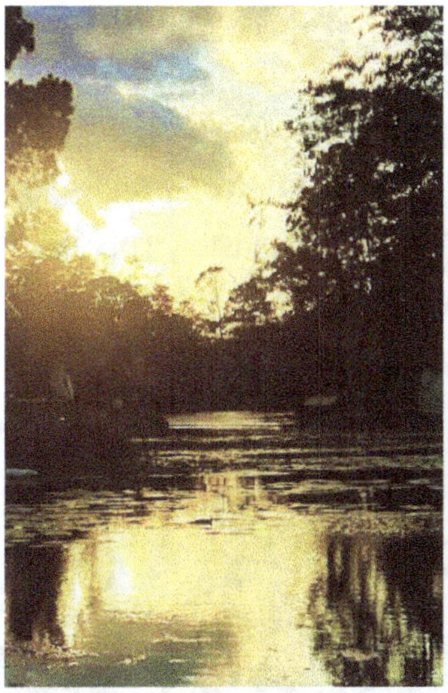

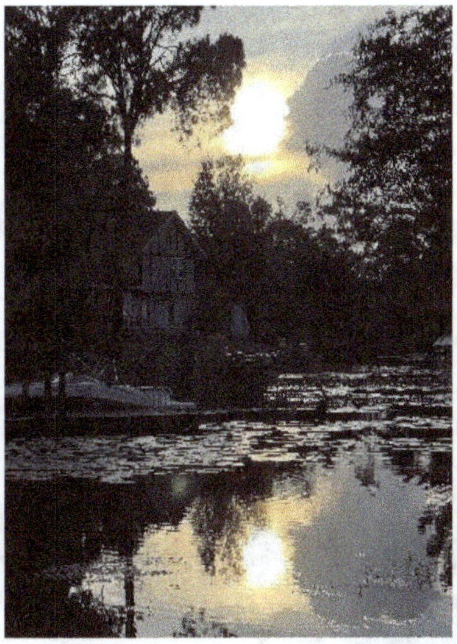

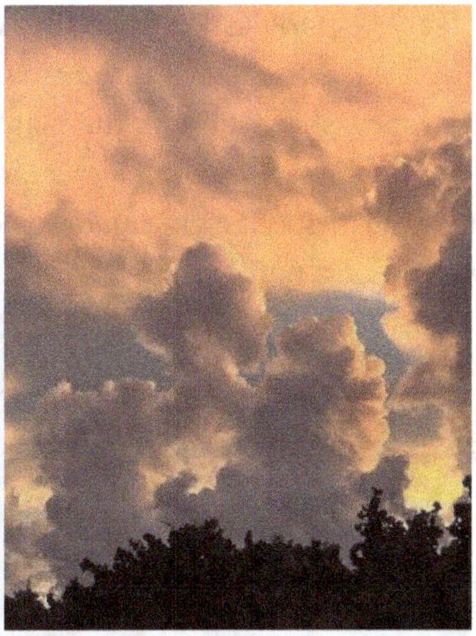

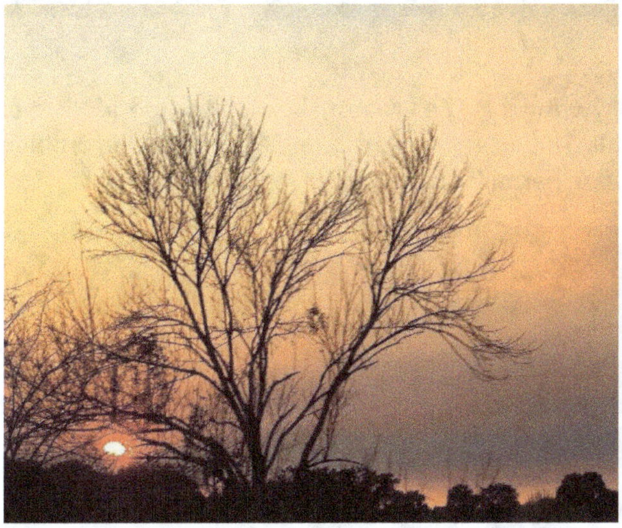

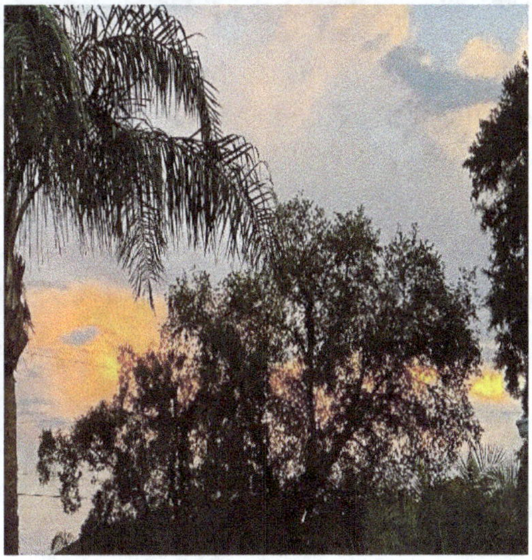

Leave the Light On

8/11/2021: Right before dawn, my eyes noticed a vision in the Western sky; I shot up at it. Afterwards, I realized it was the celestial body called Saturn.

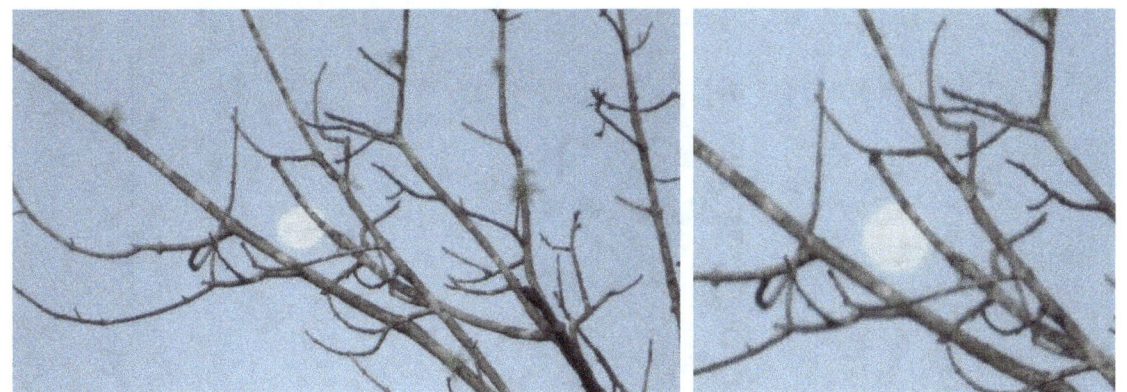

Don't fear the darkness. Even as The Central Light of The Universe dims after dusk, The Creator leaves nightlights on in The Heavens to help show mankind the way to His Realm. Other planets, meteors, stars, and the moon shine through the night. In June of 2022, five planets aligned and became visible for the first time in about a thousand years; they were Venus, Jupiter, Saturn, Mars, and Mercury. In 2020, for the first time in about eight-hundred years, near Christmas, The Star of Bethlehem visibly sparkled. What a miracle to be a part of this generation! Pictured is some of The 2022 Vision, only.

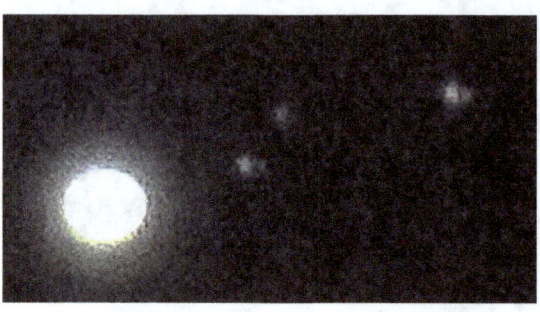 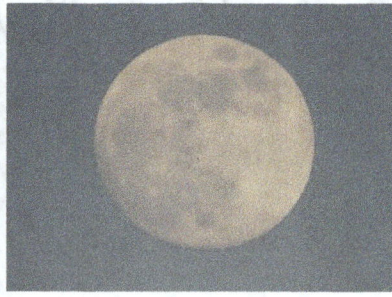 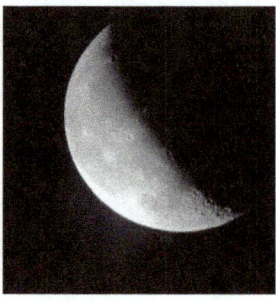

Skywriting that Turns a Mind's Light On

Some cloudy mist in The Heavens appear to be skywriting. Is The Creator showing the world His thoughts and the way to His everlasting and peaceful Realm? In Heavenly Paradise, "MAY" all your problems be little ones. MAY The Alpha and Omega's Light tan be harmless to your soul for an "E"ternity "!"

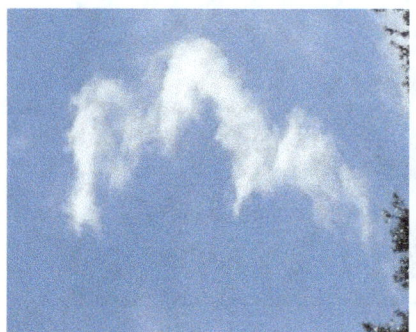 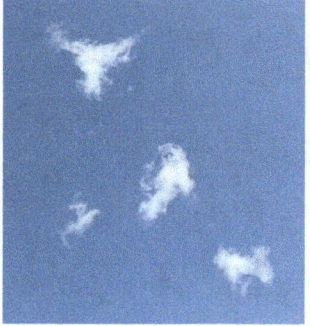 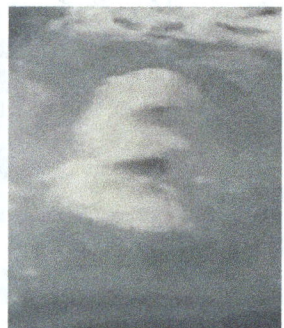 

Go Figure(s)

What exactly is happening in our time? With the help of God through the teachings of The Bible and Jesus as well as the guidance of The Holy Spirit, go figure it out. Your soul senses The Truth; let it be your moral and spiritual compass.

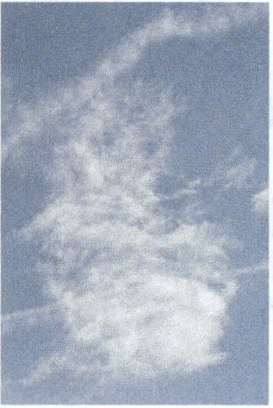 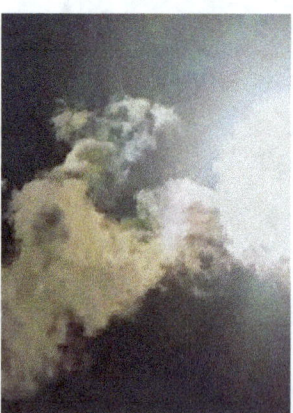 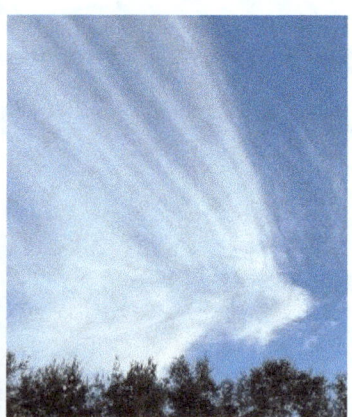

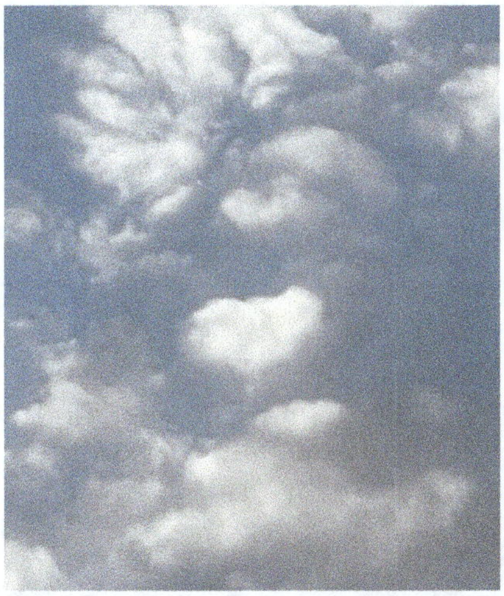

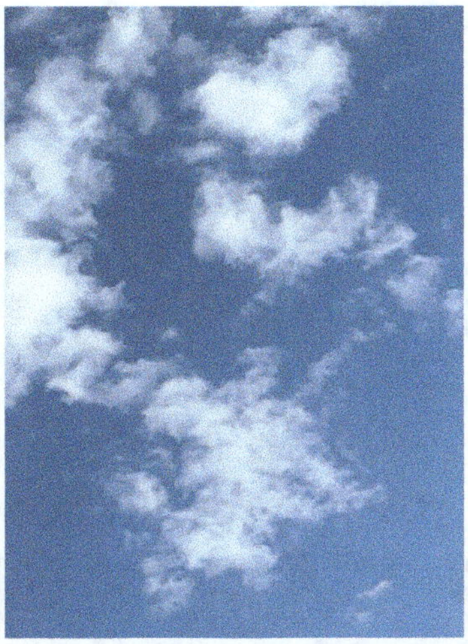

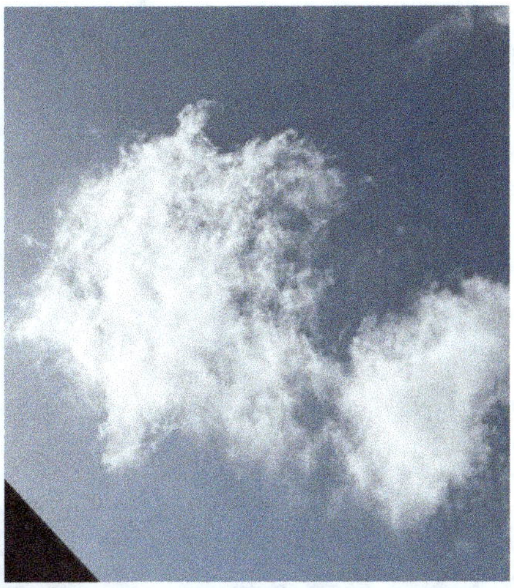

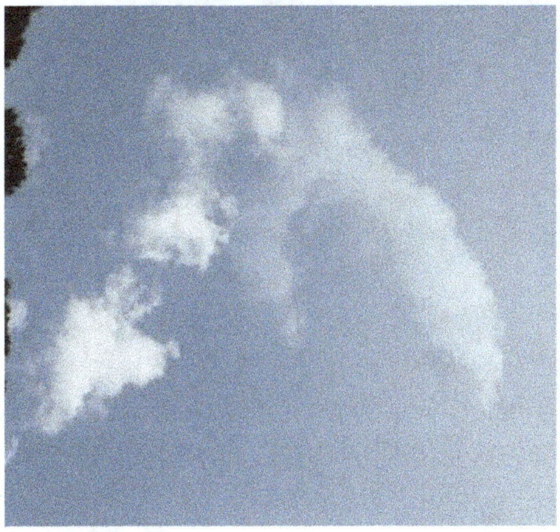

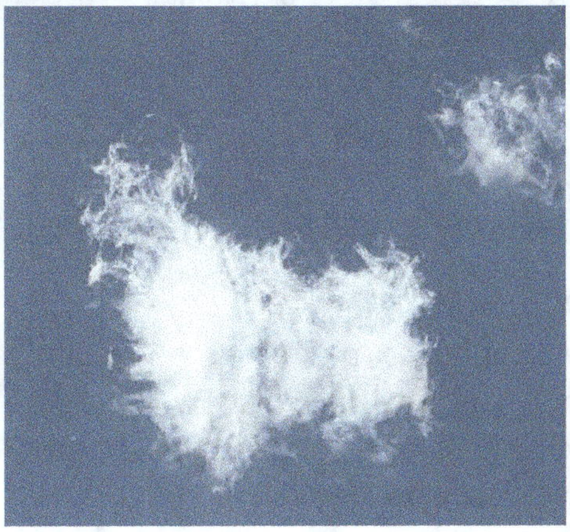

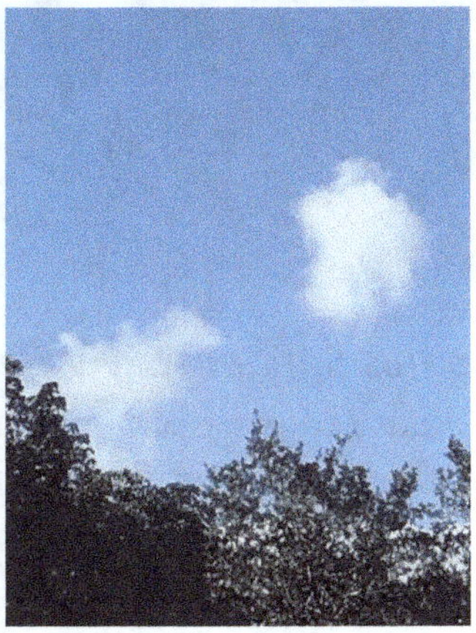

My Word
While looking through my photo diaries, I hope The Spirit in the sky brought joy to your soul as well as faith, hope, and love. "UN"ited we stand with Love.

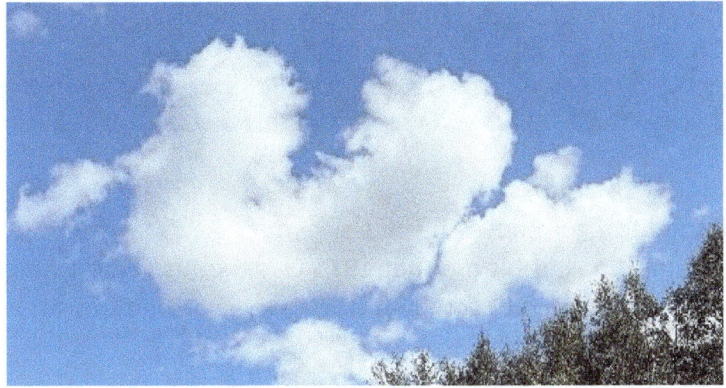

Heaven, Thanks
Thank God for sharing His heavenly visions in His skywriting in and other scenes.

12/2: I hope God continues to guide you through. Thank you for paying attention.

12/7: On this day, misty clouds appear to be communicating that "7" or Biblical Perfection aka God aka "Y"ahweh wants mankind to keep looking up.

 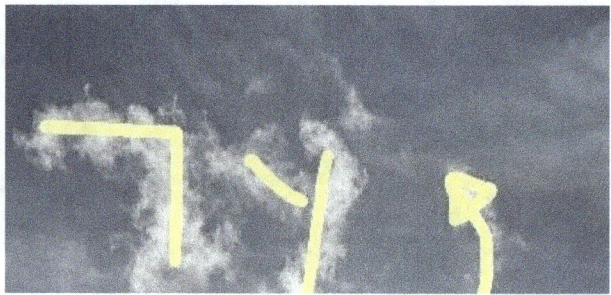

Is this Random Skywriting?
Choose to unite with the "V"ictorious "S"pirit of Jesus The Christ. He reopened The Pearly Gates to His Father's Kingdom for everyone following His Words in The Bible. If a soul honestly attempts to obey and live His Law of Love, that person will enter His Father's, Eternal Realm. The Christian Messiah came to redeem" U" and "I." That Savior came to save the world.

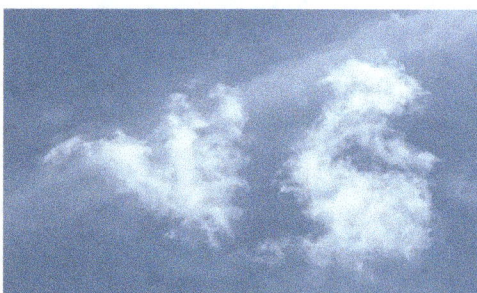 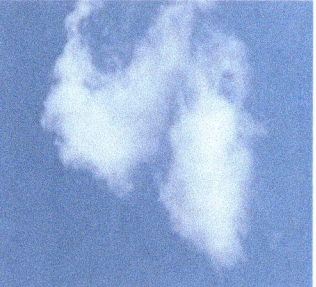

Every Picture Tells a Story; Don't it?
By the way, I tried and tried to figure out Yahweh's skywriting a "71." After mulling it over and nearly dropping that cloud from this book, it hit me that 1971 was the first time I was on the edge of a riot, violence, or war-like event. It started with some mean girls telling some African American ones that the bathroom near the gym was "Whites, Only."

My oldest sister and I told our parents about our day; Mom sent us to class even after a dire warning that all whites, especially females, would be killed if they dared to show up on the campus the next day. My mother told us that not going to school meant that we were a part of racism. The next day, very few faculty and students walked those hallowed halls. Each class, we were left alone to think about or discuss the events that emptied classrooms. There were only a handful of brave teachers and substitutes to mingle with the scarce student population that morning after the trauma aka riot. We talked and learned from our peers- all of those courageous or fearless enough to attend school. We compared life without judgement. In fact, most of the teens that came back to Miramar High that day talked about Martin Luther King's Dream and our life views finding commonality regardless of our skin color.

We, also, chatted about the kids too scared to show up due to the fight they started or witnessed. Looking back on that experience, it all makes sense in today's world. The bullies are usually cowards. More than likely, those tyrants kick sand in your face in order to know why you are mad at them instead of hoping you will get to know and like them. They live up to their low expectations and self-image. Sadly, too often, the mean souls are the leaders of the selfish in each generation; they win by intimidation. I wrote about this youthful experience in <u>Race Against Time</u>.

Are we at the worst point in His Story?

Apparently, some, good souls make The Almighty smile. However, many years ago, I was warned by The Presence that I was a part of the most selfish group of people to date. Keep the faith because God may smile upon you, too. I'm the living proof that He can guide a soul to safety and sanity even when the world is falling apart. Remember, I was not killed in 1971 even though I am a white girl that attended class the day after bloody violence raged on campus and a grave warning was issued that my skin color would get me killed.

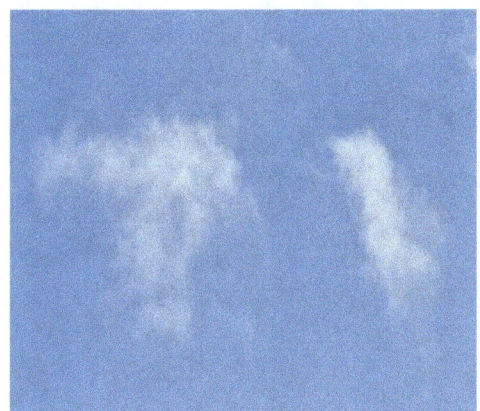

This photograph is from 2/23/2022 ...

By the way, I've lived an interesting life including being born legally blind to the point of needing surgery to go to school, having a dad with mental health issue that caused dysfunction in my childhoods, almost losing my arm to amputation, and so on. But I'm positive that God took me through the bad times shielding me against worse evils. FYI, my nonfictions where I scribe for The Supreme Being can be found online through Amazon KDP. In addition, my children's picture storybooks and novels or truth stretching fictions can be purchased online.

www.ingramcontent.com/pod-product-compliance
Lightning Source LLC
Chambersburg PA
CBHW080941220526

45465CB00008BA/3111